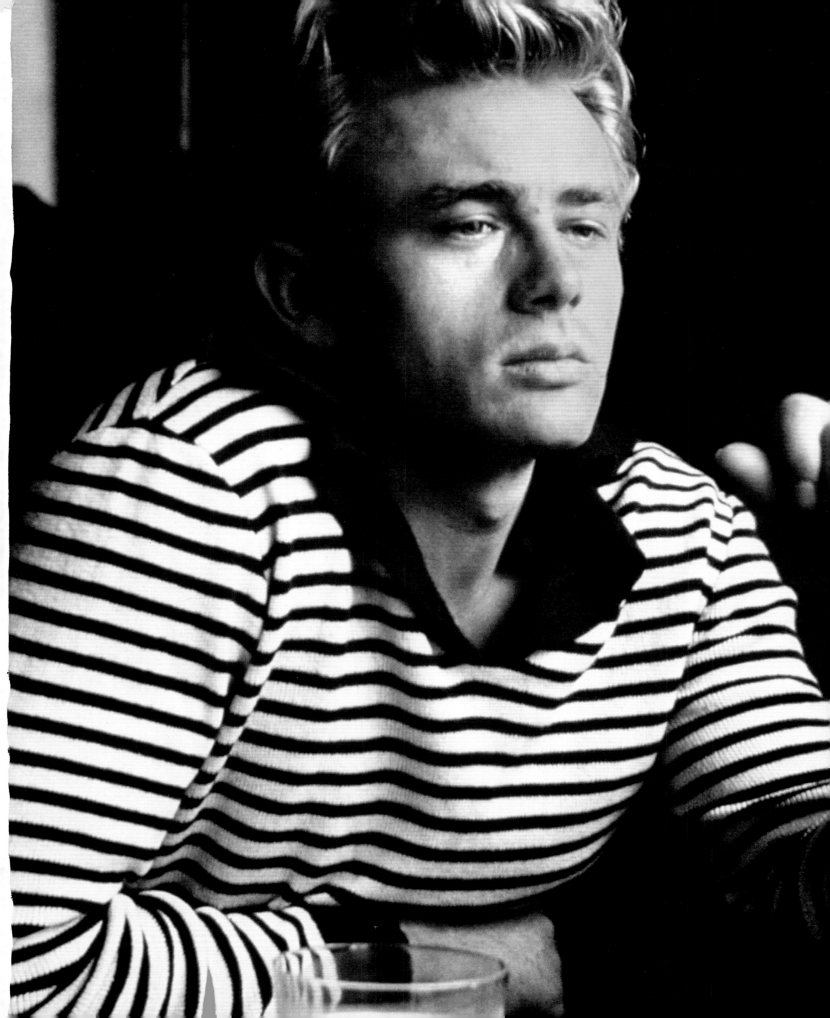

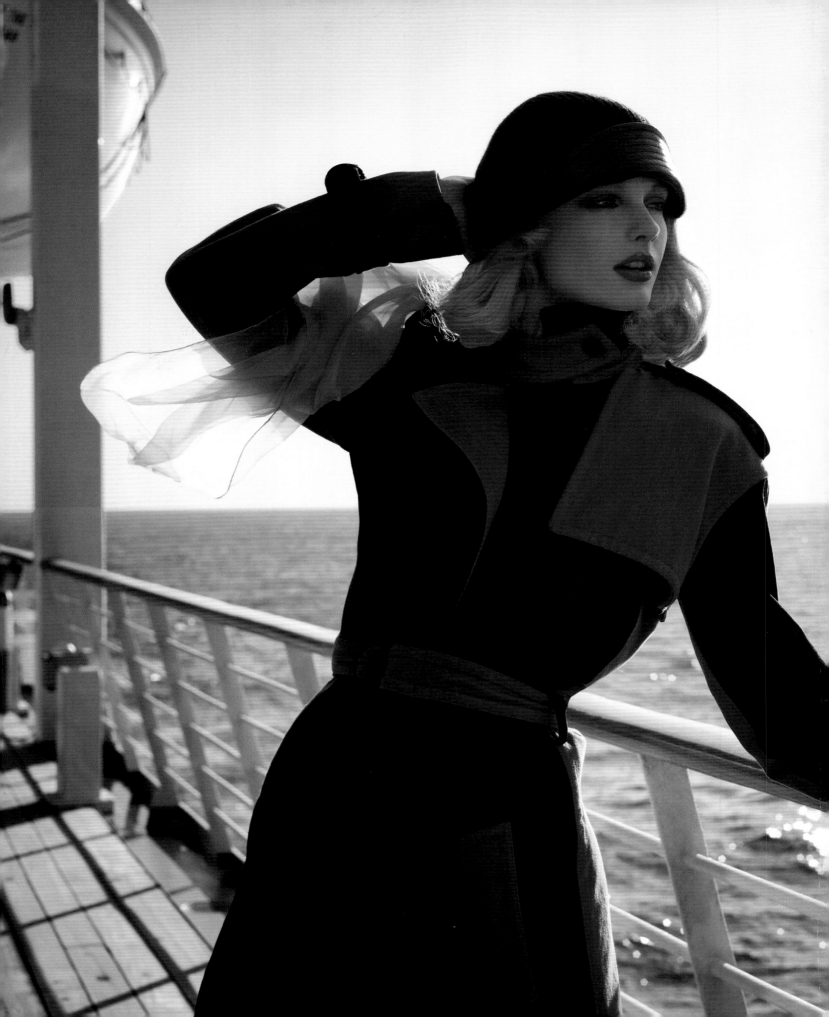

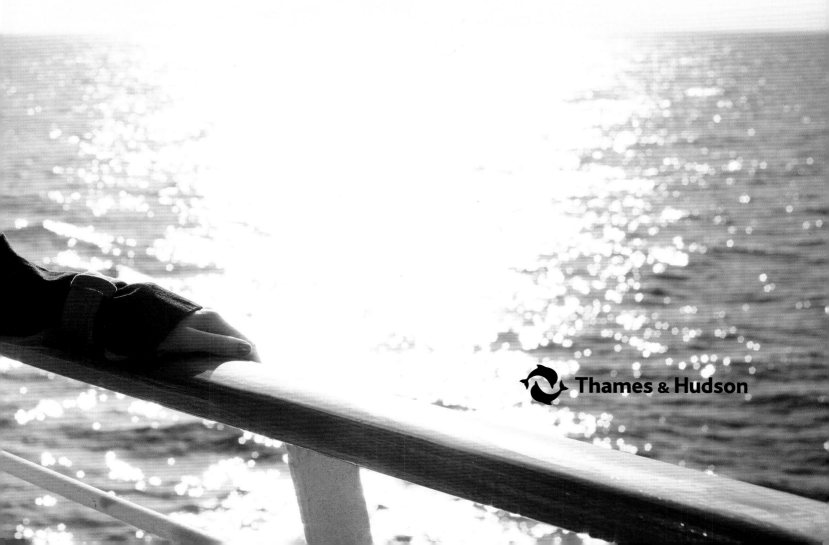

# NAUTICAL CHIC

AMBER JANE BUTCHART

Thames & Hudson

**Frontispiece:** *James Dean in nautical stripes, 1955.*
**Title page:** *Model Patricia van der Vliet wears
a Celine coat, Louis Vuitton hat and Charvet
scarf. Photographed by Sofia Sanchez and Mauro
Mongiello for the* Wall Street Journal, *July 2011.*
**Contents page (left to right):** *Alexander McQueen
spring/summer 2012 (p. 211c), Olympia Le-Tan
spring/summer 2014 (p. 66), Gieves (now Gieves
& Hawkes) late 19th century (p. 27), Jean Paul
Gaultier spring/summer 2008, Chanel cruise
collection 2010, presented in Venice (p. 14).*

First published in the United Kingdom in 2015
by Thames & Hudson Ltd, 181A High Holborn,
London WC1V 7QX

*Nautical Chic* © 2015 Thames & Hudson Ltd, London
Text © 2015 Amber Jane Butchart

Designed by Anna Perotti

British Library Cataloguing-in-Publication Data
A catalogue record for this book is available from
the British Library

ISBN 978-0-500-51780-2

Printed and bound in China by C & C Offset Printing
Co. Ltd

To find out about all our publications, please visit
**www.thamesandhudson.com**.
There you can subscribe to our e-newsletter, browse
or download our current catalogue, and buy any titles
that are in print.

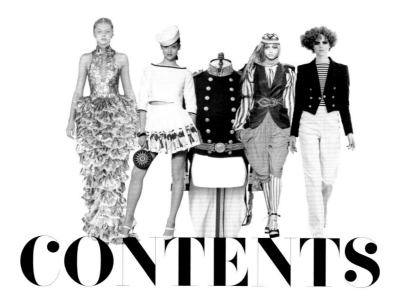

# CONTENTS

# HARPER'S *Bazaar*

INCORPORATING "VANITY FAIR"

JULY 1939

# STYLE AT SEA

*'In civilizations without boats, dreams dry up, espionage takes the place of adventure, and the police take the place of pirates.'*

MICHEL FOUCAULT, 1967[1]

Early on a summer evening at sea in 1778, the British warship *Arethusa* opened fire on the *Belle Poule*, a French frigate, off the coast of Brittany. The balance of power was precarious, with empires in flux and war in the air. *Arethusa* withdrew a couple of hours later, but both sides suffered huge losses. This brief maritime skirmish was the start of an epic moment in history. The first battle of a great European war, fought across continents; a war which would lose Britain many of her American colonies and tip France into revolution, drastically altering the history of each nation. Back in Paris, women of fashion marked the occasion with the *coiffure à la Belle Poule*, an elaborate hairstyle containing a replica of the ship itself.

Skip forward two centuries and those very headdresses were the inspiration behind Philip Treacy's 1995 ship hat created for the late fashion director and style savant Isabella Blow. Blow had recounted the 18th-century fad to Treacy, the milliner she discovered and for whom she was both muse and patron. This headpiece links not only the past and the present, but also serves to map the geography of contemporary nautical style. The maritime traditions of France, the United States and Britain have provided inspiration for the world of fashion ever since the mid-18th century, shortly before those towering headdresses set sail.[2] At the time of this early flush of nautical chic, the navy was the biggest employer in Britain,[3] Europe was busy building its empires and the United States was emerging as a new country, with its own dreams for the future. Over the following centuries, the styles and motifs of nautical dress would continually reappear in fashionable clothing.

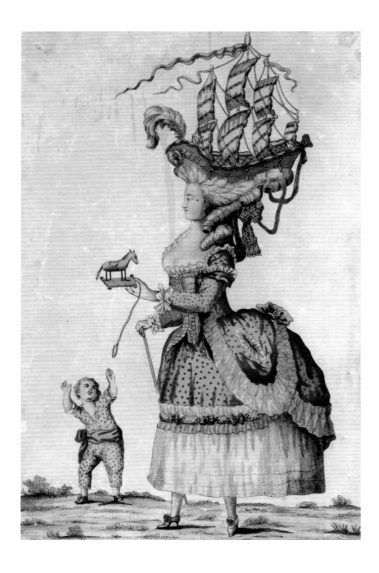

Throughout history, sea power and trade have been invaluable to nations, dynasties and regions, among them Persia, Polynesia, Egypt, Scandinavia, India, Venice, China, the Netherlands, Spain and Portugal. Yet it is France, the United States and Britain whose naval uniforms and maritime clothing have had a lasting legacy around the globe. From tailoring to sportswear, and from haute couture to the high street, these countries are the key producers and exporters of nautical style. Intertwined with politics, imperialism, war, leisure, trade and sport, marine passions and seafaring endeavours have made the journey from lifeblood to lifestyle.

The ocean has been inspiring artists for centuries. From Turner to Tracey Emin, the fruits of the sea have long fed creative minds, as well as hungry stomachs. Yet a comprehensive look at the nautical influence on dress remains somewhat uncharted waters. Seafaring style has had an enduring influence on modern clothing. Beyond the extravagance of shipshape hats, 21st-century catwalks are awash with nautical chic, from the modernist elegance of Chanel to the kitsch of Jean Paul Gaultier. Cruise and resort collections are an established part of the fashion calendar, and a wide variety of maritime garments are now ubiquitous, from basics such as the T-shirt to chic classics such as the marinière striped top. This book tracks the trend of nautical style from its inception in the 18th century to its current position as a perennial runway favourite through its five most enduring characters: Officer, Sailor, Fisherman, Sportsman and Pirate.

The Officer traces the birth of British naval uniform in an 18th-century coffee house through to the regimental glamour regularly shown on Parisian catwalks by the likes of Balmain. Fashionable styles influenced early uniform, and the relationship between war and fashion continues to be complex. The tailoring traditions of London's Savile Row have distinguished links with naval uniform, while ornamental features such as the epaulette have become stylistic shorthand for military spectacle and are used by fashion designers and flamboyant performers alike. Contemporary outerwear is equally indebted to the navy. The duffle coat crossed into civilian wear on pacifist protest marches and the pea coat was key to Yves Saint Laurent's 1960s democratization of fashion.

The Sailor charts the journey from national hero to homoerotic icon and fashion favourite, as reinvented by a host of designers from Mary Quant to Jean Paul Gaultier, Kenzo,

*Page 6: Wide sailor-style pants capture the essence of nautical chic in leisurewear. Illustrated by A.M. Cassandre for the cover of the summer travel issue of* Harper's Bazaar, July 1939. Above: *The ship that launched a thousand hats. Named after a French frigate, the elaborate* coiffure à la Belle Poule *headdress became an early example of nautical chic when it caught on in Paris in 1778.* Opposite: *Originally inspired by 18th-century headdresses, Philip Treacy revived his ship headpiece with the 'Silver Ghost Hat' for spring/summer 2013.*

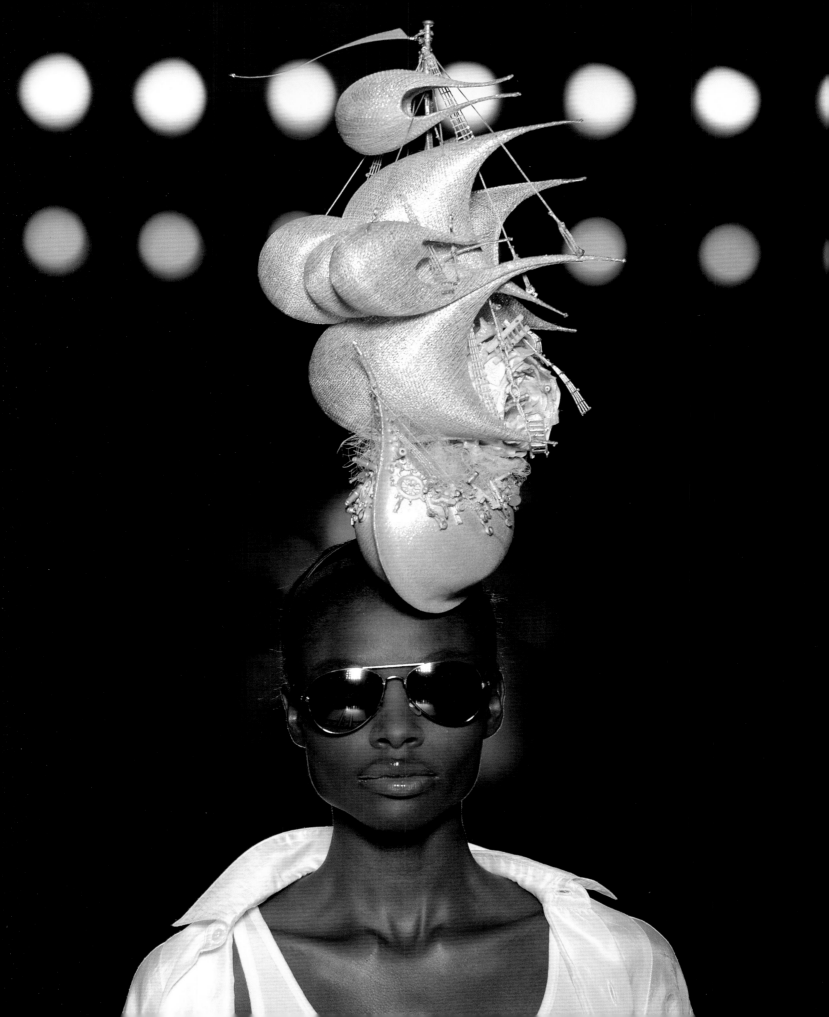

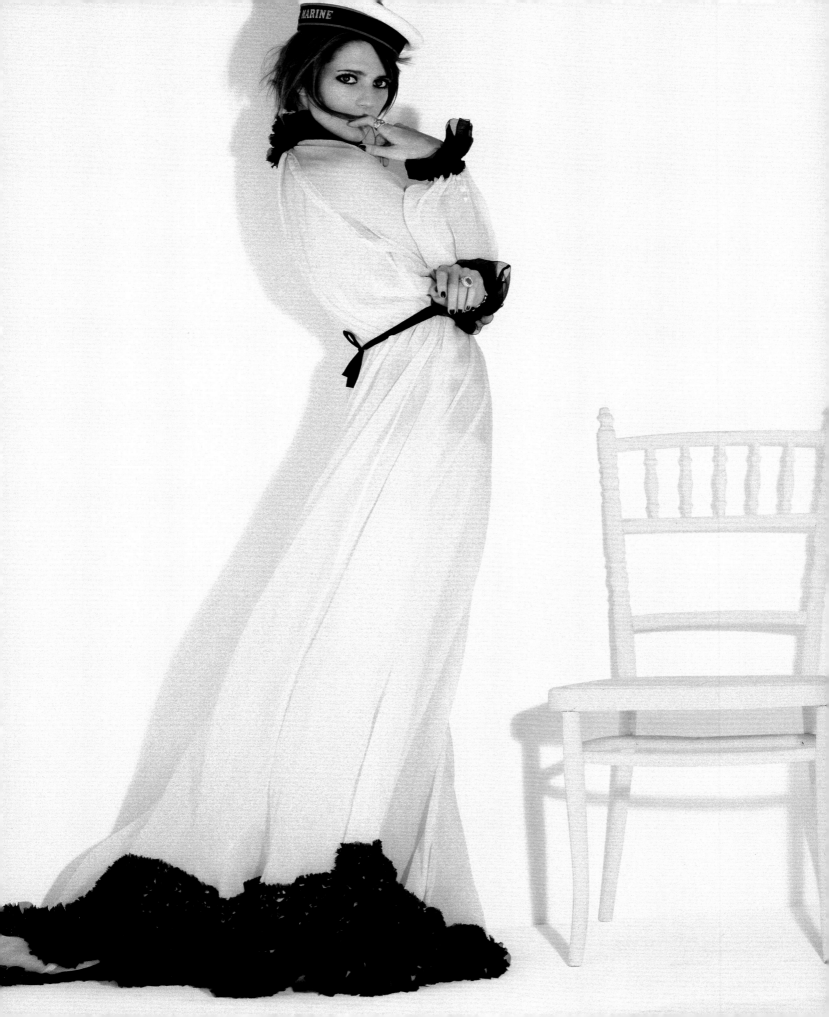

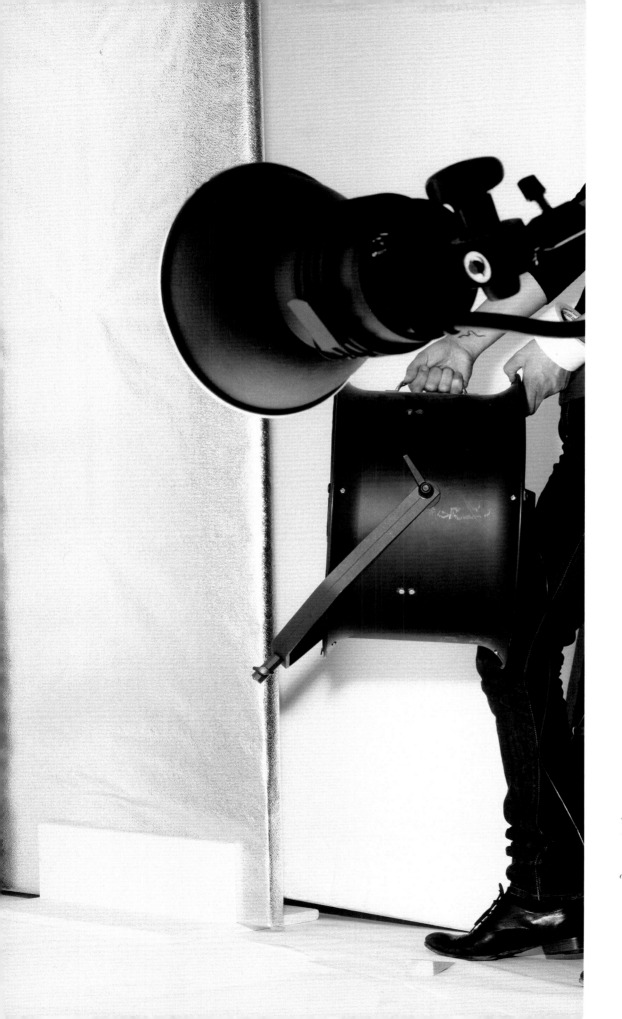

Sailor style as a fashion favourite. Mischa Barton wears a D&G silk chiffon dress from their pre-fall 2009 collection, accessorized with a vintage sailor hat. Photographed by Giampaolo Sgura for Italian Glamour, *June 2009*.

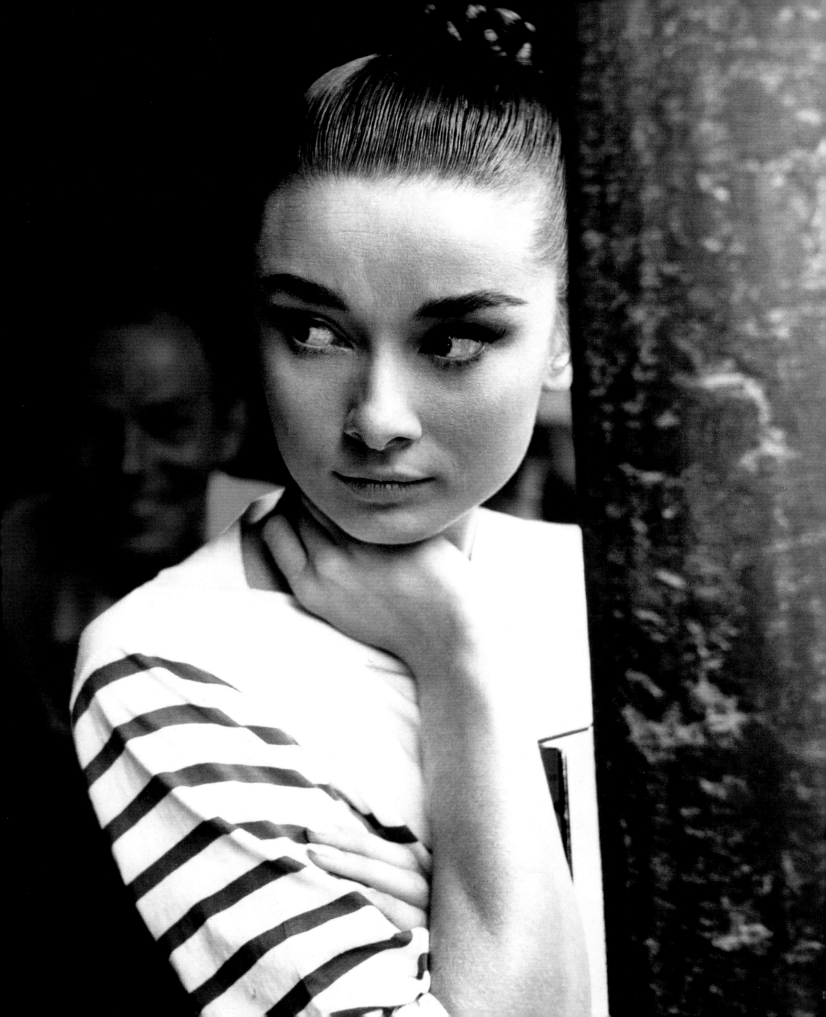

Miu Miu, Dior, Schiaparelli and Yohji Yamamoto. Following the introduction of the first official sailor uniforms in the 19th century, the iconic square collar and bell-bottom pants have become nautical icons the world over. The American sailor has given us the white 'dixie cup' hat, a favourite item in Hollywood musicals and on the fashion runway. Mixing blue-collar masculinity with seaside kitsch, sailor style has an enduring appeal that is both playful and chic.

The Fisherman tracks the story of occupational dress through to the realm of high fashion as the beach shifted from being a place of work to a place of fashionable leisure. Workers at the coast have inspired couture from designers such as Chanel and Balenciaga and, in their constant battle with the elements, fishing communities have developed their own garments that have become favourites on dry land. The French coast has played a big part in the spread of nautical chic. From bohemian visitors along the Riviera to fishermen and sailors on the shorelines of Brittany, items that were once workwear have become fashion classics.

From the mid-19th century, the Sportsman showed that seafaring lives could also be lives of luxury and recreation. During America's Gilded Age, leisure pursuits at the coast and at sea became associated with aspirational lifestyles along the New England shores of Martha's Vineyard, Nantucket and Newport, as the yachting dress code of blazer and flannels came to represent the sartorial equivalent of the American Dream. The ocean liner created a new type of luxurious travel, one that thrived on fashionable display on the promenade decks. Sportswear became the defining feature of American style, a look that rose to prominence on Ivy League campuses and was spread around the world through East Coast lifestyle brands such as Ralph Lauren, Tommy Hilfiger and J.Crew.

Opposite: *Audrey Hepburn on the set of the movie* War and Peace, *wearing a nautical striped top by the American luxury company Mark Cross, 1955.*

The Pirate embodies the spirit of romance and adventure more than any other maritime figure. From the excessive designs of Jean-Charles de Castelbajac and John Galliano to Alexander McQueen's skulls, the motifs of the pirate hint at the exotic and dangerous side of life on the ocean waves. While the historical aspects of pirate dress are rooted in the 1660s during the Golden Age of Piracy, fictional pirates – from Captain Hook to Jack Sparrow – have shaped our view of buccaneer style. The mythical mermaid regularly adds aquatic allure to the catwalk and was also a favourite emblem for sailor tattoos. In 1981, pirates got political as Malcolm McLaren and Vivienne Westwood channelled them through the lens of the French Revolution, cementing the idea of the pirate as an anti-establishment rock 'n' roll outlaw. The continual lure of the sea as imagined through the dress of these characters lays the foundation of our 21st-century obsession with nautical chic. Welcome to the story of high fashion on the high seas.

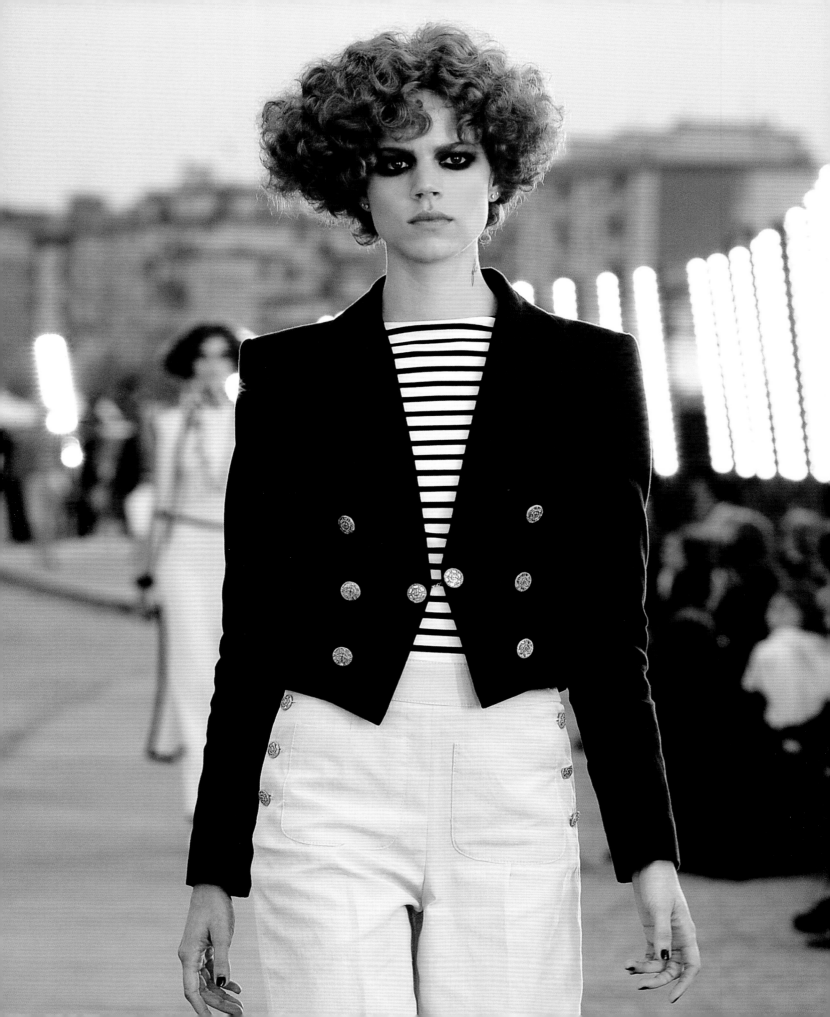

# CHAPTER 1

# THE OFFICER

From 18th-century London to the catwalks of Paris, the figure of the Officer cuts a regimental dash in strict tailoring and lavish embellishment. The officer's uniform is regularly reimagined by design houses such as McQueen and Givenchy, playing with ideas of power, prestige and spectacular adornment.

*'Even the most
gay feminine attire
scarcely equals the
gorgeousness of certain
military uniforms.'*

JOHN CARL FLÜGEL, 1930[1]

The power of decoration and uniform has been linked for centuries through naval style and continues to provide endless inspiration for the world of fashion, whether reflected in the tailoring of Alexander McQueen or in the ornamentation seen on the catwalk at Balmain. The very first naval uniforms were used as an expression of both professional and social status; fashion had a big influence on these earliest naval uniforms, based largely on clothing worn at the French court. The naval uniform established for British officers in the 18th century was more concerned with visually preserving social rank than addressing the specific functional requirements of life at sea. While the navy was more meritocratic than the army, commissioned naval officers were drawn from further up the social scale than the enlisted sailors of the crew who were working seamen, sometimes press-ganged by force into joining the fleet. Concerns about the use of dress to obscure class origins and encourage social mobility were prevalent among the upper classes, and officers were keen to enshrine their status into the fabric of their clothing.[2] As the role of the Royal Navy expanded, from fighting to scientific expeditions, protecting trade routes and imperial missions, it became increasingly important that naval officers were identifiable overseas. This expression of institutional identity used the trappings of insignia to signal rank and maintain order in a spectacular display of sartorial supremacy.[3]

## AN OFFICER AND A GENTLEMAN

In 1746, a group of British naval officers petitioned government for a standardized uniform. The petition plans had been forged at Will's Coffee House in London's Covent Garden, well known for its naval clientele, and the Admiralty – the governing body of the Navy – responded with a request for officers to submit their own designs, so that the most appropriate could be chosen by the King. The uniform elected was likely to have been based on the option provided by Captain Philip Saumarez, who had served in the navy for two decades and had recently completed an around the world voyage.[4] This uniform became the standard in 1748, and introduced items such as the heavily laced and spangled dark blue jacket with fashionable deep boot-cuffs for the admiral's formal dress uniform, and a less ornate, dark blue frock coat with smaller 'mariner's cuffs' for the informal undress uniform of the captain. The more spectacular your uniform, the higher up the ranks you sat. The colour blue had long associations with seafaring in Britain, stretching back to Henry I in the 12th century,[5] and it was the colour of the coats Elizabeth I administered to the English Navy that fought the Spanish Armada. But the colour of choice for officer's uniform was not a foregone conclusion and other designs were submitted in colours such as martial red and grey.[6] The choice of blue could have been due to economics: trade with indigo-rich India had increased throughout the century, and the plant had just been introduced to South Carolina, to be harvested by slave labour. The decision could also have been influenced by the French Navy who, under Louis XIV in the previous century, had been permitted to wear a coat in blue (one of the King's colours), adorned with gold or silver lace.[7] France, arbiter of style and taste, was to have much sway over these early uniform designs.

*Page 14: Chanel cruise collection 2010, presented in Venice.* **Opposite:** *British national hero Rear Admiral Sir Horatio Nelson in rear admiral's undress uniform from the 1795 to 1812 pattern, with gold epaulettes and numerous decorations. He was promoted to Vice Admiral in 1801. Oil on canvas by Lemuel Francis Abbott, 1799.*

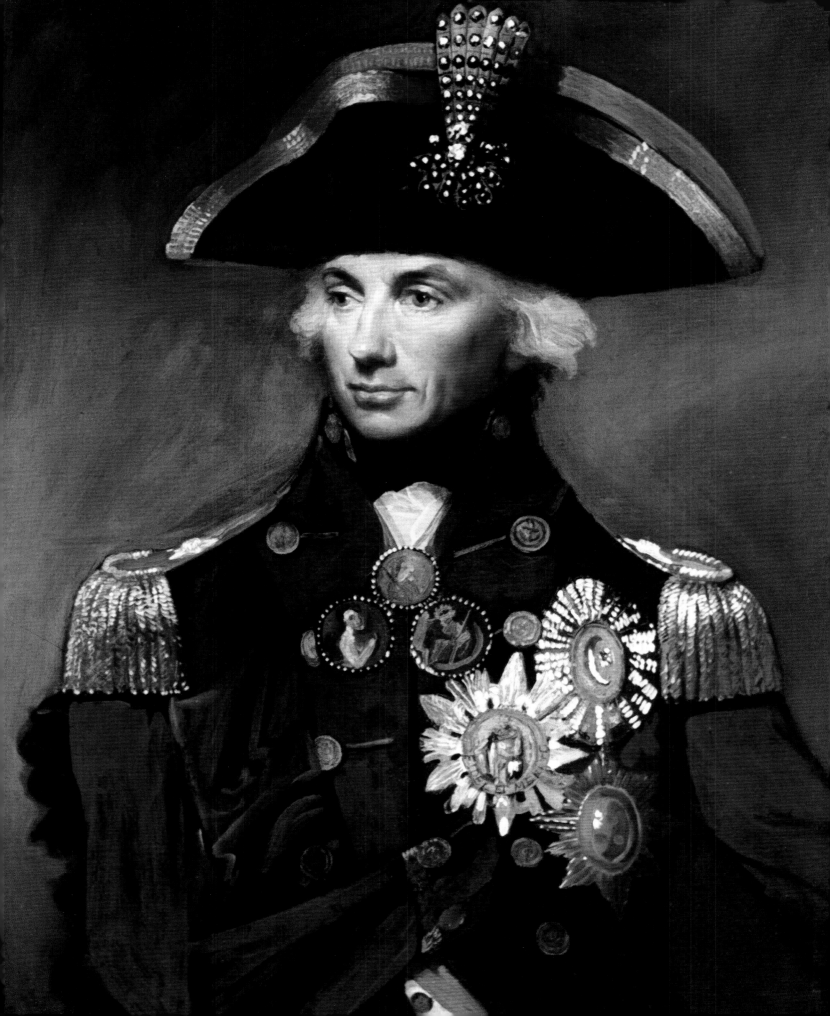

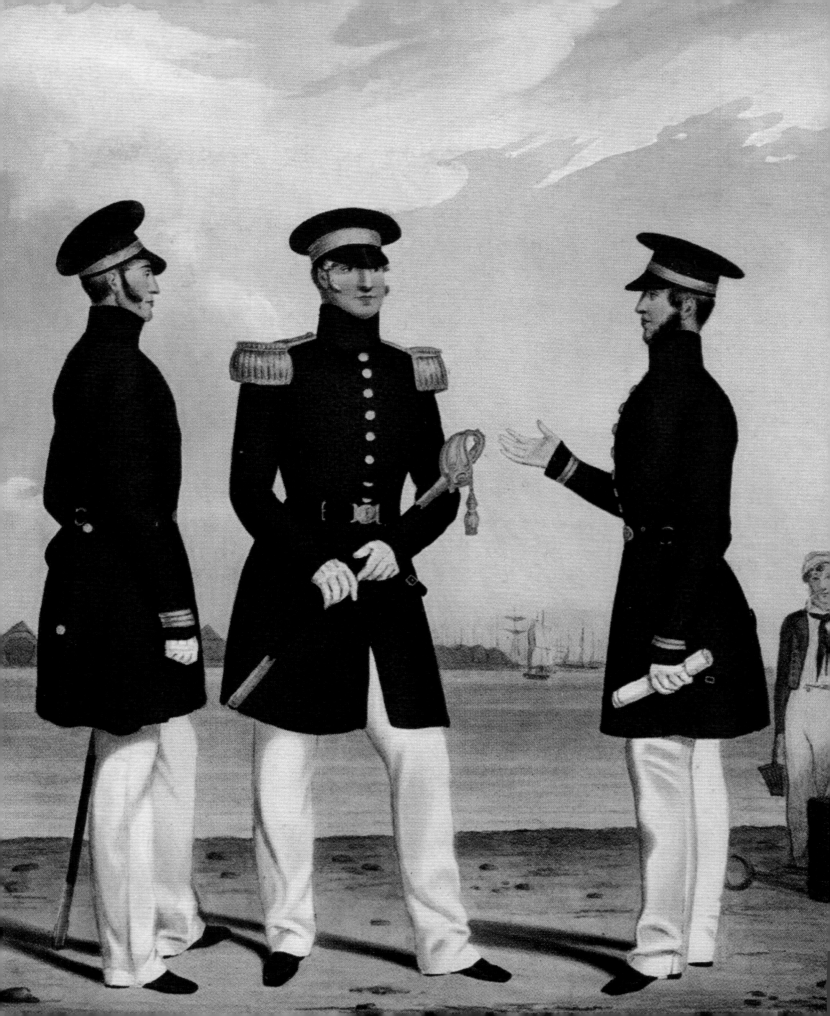

The reasons for uniform standardization were manifold, primarily due to a desire for distinction both at sea – to single out commissioned officers from the crew – and at land. These concerns weren't restricted to Britain. Full standardization of French naval uniform was initiated in 1764,[8] and after the formation of the American Navy in 1775, the issue of uniform for officers was a point of urgency. A plain uniform was issued in a bid to distance themselves from the Royal Navy, a gesture of democracy against the colonial overlords. However, the officers were not impressed and demanded something more ornate, as befitting their status. A dark blue coat with gold buttons and lace was adopted; reminiscent of the very same British forces they were fighting. Britain, whose global naval domination was established just a decade earlier at the end of the Seven Years' War,[9] would provide a template for much of the uniform adopted by American forces, and their mastery of the waves would last for almost another two centuries.

However, uniforms were not arbitrary symbols of military might, they were also influenced by the latest fashionable styles. The first official uniforms in Britain reflected contemporary men's fashions and subsequent changes also echoed the evolution of civilian style.[10] Naval uniform changed at a slower rate than fashionable dress, but there was distinct evidence of influence from the non-seafaring world. Formal dress styles

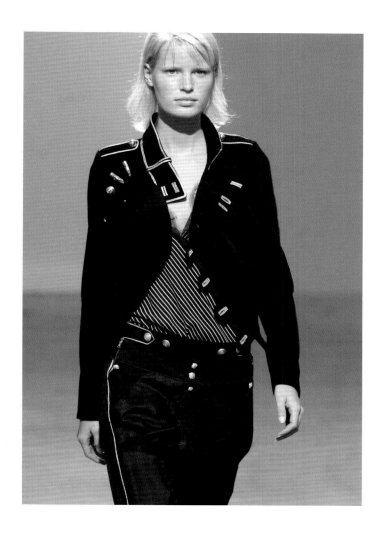

Above: *Insignia on the catwalk, including gold braid, buttons and epaulettes at Balenciaga, spring/ summer 2005.* Opposite: *The officer's uniform cutting a dash with its finery, including epaulettes that were initially introduced by the French navy. 'Captain, Flag Officer and Commander (Undress)', plate 9 of* Costume of the Royal Navy and Marines *by L. Mansion and St Eschauzier, 1830.*

mirrored French-influenced court fashions, adding social cachet to the wearer through an implied proximity to life at court. The Admiralty produced extensive guidelines on uniforms, but it was still possible to make small tailoring alterations to enhance the fashionable line of clothing without falling foul of the regulations.[11] A number of men's styles, from 18th-century Macaronis to early 19th-century Dandies, influenced the cut of uniform, whether giving it tighter sleeves or waspier waists.[12] In 1825, the first illustrated regulations were introduced, which not only demonstrated an almost fetishistic attention to detail in delineation of rank and decoration, but also bore an uncanny resemblance to fashion plates of the day.[13] As well as the coat, hat and breeches, regulations also covered items such as swords and buckles for shoes and knees. These negotiations between function and fashion were not always appreciated, and accusations of effeminacy regularly appeared in caricatures in the popular press.[14]

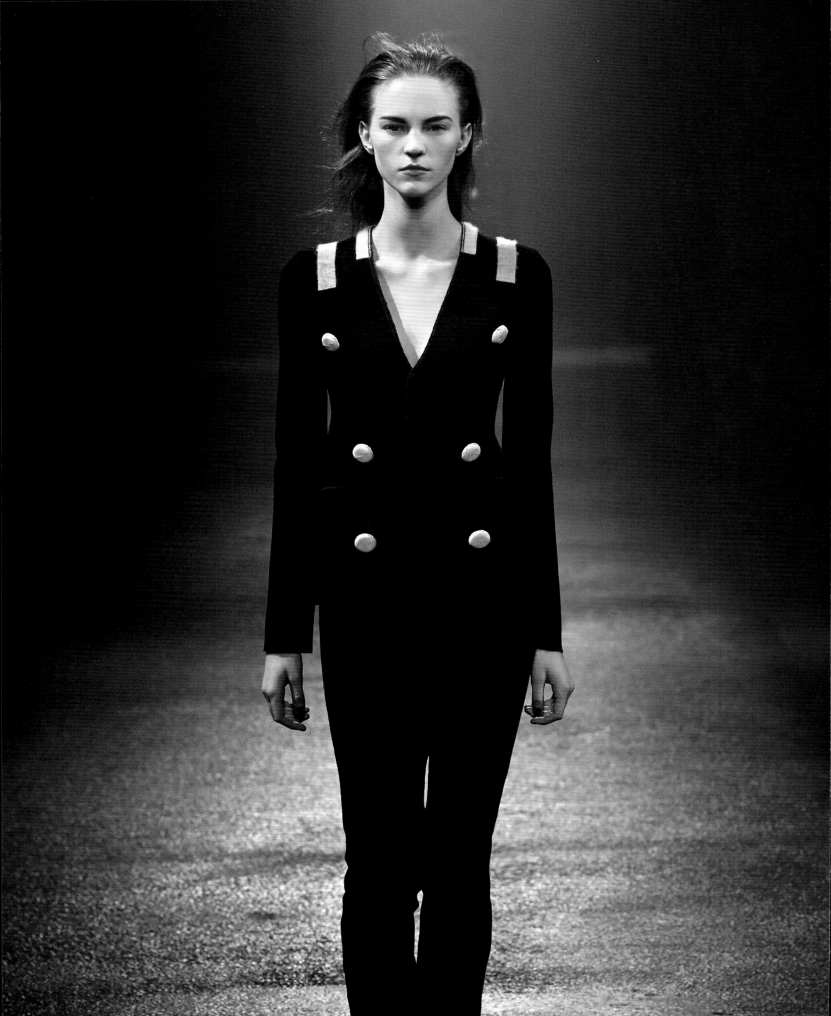

Right: *Music hall star and male impersonator Vesta Tilley as a naval lieutenant. Her patriotic songs were a rallying cry during the First World War, and this image can be found on earlier sheet music for the song 'Sweetheart May' in 1895. The midshipman was another of her favourite characters.* Far right: *The officer's overcoat is a perennial fashion favourite. Navy blue Shetland wool coat with Bermuda shorts, socks and blouse for the beach, designed by Antonio del Castillo, 1964.*

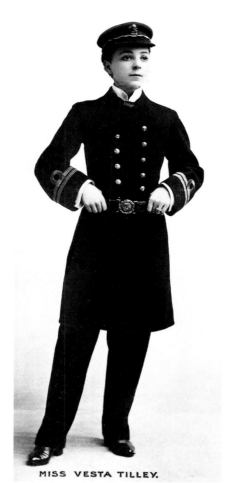

MISS VESTA TILLEY.

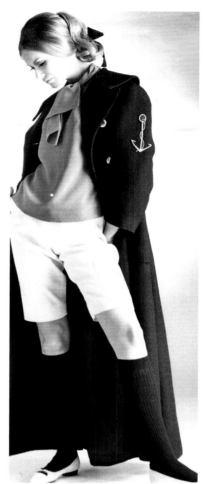

## THE ORNAMENTAL OFFICER

The lasting legacy of the Napoleonic Wars was to further consolidate Britain's place at the forefront of naval power, and to establish the sartorial splendour of uniform.[15] Throughout history, adorning and shaping the body have often been seen as the preserve of women, swathed in petticoats and bound in corsets. But the decorated officer and the woman of fashion have had much in common. Uniform's rigid tailoring sculpted the body while tight doeskin trousers or breeches emphasized the male form, at times in the early 19th century even creating the illusion of nudity.[16] The uniform was central to the ideology of power through spectacle, but also turned the wearer into a something of a sex object, to the extent that the sight of 'red coats' in Jane Austen's classic *Pride and Prejudice* is enough to send the youngest Bennet girls into a frenzy of bonnet buying.[18] Decoration is an intrinsic mark of the military uniform. Before the African campaigns of the late 19th century and the mechanized warfare of the 20th, the majority of European battlefields were populated with the ostentatious flamboyance of the bright red coats of the army, and glittering – if war-weary and smoke-tinged – insignia.

Ornamentation was not only spectacular and expensive – a visual indicator of wealth – but also a clear demarcation of social and professional status. This was designated in a number of ways, from lashings of gold lace on hats or sleeves to more subtle codes such as silver thread lining the buttonholes as an indicator of rank. Despite protests about the cost of upkeep, the predilection for such pomp and pageantry in dress endured, and, throughout the 19th century, led to associations between the military and the world of fashion, from satirical cartoons to prints of officers resembling fashion plates.[19] The *Literary Gazette* picked up on this in an 1830 article on the origins of naval uniform, noting that 'the subject of dress' was as 'important, it seems, to heroes as well as to ladies'.[20] The alignment of military regalia with female fashions had to tread a very fine tightrope in the public eye. Not only were decorated officers a visual demonstration of an idealized military might – part of the scenery of naval conquest and colonial expansion – but they paradoxically ran the risk of being overtly sexualized or satirized in the popular press.

*Opposite: Officer and sailor style recreated using designs by Nicole Farhi, DKNY, Moschino, Stephen Jones and D&G, as well as military surplus. Photographed by Boo George for* Love *magazine, September 2011.*

*'I remember the time when I liked a red coat myself very well – and, indeed, so I do still at my heart; and if a smart young colonel, with five or six thousand a year, should want one of my girls, I shall not say nay to him; and I thought Colonel Forster looked very becoming the other night at Sir William's in his regimentals.'*

MRS BENNET, *PRIDE AND PREJUDICE*, 1813[17]

## THE EPAULETTE AND THE ESTABLISHMENT

Of all the decorative trappings of insignia, it is the epaulette that has become the favourite stylistic shorthand for military pomp. Introduced first by the French military, it was taken up by British personnel who complained that soldiers and sailors failed to salute them overseas without this marker of authority.[21] This infiltration of French extravagance into British dress was not to everyone's taste, for political as well as aesthetic reasons. Naval commander Lord Nelson, for example, was sceptical of what he termed 'Frenchman's uniform'. Despite his disfavour, epaulettes were enshrined in official British regulations from 1795 until 1959.[22] Gold epaulettes were also added to the American Navy, featuring in the first official regulations of 1797, and other navies, such as Russia, soon followed suit. Epaulettes became the prevalent method of determining rank, quickly outstripping complicated earlier systems based on facings, button arrangements and the cut of lapels. Designs were specified for each position, ranging from gold or silver stars and bullion fringe to the later use of acorns and oak leaves with pearl edging.[23] Until 1856's introduction of sleeve stripes, the epaulette was the key identifier of rank in the Royal Navy.

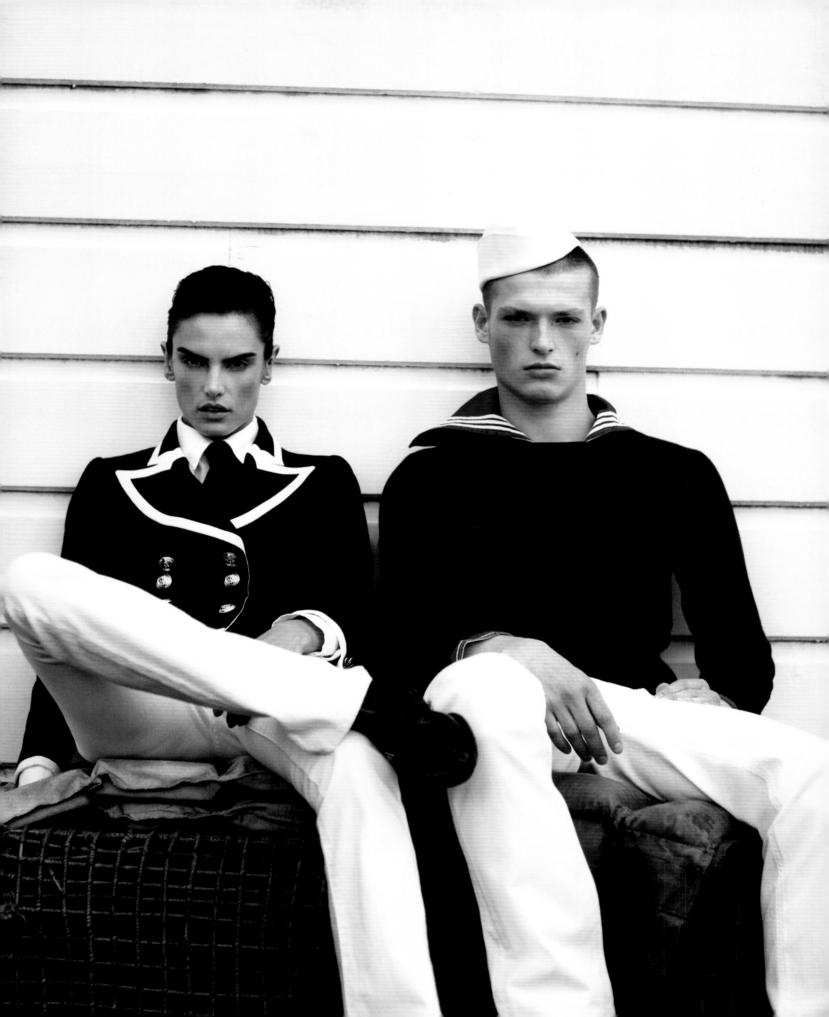

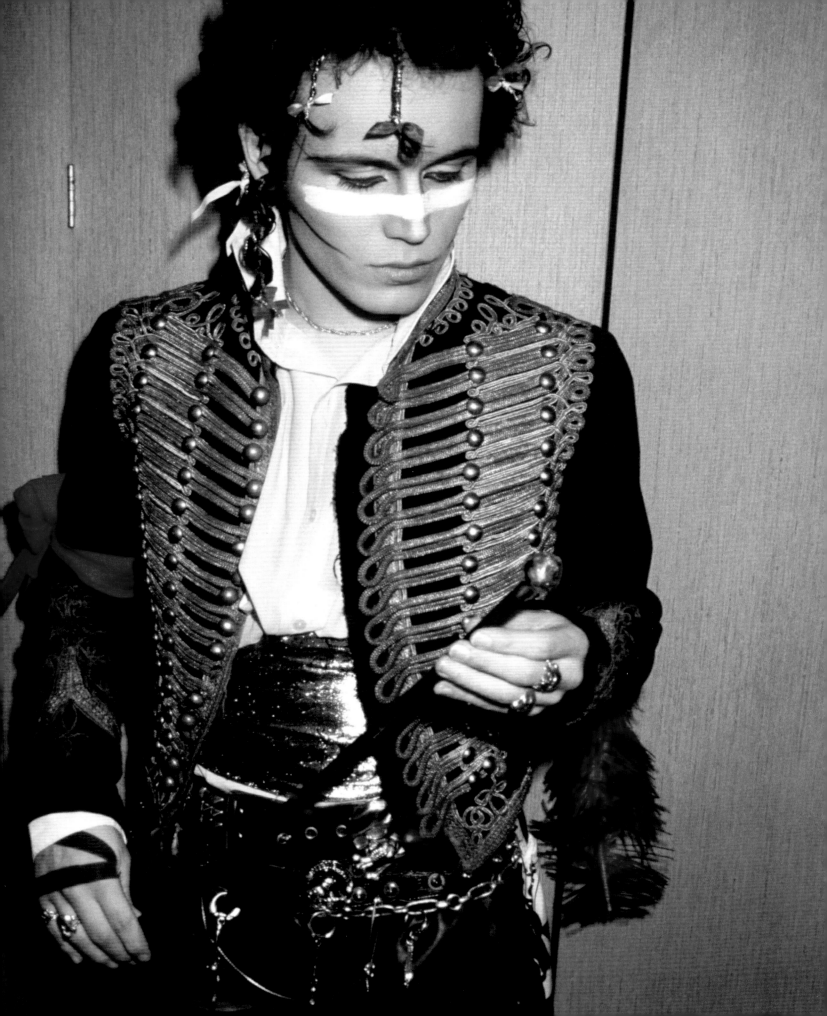

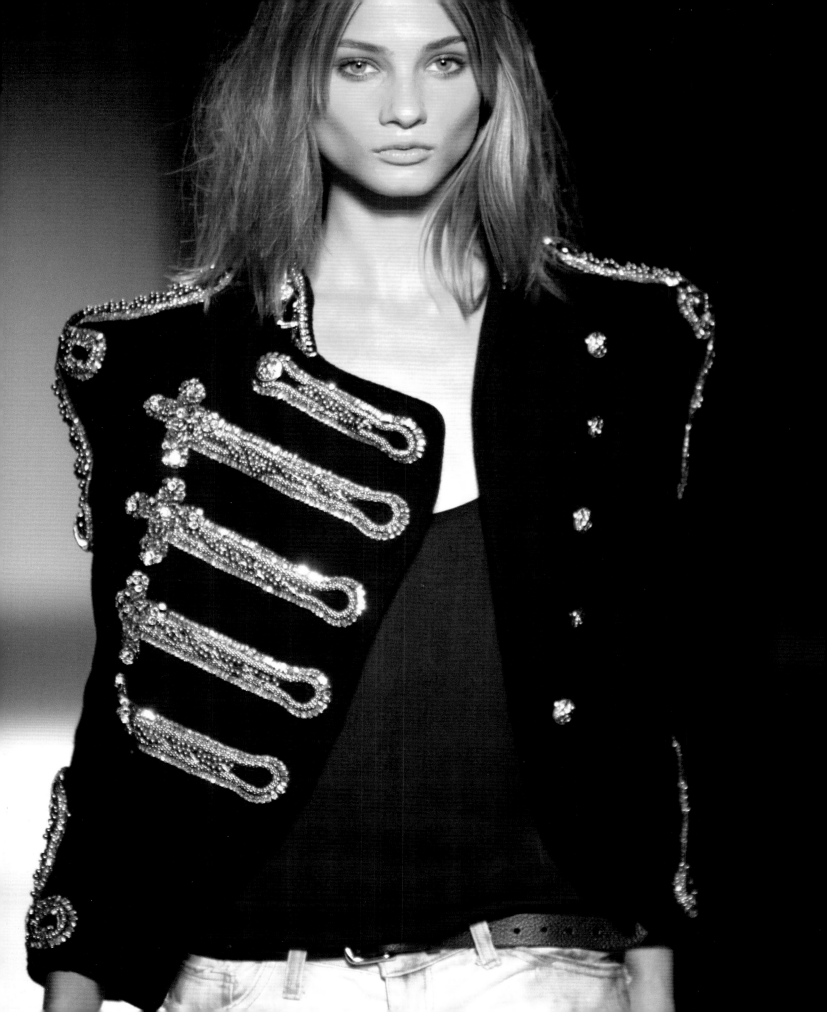

Epaulettes enhance the shoulders, serving to construct and decorate an imposing physique that is central to the idea of power through adornment. These themes of ostentatious grandeur were picked up again during the 'peacock revolution' of the 1960s that saw the heavily decorated military jacket back at the forefront of men's style. The Beatles' uniforms for the cover of *Sgt Pepper's Lonely Hearts Club Band* in 1967 were created by costume designers M. Berman Ltd, and played on the theatricality of military dress. Rendered in bright sherbet colours, they used braided cord aiguillettes and epaulettes to subvert the trappings of militarism for postwar pacifists. Concurrently, the boutique I Was Lord Kitchener's Valet was doing a roaring trade selling antique and surplus uniforms to London's fashion-savvy counterculture who had a more sceptical view of previous generations' imperial prowess. Starting out as a market stall, by 1966 the boutique had opened on London's Portobello Road before expanding to Carnaby Street and Piccadilly Circus.[24] Supplying stars such as Jimi Hendrix and Mick Jagger, I Was Lord Kitchener's Valet became a retail destination at the moment when the global fashion press was centred on 'swinging' London. The use of actual uniform for civilian fashion often led to confrontation with older generations as well as the authorities, including the Lord Chamberlain, who found the use of military items worn as a stylistic choice to be unacceptably distasteful.[25] This censure no doubt heightened the appeal for anti-establishment postwar shoppers.

The embellished officer has remained a popular look for performers, part of the historical excess of Adam Ant in the 1980s and revisited by the Strokes and the Libertines at the turn of the millennium. Military detailing also became central to Michael Jackson's wardrobe both on- and off-stage. Savile Row tailors Gieves & Hawkes – who have long-established links to the navy – provided a heavily braided uniform based on court livery for Jackson's *Bad* world tour in 1988, coupled with exaggerated epaulettes for military effect. Flamboyant uniforms were a crucial element of Jackson's costumes throughout his life, and he continues to be a key reference for military styling. Throughout 2009, Jackson was photographed wearing a naval-inspired Givenchy by Riccardo Tisci blazer studded with heavy metalware from autumn/winter 2007, as well as a luxe Balmain spring/summer 2009 jacket that featured exaggerated shoulders, widely touted to have been inspired by the King of Pop himself. For this collection Christophe Decarnin at Balmain teamed the jacket, emblazoned with crystal frogging, with distressed and torn denim, combining street style with high military glamour.

## SAVILE ROW: LONDON'S HOME OF NAVAL TAILORING

The history of formal menswear is intrinsically bound to tailoring for military service, none more so than Royal Warrant holders Gieves & Hawkes who present seasonally at men's fashion week in London and who occupy the prestigious address of 1 Savile Row. In a somewhat convoluted story, the lineage of the company can be traced directly to Lord Nelson during the Napoleonic Wars at the turn of the 19th century. The firm, as it operates today, was created in 1974 when the

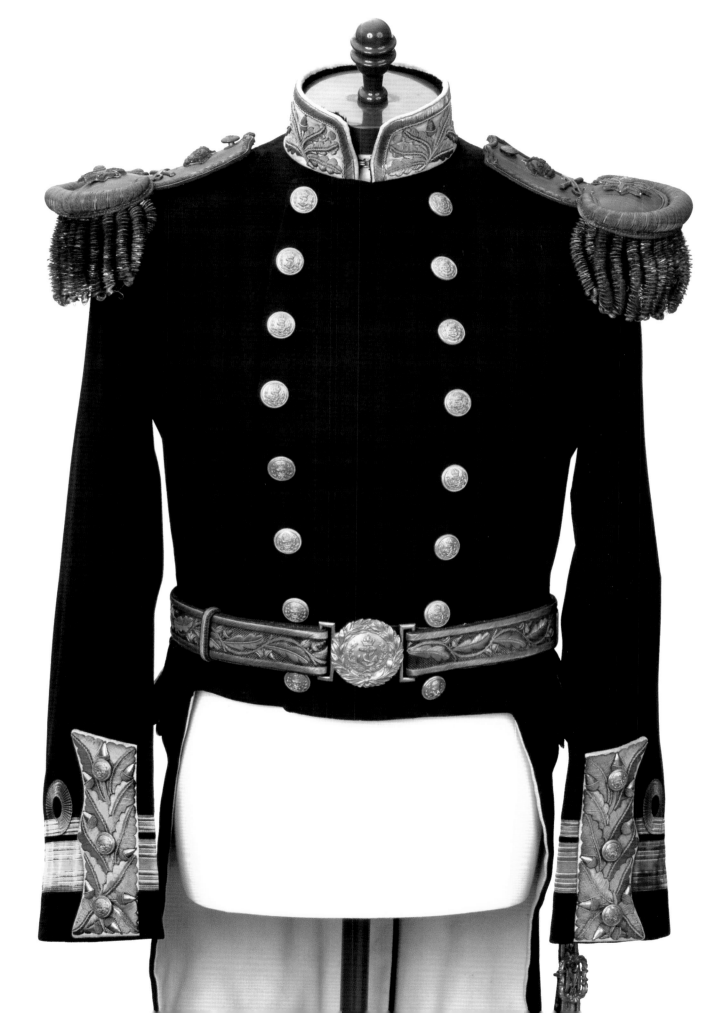

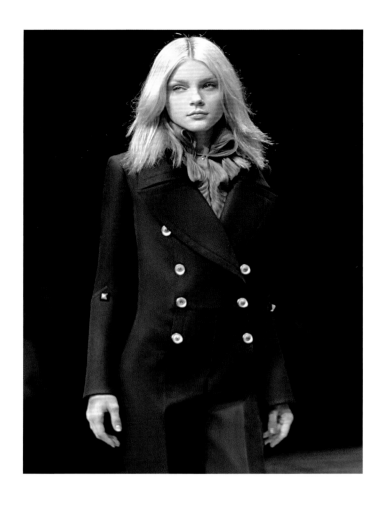

Left: *The pea coat was adapted into an afternoon dress by Yves Saint Laurent in 1966; here it has evolved yet again into a naval jumpsuit. Givenchy by Riccardo Tisci, autumn/ winter 2007.* Opposite: *Sharply tailored outerwear: military fashions by Modelia, made from Forstmann's Fabulaine fabric, 1970.*

## WAR AND WOMEN'S DRESS

tailors Hawkes & Co – with its military heritage – merged with the naval tailor Gieves & Co. But the origins of each goes back a further two centuries. In 1785, a tailor called Melchizidec Meredith, known as 'Old Mel', set up a business in Portsmouth catering for the naval trade. He made items for Nelson as well as his Trafalgar ally Lord Collingwood. Old Mel's son later sold the business to Joseph Galt, and James Gieve joined in 1852. Shortly afterwards the newly-named Galt & Gieve took a floating tailor shop to Sevastopol to service the fleet during the Crimean War. Their prestige grew due to the high quality of their indigo-dyed merino wool and, by the 20th century, Gieves & Co. was tailor by appointment to the Royal Navy. Hawkes & Co has an equally prodigious heritage, including having made the plumed bicorn hats worn by the Duke of Wellington at the Battle of Waterloo. In 1953, Gieves & Co also tailored the Admiralty-commissioned Boat Cloak for Queen Elizabeth II, which was subsequently photographed by Cecil Beaton and, later, Annie Leibovitz for *Vanity Fair*.[26]

The complicated interplay between fashion and the military always reaches a crescendo during times of war, when motifs from uniform and even specific battles are adopted into womenswear. The boxy lines of the Second World War are a familiar example from the last century, when the government advocated patriotic Utility dressing and frugal, military-inspired silhouettes became the norm. But the practice stretches back much further, becoming increasingly conspicuous during the Napoleonic Wars from the end of the 18th century.[27] When Vice-Admiral Lord Nelson died in 1805 at the Battle of Trafalgar he was at the height of his fame. France, under Napoleon, and Britain were engaged in series of wars that would continue for another decade, and this was a pivotal battle. Not only did it take Nelson's life, but also the ensuing victory put an end to Napoleon's plans to invade Britain and secured British trade routes. Nelson died a naval hero while waging his most successful campaign and, in the wake of his death, a booming souvenir industry developed, including

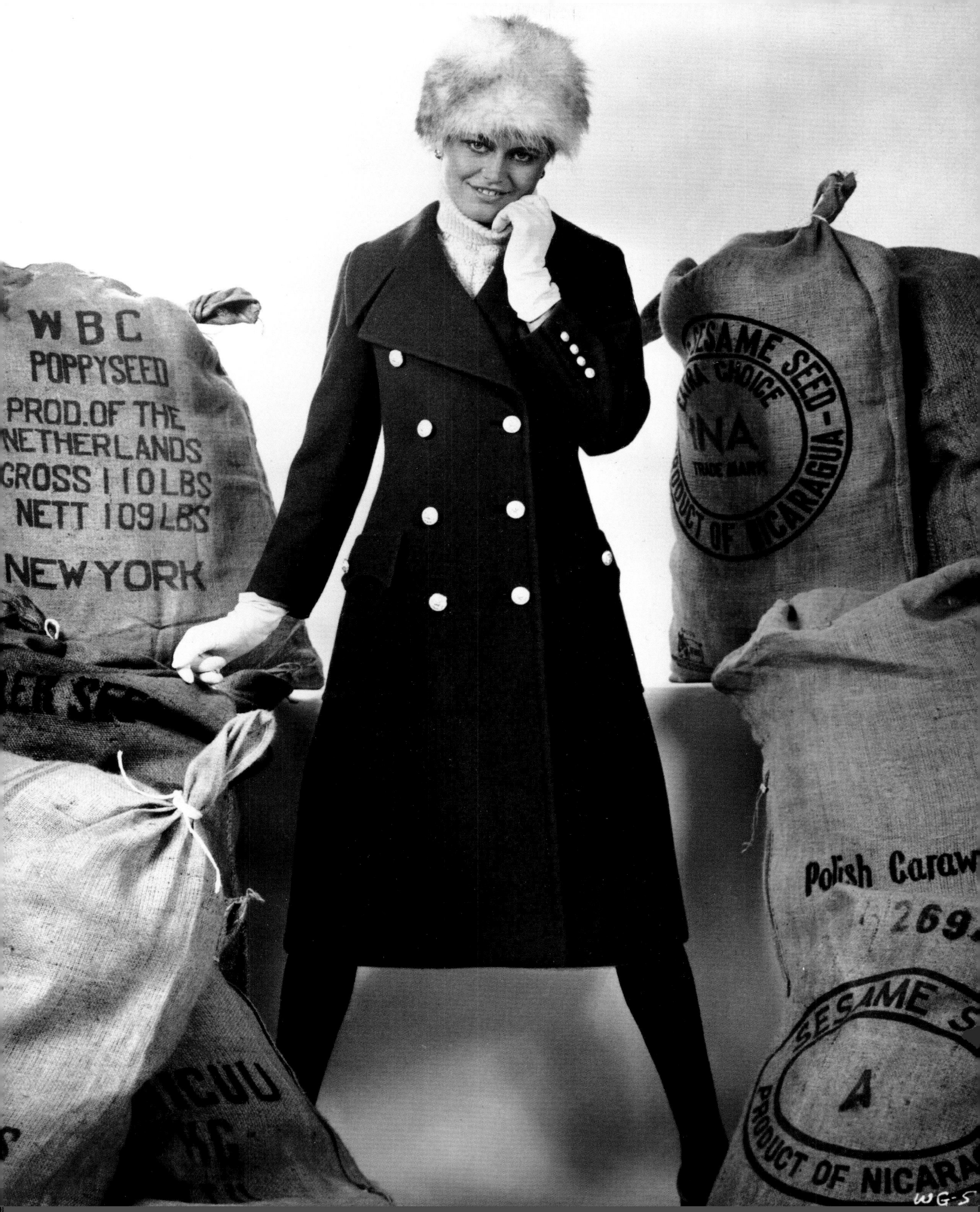
WBC
POPPYSEED
PROD. OF THE
NETHERLANDS
GROSS 110LBS
NETT 109LBS
NEW YORK
SESAME SEED -
INA
TRADE MARK
PRODUCT OF NICARAGUA
A
WG-5

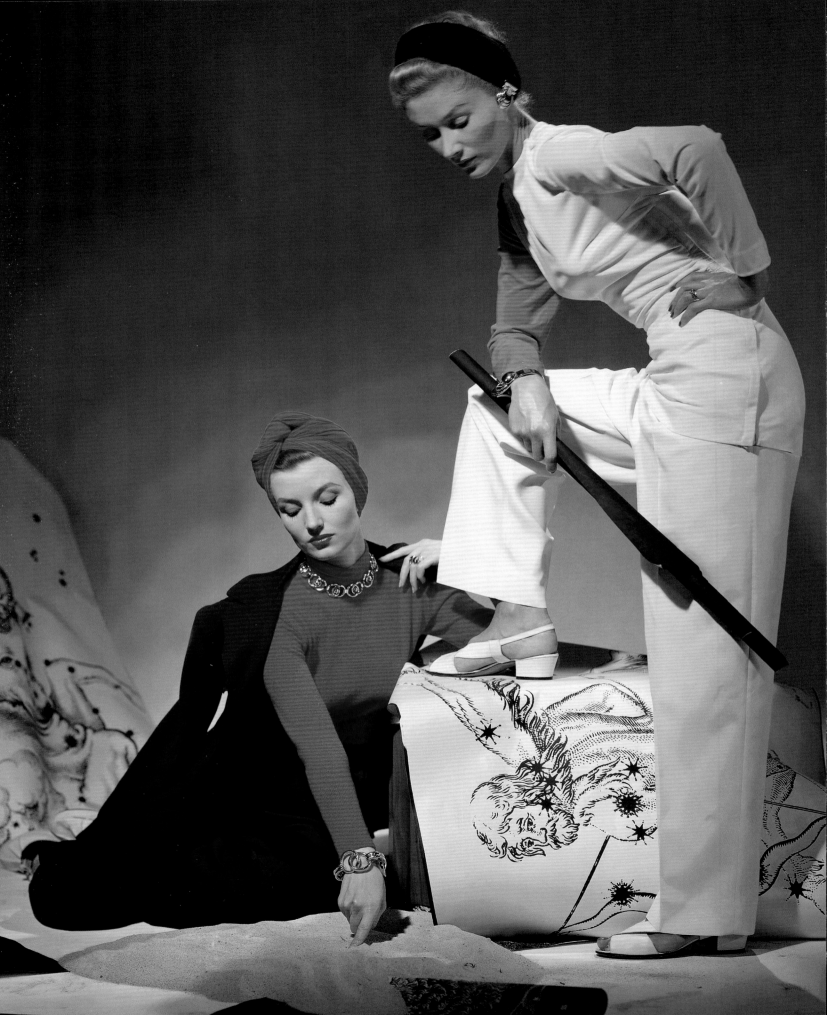

Opposite: *Military precision is softened with turbans and jewelry as naval tailoring is brought into high fashion. Blue whipcord suit (left) and navy uniform with one pink arm and sharkskin slacks (right). Photographed by John Rawlings for US* Vogue, *December 1940.* Right: *Marlene Dietrich was referred to as 'the best dressed man in Hollywood' due to her predilection for wearing formal menswear in her roles. She played a cabaret singer with a penchant for naval officers in* Seven Sinners *(1940).*

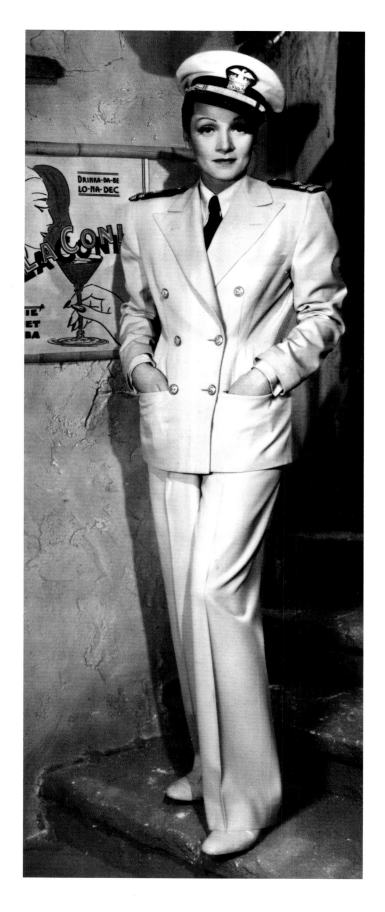

everything from commemorative medals to earthenware jugs and Staffordshire pottery.[28] Having ventured to sea at the age of twelve, a cult of hero worship was spun around Nelson on his death as, in Colin McDowell's words, 'the perfection of masculinity: the romantic man of action'.[29] Textiles played a big part in the commemoration of Nelson. From snuff handkerchiefs to 'Trafalgar chintz' furnishing fabrics, the craze for Nelsoniana was found both on the body and in the home.[30]

One such souvenir is a silk ribbon celebrating Nelson's victory at the Battle of the Nile in 1798. The ribbon is printed with fouled anchors and the insignia and motto for the Order of the Bath, to which Nelson belonged. Ribbons were used throughout the 18th century, worn as trimmings on gowns or hats, or bunched and used as accessories to decorate an outfit. Due to their diminutive size, they were affordable to a wider variety of people; women who couldn't afford Spitalfields silks could afford the printed ribbon equivalent and so could keep abreast of fashion, much like accessories operate for fashion houses today.[31] Other fashion items such as fans were also produced as souvenirs of the victory.[32] Nelson's victory at the Battle of the Nile spurred much interest in Egyptian-influenced clothing and textiles, and this interest was also felt in France. Although France was defeated, the Egyptian campaign affected fashions and resulted in a widespread trend for turbans.[33]

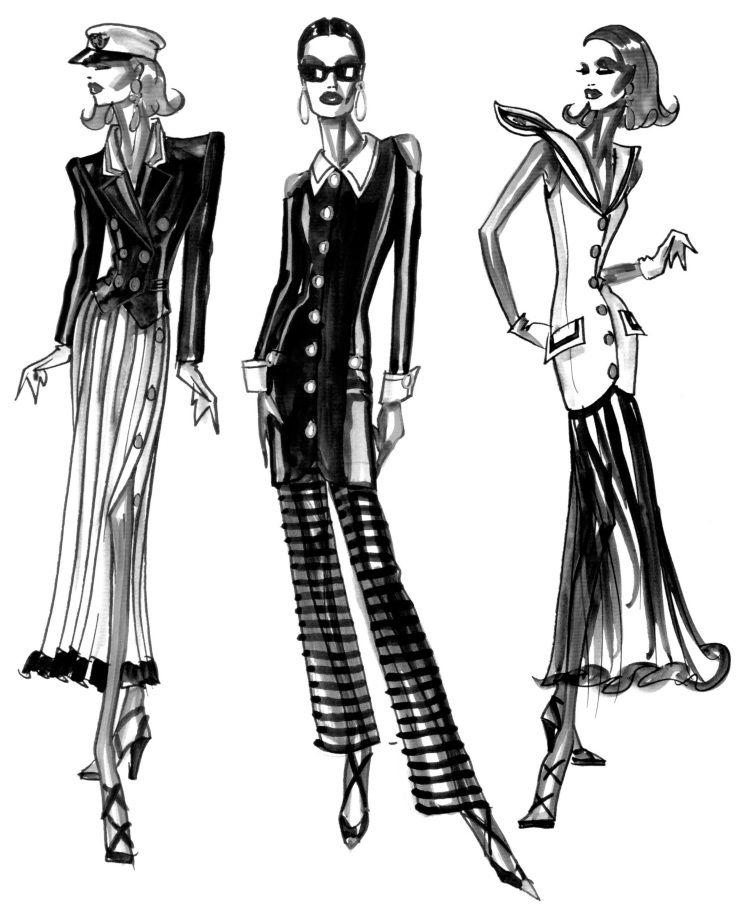

The Napoleonic Wars failed to spark major nautical trends in France, as the officer class of the navy had been somewhat depleted due to the Revolution. This ensured French naval power was reduced in the following years, and military might was found on land rather than at sea. However, Napoleon's reign did have a marked influence on the fashion industry. At the turn of the 19th century, there was a renewed interest in dress, as evident in the birth of the magazine *Journal des Dames et des Modes* in March 1797.[34] When Napoleon came to power in 1799, he sought to bolster the national industry, encouraging textile production as it was vital for the nation's economic, and therefore military, success. At his Imperial court, Napoleon initiated a level of magnificence in dress not seen since before the Revolution. This extended throughout society as he reintroduced uniforms for all officials, creating work in textile centres such as Lyon. The use of gold and silver embroidery and trimmings emphasized that, in post-Revolutionary France, power was still very much equated with decoration.[35]

After Britain's victory in the Napoleonic Wars in 1815, the style conscious adopted 'Waterloo blue' as a fashionable colour, named for the final battle of the conflict.[36] This reappropriation of combat zones into fashionable accoutrements wasn't always met with approval. An *Illustrated London News* article at the time of the Crimean War in 1854 paints a very different picture, 'An attempt was, it is true, made a short time since to bring in "Alma sleeves", and "Inkerman bonbons"; but the public good taste quickly rendered justice to these injudicious novelties.'[37] Relating to battles fought earlier that year, the implication was that transposing military missions into the latest styles bordered on the distasteful. But that didn't stop fashionable women from adopting regimental elements into their ensembles.

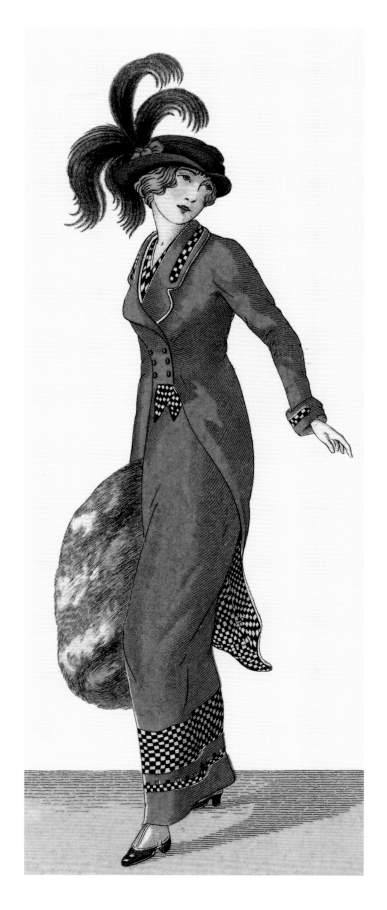

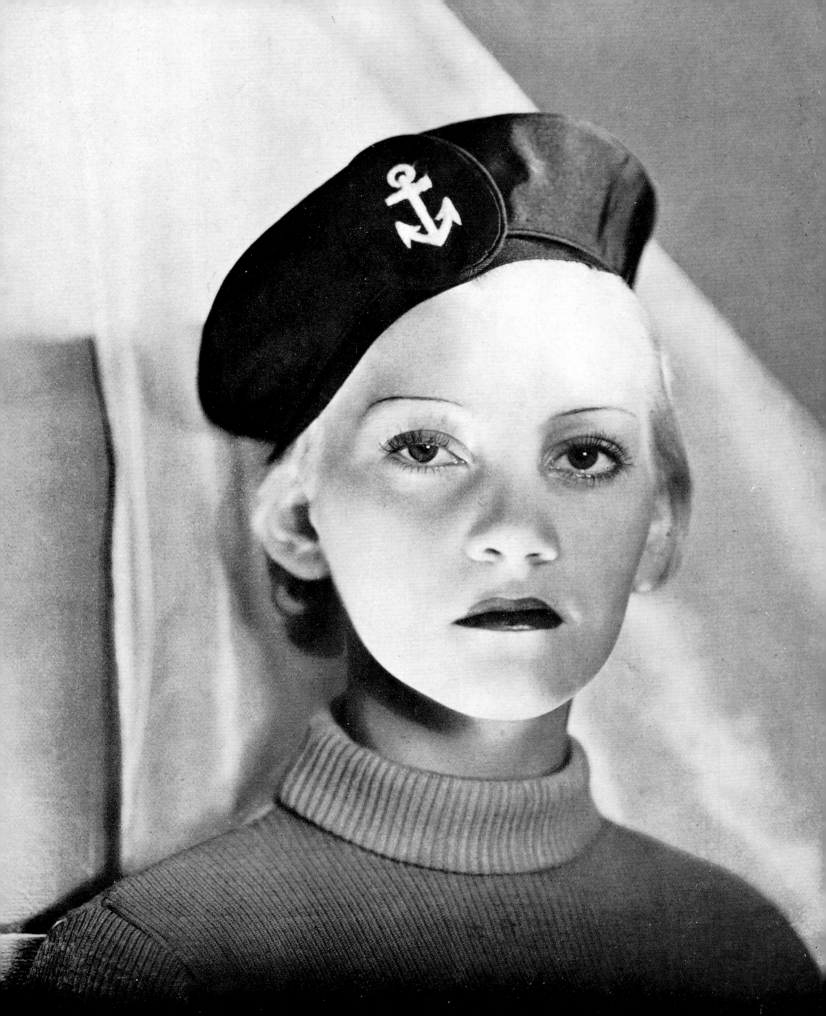

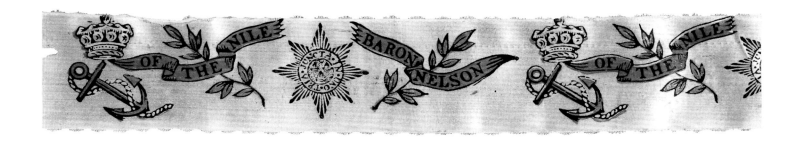

# ACCESSORIES PLUG NAVY THEME

Scarves, pins, bags, bracelets, prints, gloves, clips, necklaces, vests, lipsticks, cigaret cases, cuff links, tiepins— long is the list of accessories which the fashion world calls upon to plug a theme. Shown here are only a handful of the scores of suggestions sent to LIFE by enthusiastic designers. Notable among the omissions (due to space limitations) are fabric prints with ropes and barrels and port-hole parasols (holes around edge), and several scarf designs. Some of them are gay with borders of U. S. Navy flags. Others have centers of battleships and Navy quotations.

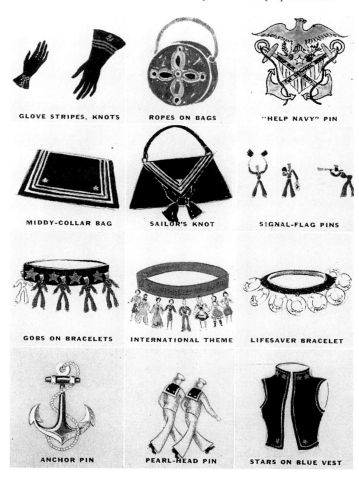

Women had been wearing tailored clothes for riding since the 17th century. The riding habit, or redingote, became a fashion staple in the 18th century, and often incorporated elements such as the mariner's cuff, a feature of captains' and midshipmen's uniforms. The tailored, military lines and square shoulders of British Utility clothing during the Second World War has been well documented,[38] but naval influences were also rife. In an article from 1943, *Life* magazine chronicles 'a popular wartime hat fashion' inspired by General Montgomery's beret, and also notes the 'Pierre', modelled after the French sailor's pompom beret.[39] An earlier issue from 1940 has a four-page article on the naval influence on fashion, featuring everything from clutches embroidered with Admiral's swords to anchor and rope designs to be painted onto stockings with waterproof paint. Boat-adorned belts are emblazoned with suggestive phrases like 'We are ready for a fight or a frolic,' and new colours 'marine olive' and 'Pearl Harbor gray' are noted.[40] The interplay between the navy and fashion is also evident in the uniforms of the Women's Royal Naval Service (WRNS). In 1951, couturier Victor Stiebel was enlisted to design the mess dress, creating a smart long skirt paired with a bolero in black Ottoman rayon.[41]

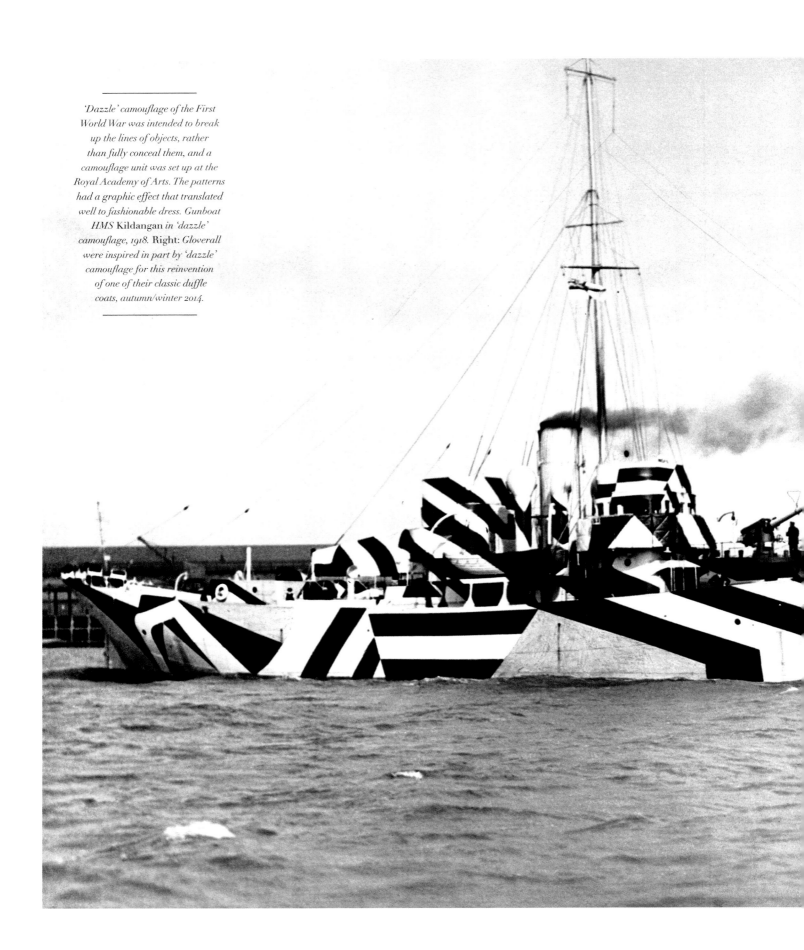

*'Dazzle' camouflage of the First World War was intended to break up the lines of objects, rather than fully conceal them, and a camouflage unit was set up at the Royal Academy of Arts. The patterns had a graphic effect that translated well to fashionable dress. Gunboat* HMS Kildangan *in 'dazzle' camouflage, 1918.* Right: *Gloverall were inspired in part by 'dazzle' camouflage for this reinvention of one of their classic duffle coats, autumn/winter 2014.*

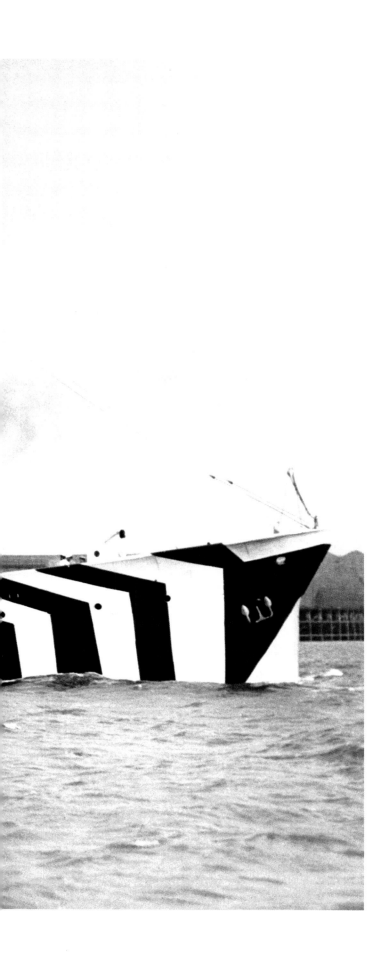

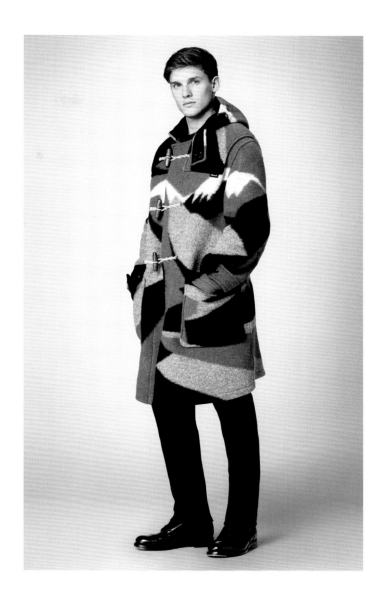

## DAZZLING FASHIONS

The specific circumstances of technology and modern art combined during the First World War, resulting in the first use of camouflage in warfare, and subsequently the earliest instance of it being repurposed for fashionable dress. Advances in aerial photography meant weaponry and vehicles required obscuring from enemy view. In France, the idea was pioneered by Lucien-Victor Guirand de Scévola, a society portraitist who painted canvas sheets to throw over inactive artillery before going on to lead the French camouflage workshop.[42] Britain raised its own camouflage division and, in 1917, the seascape painter Norman Wilkinson led a proposal to the Admiralty for a disruptive pattern that became known as 'dazzle'. The aim of this camouflage was to break up the lines of objects making them harder to hit; creating an optical illusion rather than concealing the target. Many camoufleurs were also modern artists: Vorticism was a big influence on British designs and a camouflage unit was set up at the Royal Academy of Arts.

In 1917, orders were given to paint the entire mercantile marine fleet, each with a unique dazzle pattern.[43] Merchant ships were used during wartime to transport soldiers, as well as import food and materials, so it was vital to disguise them for fear of attack. Ships were decorated in fittingly dazzling designs, in black, white, blue and green colourways, and by the end of the war the American Navy had also 'dazzled' over 1200 of their merchant vessels.[44] Just four months after the armistice, the Chelsea Arts Club in London held their annual summer ball at the Royal Albert Hall. Inspired by the graphic patterns of camouflage – and no doubt by its links to the art world – it was named the Dazzle Ball and this new military design scheme was reflected in the extravagant costumes. Over the next couple of years this motif reappeared on garments and the resulting fashions were reported and syndicated across North America, from Washington to Winnipeg.[45] 'Dazzle hats' graced heads in London,

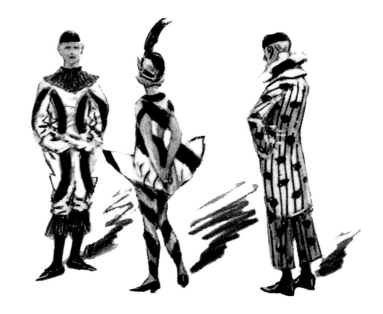

Above and opposite, above: *Held at the Albert Hall, the Dazzle Ball featured incredible graphic costumes inspired by the camouflage of the First World War and reminiscent of* Commedia dell'arte *costume. The paper reported, 'During the evening a shower of "bombs" in the shape of coloured balloons descended on the devoted heads of the dancers, and added greatly to the hilarity of the occasion.' From 'The Art of Naval "Camouflage" Applied to Fancy Dress: The Chelsea Arts Club "Dazzle Ball"' in the* Illustrated London News, *22 March 1919.*

Opposite, below: *Dazzling fashions. 'The camouflage bathing suit has made its appearance in England and has excited attention if not admiration.' 'Dazzle' swimsuits in Margate, from the* New York Sun, *15 June 1919.*

while bold dazzle swimwear, imported from the shorelines of Britain, proved especially popular on the beaches of Coney Island, New York. The garish patterns were a popular topic, as the *New-York Tribune* wryly observed, 'The newest things in bathing suits brighten the beach at Margate, England. The "dazzle" designs of gayest hue defeat the usual purpose of camouflage, that of promoting low visibility.'[46]

The graphic patterns of dazzle camouflage continue to inspire. London-based designer Christopher Raeburn repurposes surplus fabrics in an original take on military chic. He began creating anoraks and parkas from British Army parachute silk, and has since taken inspiration from the Maunsell Forts (Second World War naval defences), 1950s flight escape maps and Siberian army officers. His spring/summer 2011 'Dazzle' collection looked to this distinctive form of naval camouflage. Dazzle camouflage also provided the inspiration for the patterns on Gloverall's autumn/winter 2014 duffle coats, the duffle coat being yet another item with naval origins.

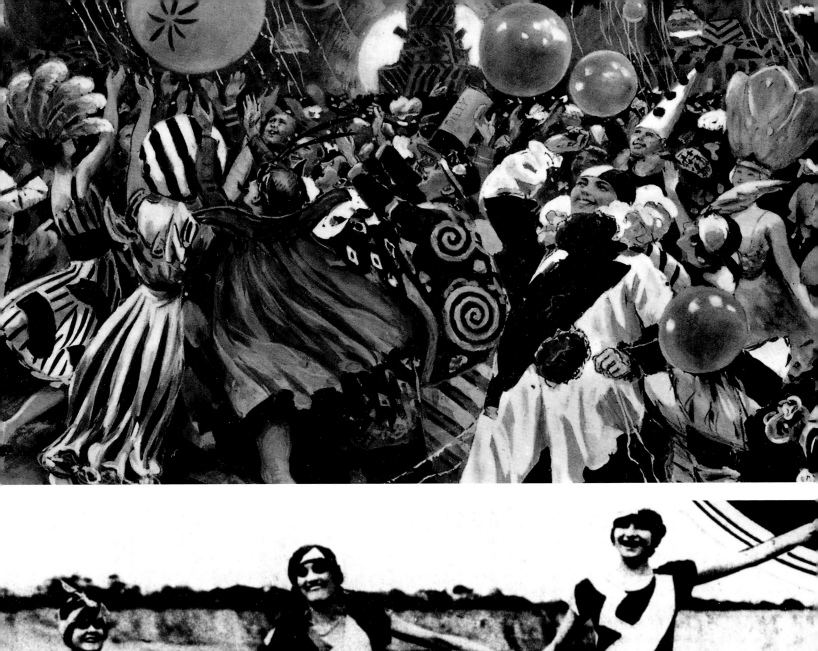
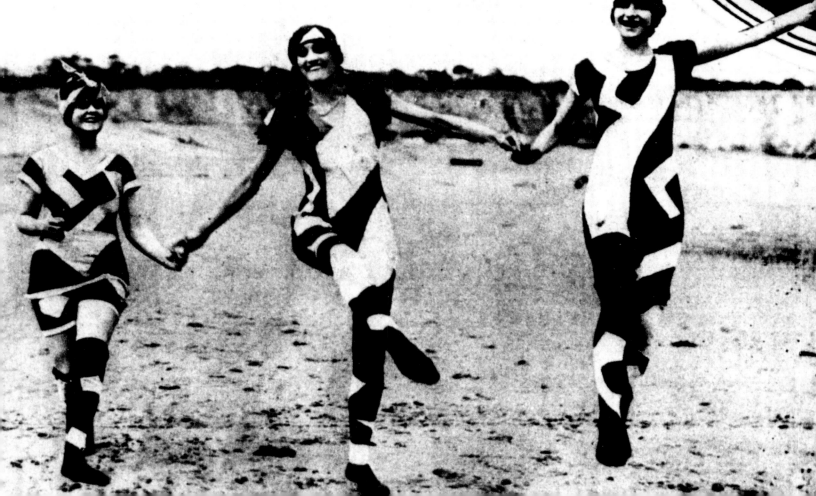

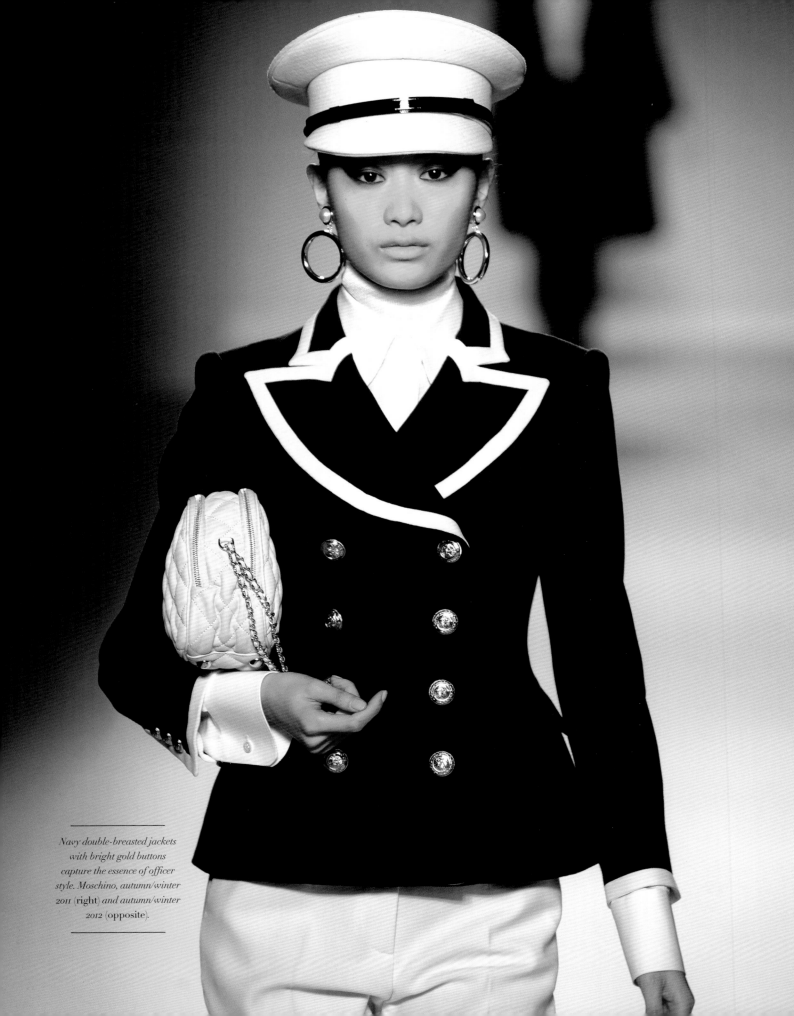

*Navy double-breasted jackets with bright gold buttons capture the essence of officer style. Moschino, autumn/winter 2011 (right) and autumn/winter 2012 (opposite).*

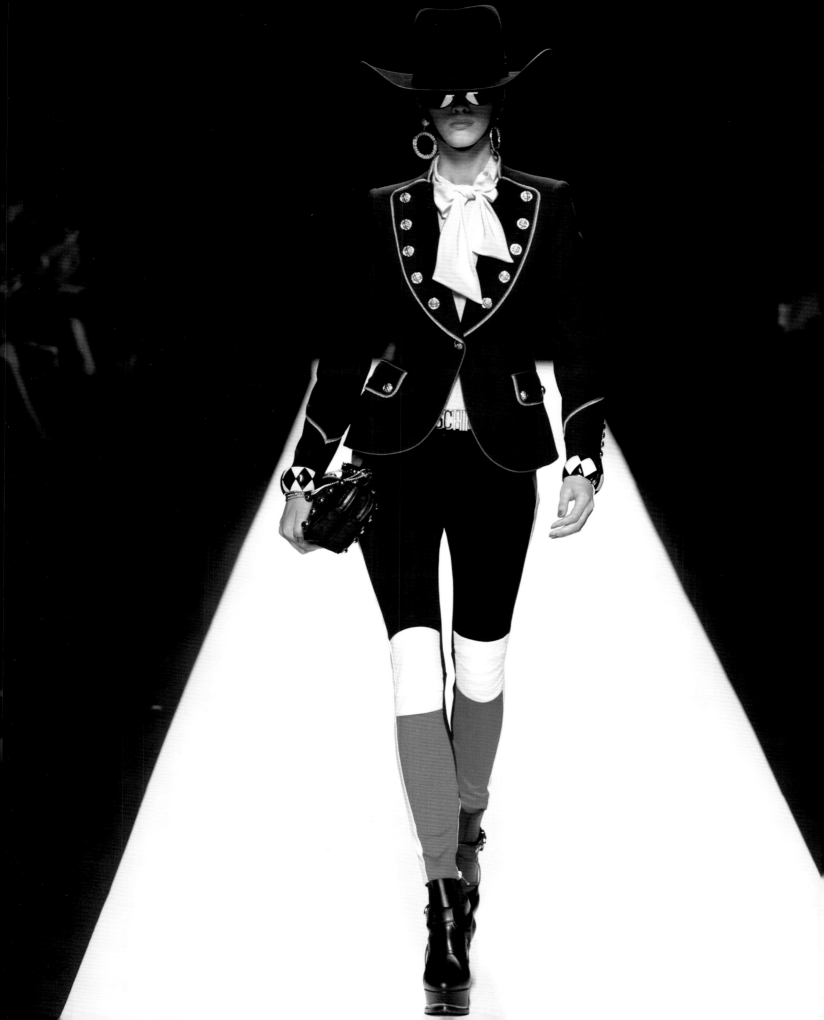

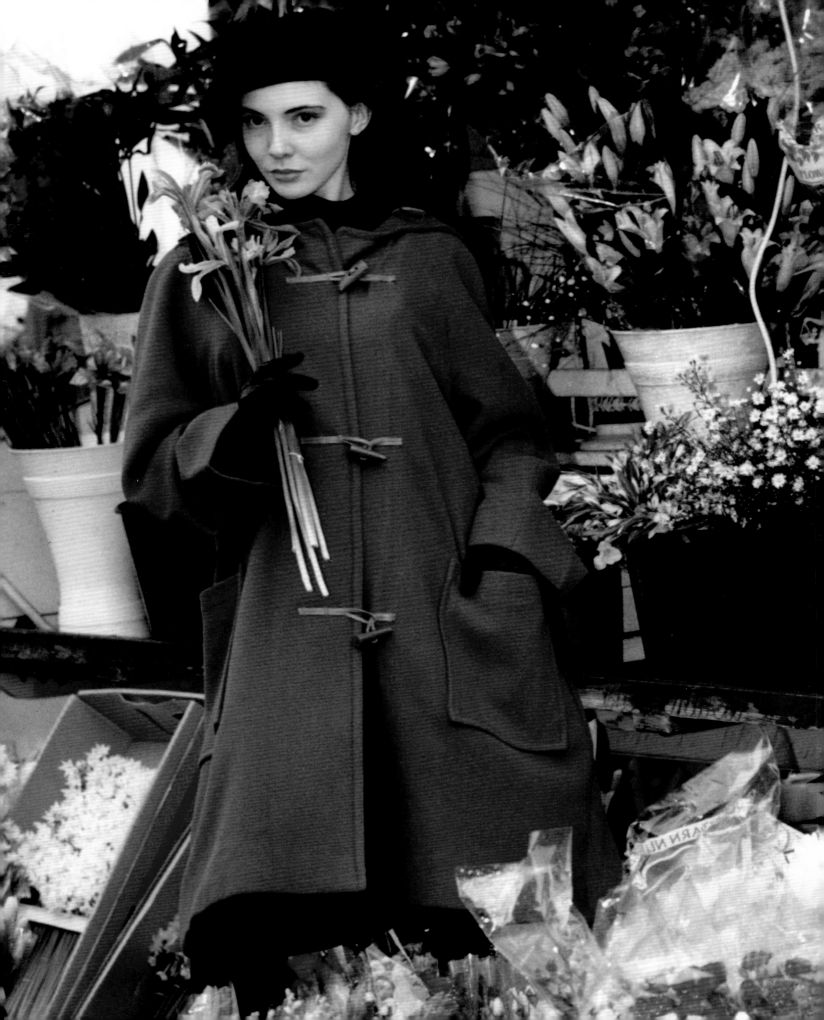

## UTILITARIAN CLASSIC: THE DUFFLE COAT

In the 1890s, the Ideal Clothing Company (now called Original Montgomery) began making duffle coats to a design specified by the Admiralty, which the company later adapted.[47] The coats were provided in loose sizes so they could be commandeered by any seamen, pulled on over the uniform when temperatures dipped. Not initially an officer's item, during the First World War the duffle's popularity spread to officers in the army and the Royal Flying Corps, despite the fact that the distinctive toggle fastening, patch pockets and hood were much more utilitarian than the slim tailored lines associated with officer's dress coats. During the Second World War the duffle was taken up by Field Marshal Montgomery, still one of the coat's most well-known wearers. After the war, the duffle quickly made the journey from military issue to civilian fashion.

British company Gloverall was founded in 1951 by Harold and Freda Morris, who had previously run an industrial clothing specialist that sold items including gloves and overalls. After the Korean War, they were approached by the Ministry of Defence to sell ex-war department duffle coats. Due to their success, they began making their own version in 1954, adapting the design to streamline it for a civilian market. They also replaced the wood and rope fastening with horn and leather toggles. The availability of cheap surplus duffle coats made them a popular choice for students in the 1950s, and they quickly became associated with left-wing politics, especially after they were worn by protesters at the Campaign for Nuclear Disarmament marches in the 1950s. This connection, coupled with their traditional use as an enlisted men's item that was adopted by officers, led to the duffle becoming a symbol of resistance to authority; a countercultural item that offered a show of solidarity with working men, allegedly one of the reasons that Jean Cocteau was a fan. At this point, it also crossed the Atlantic to become a college campus favourite in the States, helped along by John F. Kennedy who wore one for winter sailing.

In 1987, the Ideal Clothing Company changed its name to Original Montgomery in honour of the centenary of Field Marshal Montgomery's birth. They continue to make their duffle coats in the UK. Gloverall have recently undertaken a variety of collaborations to produce updated versions of the duffle for a fashion-forward customer. Vivienne Westwood, YMC, Fred Perry, J.Crew, and Junya Watanabe have all given the classic design their own twist, while an alliance with Gieves & Hawkes produced a coat along more traditional naval lines. The company shows at men's fashion week in London and, for autumn/winter 2014, head designer Mark van Beek explored the brand's heritage, finding inspiration in images of protest marches, as well as looking at 'dazzle' camouflage.[48]

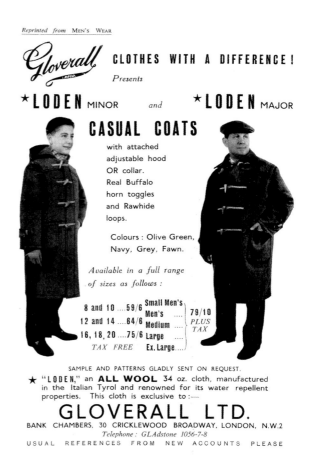

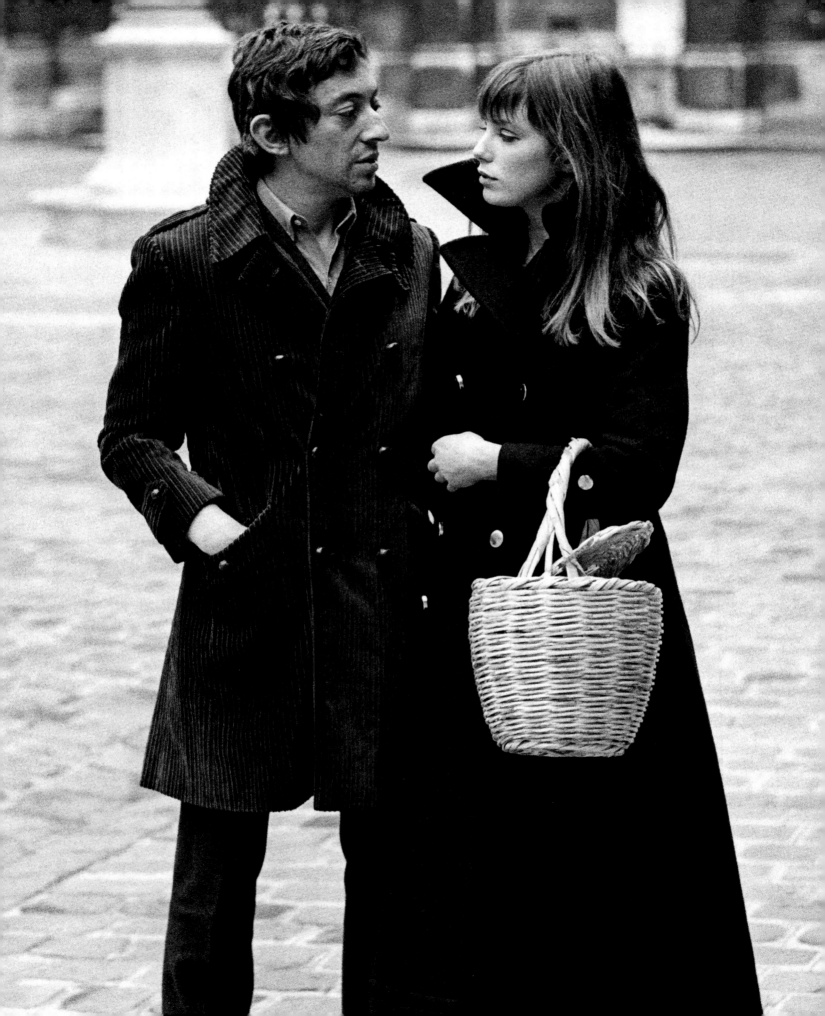

## ELITE TO STREET STYLE: THE PEA COAT

For all the militaristic obsessions that the fashion world has, no one garment has passed into the annuls of chic essentials quite like the pea coat. The origins of the term are difficult to pin down, but there is general agreement that 'pea' refers to the type of coarse twilled blue cloth that was used, either named '*pij*' in Dutch, or 'pilot' in English.[49] This type of garment dates back to the first half of the 18th century, and featured in navy lists in the *London Gazette* as early as 1757,[50] while it can be found in American uniform for officers from 1841.[51] Today, Sterlingwear of Boston and Schott NYC, contractors to the American Navy, sell their pea coats to civilians for customers looking for authentic naval style. The pea coat's transition from seafaring life to style staple occurred in 1962. Just two years before, Yves Saint Laurent had been sacked from Christian Dior for his radical designs. Keen to bring fashion into the modern age he set up his own business, with Pierre Bergé as a partner. The first collection, spring/summer 1962, showed the *caban* as a star piece: a pea coat with gilt buttons which, in its original form, had been added to the uniform lists of the French Navy in 1845.[52]

Typifying his attitude towards style, Yves Saint Laurent took the functional nature of the garment and translated it for chic Left Bank bohemians, as epitomized by Serge Gainsbourg and Jane Birkin, who were often photographed in matching pea coats. The nautical theme became a recurrent motif for Saint Laurent: the costumes he designed for Catherine Deneuve in *Belle de Jour* (released 1967) also drew on naval style, featuring double-breasted boxy coats and epaulettes, inspired by a trip to Kaufman's Army & Navy surplus store in New York.[53] Military surplus pea coats had been worn as a cheap option by students, much like the duffle. This also fed into Saint Laurent's summer 1966 collection that featured a sailor's smock, pants and cap and a recreation of the *caban* as an afternoon dress.[54] Later that year he opened his Rive Gauche prêt-à-porter boutique on the Left Bank, heralding his desire to democratize fashion and the beginning of the ready-to-wear revolution. Couture would never be the same again, and a style classic was born.

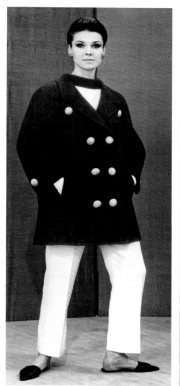 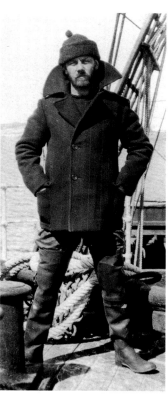

Opposite: *Singer and songwriter Serge Gainsbourg with singer and actress Jane Birkin adding Left Bank chic to the pea coat's increasingly bohemian image. Paris, 1969.*

Above, left: *The first Yves Saint Laurent* caban *pea coat, haute couture autumn/winter 1962.* Above, right: *The pea coat in action – here a single-breasted model. Crewmember W.F. Howard on board RRS* Discovery, 28 December 1930.

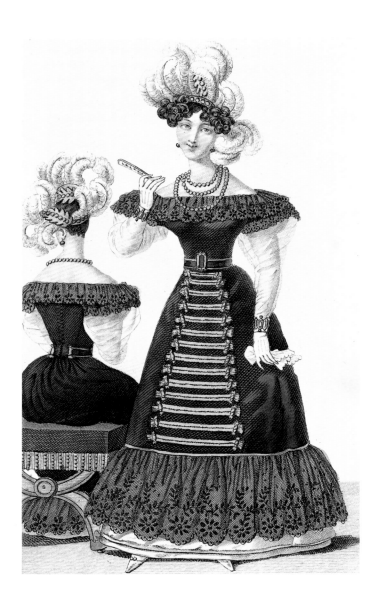

Above: *The use of gold braiding
as decoration has a long history of
crossing into fashionable women's
wear, here in a velvet dress with
blonde lace. Paris fashions in*
Petit Courrier des Dames,
*illustrated by Julie Ribault, 1827.*
Opposite: *Black wool jacket with
gold bullion cord, again showing
the Hussar influence as well as
the naval officer. Alexander
McQueen's 'Dante' collection,
autumn/winter 1996.*

## THE CONTEMPORARY OFFICER

Officer style remains immediately recognizable through
strict tailoring and ornamentation, elements that continue to
be referenced on the runway. Tailoring was brought to the
catwalk by Alexander McQueen in a characteristic mix of cut,
embellishment, and historical detail. In 1984, McQueen served
two years of an apprenticeship at Savile Row tailor Anderson
& Sheppard, and the techniques of the trade informed his
work for the rest of his life. He later worked for bespoke tailor
Koji Tatsuno specifically to learn how to cut a frock coat, an
item that would become a signature of McQueen's work.[55]
The use of tailoring to enhance the body, so intrinsic to the
officer aesthetic, held much interest for McQueen, who spoke
of using cut 'to draw attention to our unrelenting desire for
perfection'.[56] Items influenced by menswear tailoring featured
in his 'Joan' collection from autumn/winter 1998, alluding to
Joan of Arc's cross-dressing. Meanwhile, for autumn/winter
1996's 'Dante' collection, inspired by the poet, McQueen used
traditional skills to create a modern aesthetic, including a coat
cut along exaggerated military lines, made of black wool felt
embroidered with gold bullion cord. Naval looks were later
deconstructed in Nicolas Ghesquière's spring/summer 2005
Balenciaga collection, where experimentation with tailoring
resulted in fluid sailor-style trousers finished with gold braiding.
Navy was the predominant colour and multi-layered dresses
were edged with gold buttons, magnifying the links between
fashionable dress and the trappings of insignia. For Givenchy's
ready-to-wear autumn/winter 2007 collection, Riccardo Tisci
took a 1920s Japanese marine jacket as his inspiration, and
the resulting collection featured fishtail hems and deep pile fur
in dark blue, aligning naval uniform with luxe opulence. The
combination of sharpness of cut and glitzy ornamentation that
is central to officer's naval uniform remains a runway favourite,
and provides a template for addressing and reworking themes
of wealth, power and prestige within fashionable dress.

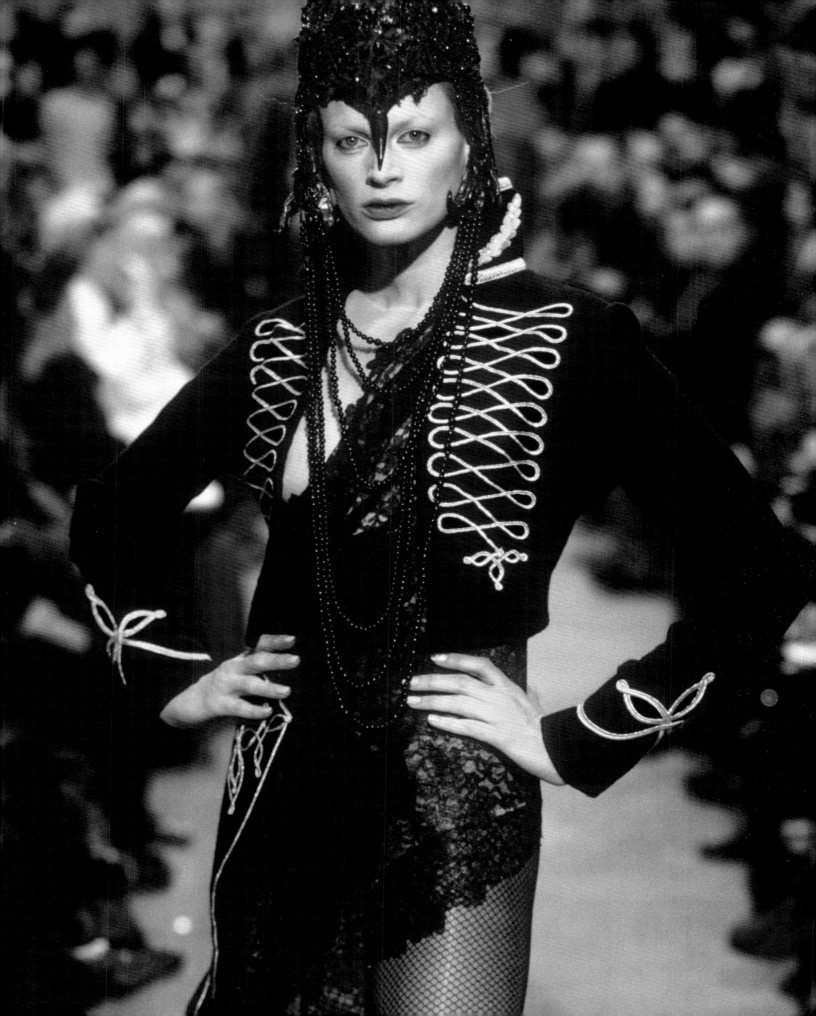

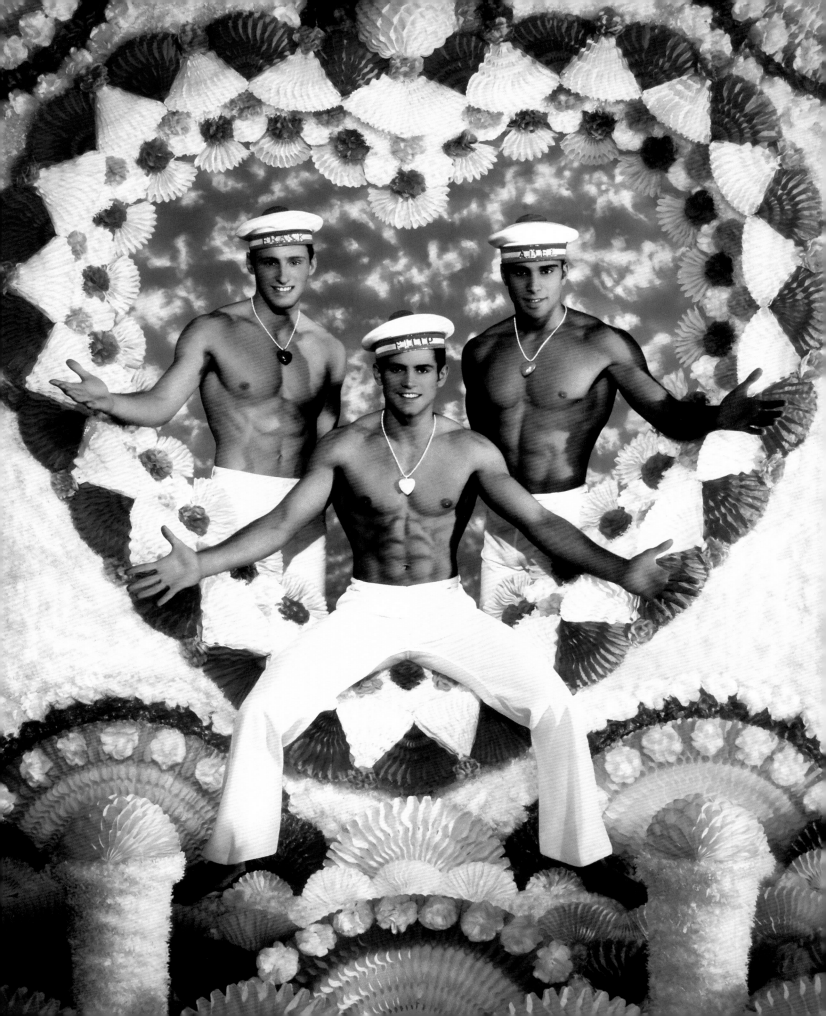

# CHAPTER 2

# THE SAILOR

The Sailor is a transient character, remodelled for each era. He has been both a 19th-century hero and a hypermasculine gay icon. The iconic sailor suit has been reimagined on the catwalk by designers as diverse as Chanel, Jean Paul Gaultier, Yohji Yamamoto, Mary Quant and Dior, each drawing on the mutable legacy and timeless appeal of sailor style.

'As for me, I am tormented with an everlasting itch for things remote. I love to sail forbidden seas, and land on barbarous coasts.'

HERMAN MELVILLE, *MOBY-DICK; OR, THE WHALE*, 1851[1]

The fashion world has flirted endlessly with the nautical motifs of the sailor suit since its adoption into womenswear in the 1870s. Elements of seamen's uniform such as the square collar and the anchor motif were featured in the fashions of *The Queen* magazine and on the pages of *Punch*. Sailor chic was given the royal stamp of approval when Princess Alexandra, the future Queen Consort of the United Kingdom, wore a sailor-inspired suit to Cowes yachting week in 1884. Olympia Le-Tan's spring/summer 2014 collection featured the 'timeless and chic' sailor suit and celebrated life on the ocean waves, with inspirations drawn from the uniforms at the US Naval Academy in Rhode Island and Portsmouth in the UK.[2] Design houses as disparate as Chanel, Lanvin, Mary Quant, Givenchy, D&G, Laura Ashley, Jean Paul Gaultier, Yohji Yamamoto, Miu Miu, Dior, Kenzo and Schiaparelli have repurposed the sailor suit. The sailor is ripe for conjuring up a rich host of associations, ranging from maritime adventures to rugged masculinity and homoerotic kitsch.

Page 48: *The sailor is a perennial feature in the photography of Pierre et Gilles, who frame the rugged sailor's torso within a kitsch aesthetic to create a camp spectacle.* Vive le marine, *1997.* Opposite: *This satirical cartoon from* Punch *magazine mixes the Ballets Russes with sailing at Cowes, and also highlights the tightness of sailor trousers, 1934.*

## UNIFORM AND UNIFORMITY

The humble British sailor had to wait for over a century from the regulation of officer's uniform before his own dress was standardized in 1857. However, certain styles and items could immediately mark out a seafaring man.[3] Short coats were worn, as opposed to the more hazardous tailcoats that could get caught in the rigging, and the 'tarring' (early attempts at waterproofing) of items from rope to clothing and pigtails gave the British sailor the nickname Jack Tar. But it was really the slop chest that led to a degree of uniformity for sailors in many European navies. The practice of the slop chest – ready-made clothes available on board to replace garments that had worn out – was also a feature of life at sea for French and American navies and, in Britain, dates back to the 17th century.[4] The original supplies consisted of a number of items still associated with maritime life, including red caps, blue neck-cloths and blue wool jackets. The availability of these items – paid for from the sailor's own pocket – ensured that a mariner's working uniform had a loose uniformity even before it was centrally regulated. However, it was the captain of the ship who officially determined the uniform of his crew, and he was free to indulge his own idiosyncrasies if he was prepared to foot the bill. A notable case was A.P. Eardley-Wilmot, who was appointed Commander of the *Harlequin* in 1851 and didn't miss this sterling opportunity to deck out the crew of his gig boat as 'multi-coloured Harlequins'.[5] While this practice was likely limited to the gig boat (essentially a taxi to take the captain to and from the main ship) rather than the full crew, stunts like this fed into the idea that working seamen should have a regulated uniform alongside their officers.

Official sailor's uniform was established in Britain in 1857 and it was fully standardized in France the following year. In reality, it regulated what was already the norm on many ships. Based on the uniform of Queen Victoria's Royal Yacht, the British uniform included a blue serge frock and trousers, as well as a summer uniform of white cotton with square 'sailor' collar, ever since the ultimate marker of the seaman.[6] Sailors on board the Royal Yacht were more uniform in appearance than the majority of seamen, due to the prestige of their ship and the presence of royalty. Their summer garb had been immortalized a decade earlier in a portrait by Winterhalter

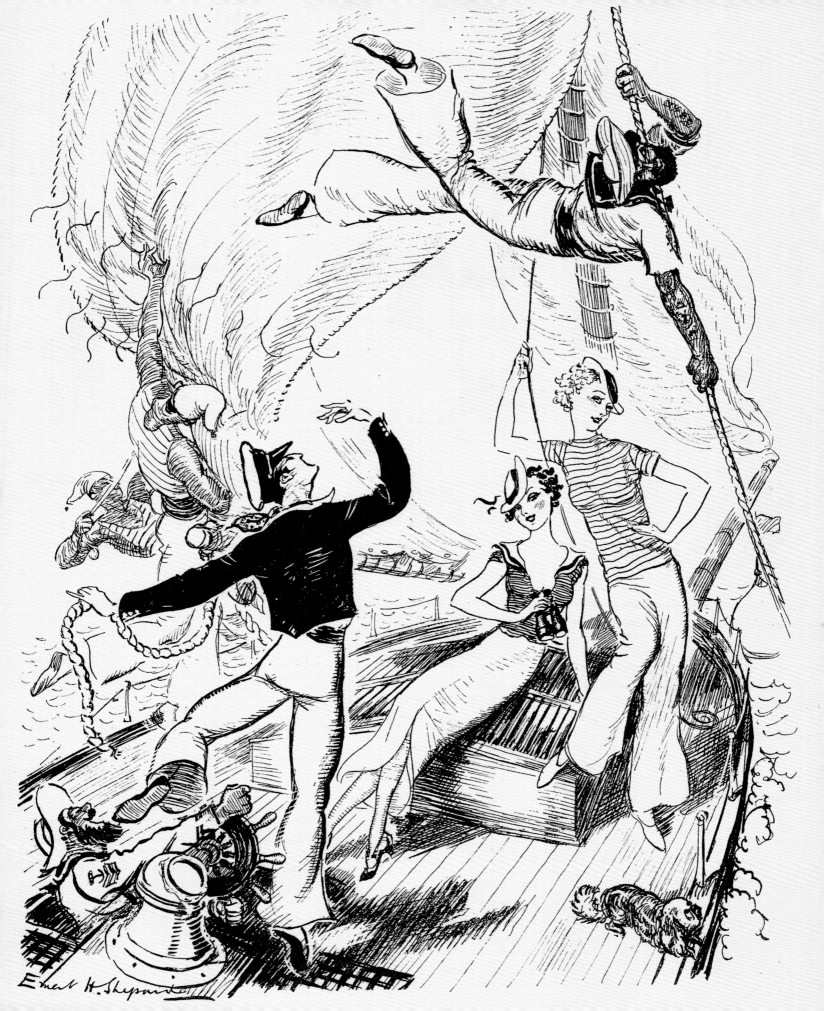

of Queen Victoria's son, Prince Albert (later Edward VII) aged four, wearing a replica outfit created by the ship's tailor. By the 1860s, the practice of dressing children in sailor suits was spreading rapidly.[7] The sailor suit for children has remained a popular choice across the world in many contexts, from Japanese school uniform to Catholic First Communion ceremonies and page boys at Christian weddings.

The iconic square collar has somewhat murky origins. While forerunners have been traced back to the 17th century,[8] the collar as we know it began to take its distinctive shape in the late 18th century.[9] Various myths about the collar persisted: the three rows of tape at the edge of the collar were believed to symbolize Nelson's sea victories, while the black silk handkerchief worn at the neck was attributed to mourning for Nelson's death.[10] Neither of these accounts is true: the Admiralty considered having two rows of tape instead of three, while the black neckerchief actually predates Nelson. Similar myths regarding naval uniform have circulated the world over. There was briefly a theory that the same black silk necktie in American sailor's kit was introduced to commemorate the Spanish-American War of 1898 when, in reality, it took its lead from British uniform.[11] By the mid-19th century, the square sailor collar was a powerful symbol of seafaring life at a time when imperial expansion and naval domination were intrinsic to British national identity. The easily identifiable collar became a symbol used throughout 19th-century visual culture, as both the defining feature of the sailor, and concurrently a key detail that crossed into children's clothing and women's fashion.

Above: *Scenes depicting the sailor's return were reproduced on a myriad of cultural products. Hand-coloured lithograph, c. 1847.* Opposite: *The square collar has at various times symbolized innocence, heroism and homoeroticism. Here Jennifer Garner wears a Yohji Yamamoto sailor blouse, photographed by Gilles Bensimon for* American Elle, *January 2007.*

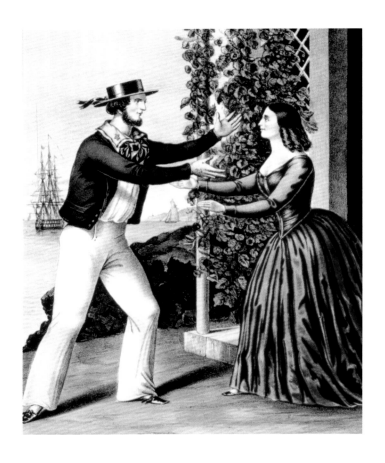

## THE HEROIC SAILOR

By the time details of the sailor suit began to cross over into fashionable women's dress in the 1870s, the sailor had gone through a necessary rebrand – to use modern parlance – both professionally and socially. The 18th-century seaman was seen as untrustworthy, philandering and uncouth. His low social status, the abundance of grog on board and the old cliché of 'a girl in every port' was a reputation that was hard to shake, as laid out in the ballad 'Advice to Young Maidens in Chusing of Husbands':

> *You pretty maids of Greenwich, of high and low degree,*
> *Pray never fix your fancies on men that go to sea…*
> *For up and down in sea-port town they court both old and young:*
> *They will deceive; do not believe the sailor's flattering tongue.*[12]

This changed as the 19th century rolled around. Throughout the early part of the century, British sailors were still employed on a per-voyage basis, hired as a ship was fitted for service and let go on its return. Press-ganging

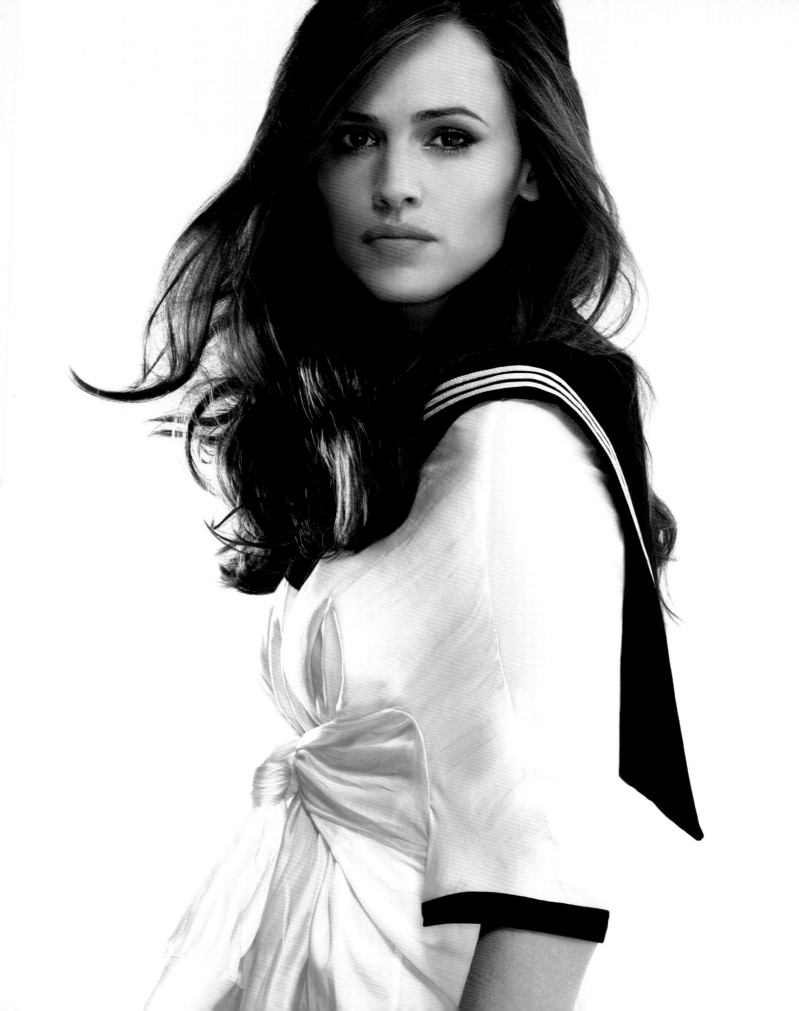

sailors for work – the coercing of men to join – was no longer acceptable. The French system had always been far more reliant on enlisting men and, as this idea spread to the Royal Navy, fleets had to be manned through recruitment campaigns rather than force. This, along with the growing imperial zeal in Britain, led to an image overhaul for the sailor that included uniform regulation. The culture industries were quick to help out, and countless paintings and prints were produced depicting saccharine scenes such as the sailor's return, which helped to domesticate the bawdy seaman. The sailor became a popular figure in advertising, used to add a rugged dependability to products, and simultaneously the idealized sailor was exploited by authors and artists, potters, journalists and music halls.[13] The image of the sailor as national saviour was thoroughly cemented during times of crisis. During the conflict arising from the British occupation of Alexandria in July 1882, over the vital trade route of the Suez Canal, it is not the bright, glitzy regalia of officer's uniforms that shines through on successive front covers of the *Illustrated London News*, but the bearded sailor in square collar and bell-bottoms who is shown leading Britain to victory.[14]

It was not long after this that the humble T-shirt crossed over from nautical to civilian life. In 1913, a white knit short-sleeved undershirt was adopted into the US Navy regulations, including a collarless 'crew' neckline and short sleeves.[15] Earlier versions had been worn by the Oxford and Cambridge rowing teams.[16] By the Second World War, such undergarments were mandatory across all branches of the military and, by the 1950s, this early version of 'underwear as outerwear' was given credence by Marlon Brando and James Dean, those Hollywood symbols of blue-collar cool and teen rebellion.

Above: *A postcard series showing actress Gabrielle Ray in the French sailor suit was produced to coincide with the musical comedy* Lady Madcap *(1905). The show featured a routine celebrating the* Entente Cordiale *signed between Britain and France in 1904.* Opposite: *Nautical beach fashions in* The Queen, *1875 (right) and 1881 (left). The sailor hat, collar and anchor are all evident in this illustration from* Punch, *1871 (centre).*

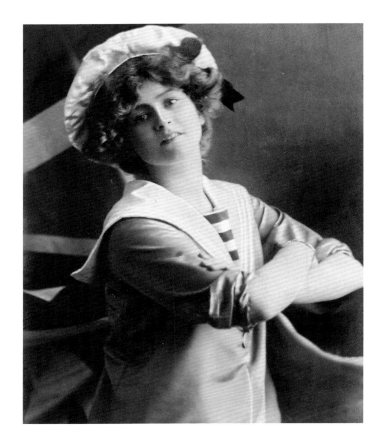

## THE SAILOR ON SHOW

As the sailor collar was increasingly incorporated into women's fashions, the uniform was being exploited for subversive potential by male impersonators of the 19th-century music halls. Novelist and performer Colette trod the boards dressed as a sailor in France, while in Britain – whether Bessie Bonehill in the 1870s or Hetty King singing 'All the Nice Girls Love a Sailor' in 1909 – the masculine nature and physical attributes of the sailor became a favourite subject for many performers looking to cross-dress on stage.[17] If women portraying sailors served to highlight the gendered nature of uniform, creating a transgressive sexual allure along the way,[18] more conventional portrayals also marked the sailor as a popular character on the stage, from Gilbert and Sullivan's smash-hit comic opera *H.M.S. Pinafore* (1878) to *The Marriage Market*, which debuted in London in 1913 and took place on the fashionable space of a yacht. The trend for actresses dressing in sailor garb was followed through into Hollywood with showgirl stars like Clara Bow appearing in *True to the Navy* (1930) and Ruby Keeler in *Shipmates Forever* (1935).

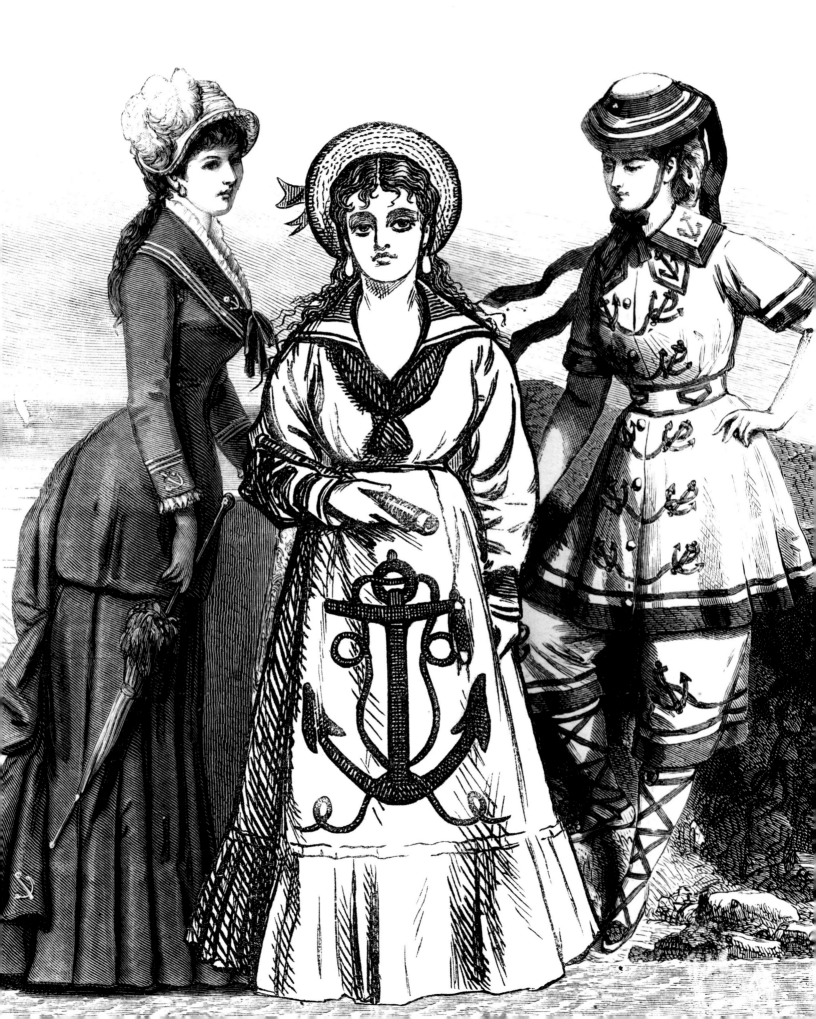

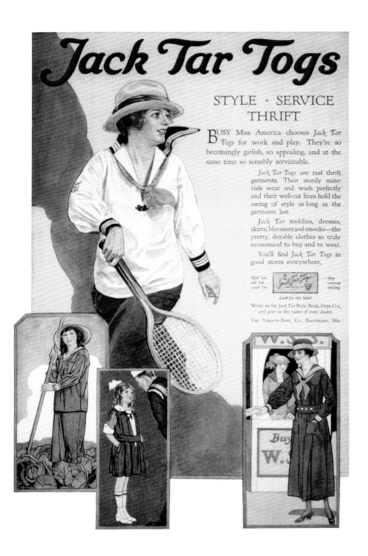

Above: 'They're so becomingly girlish, so appealing, and at the same time so sensibly serviceable.' The middy blouse in action: 'Jack Tar Togs' advertisement in Ladies' Home Journal, *1919*. Opposite: *The sailor suit as school uniform is referenced in this 'Cruisin' for a Brusin'' spread photographed by Matthew Frost for* Jalouse *magazine, April 2011.*

## THE MIDDY BLOUSE

Named for 'midshipman', the middy blouse was a smock-like sailor top with a square collar. First worn for tennis and other sporting pursuits, it became a popular feature of women's fashion in America. The adoption of the sailor collar into sportswear was prolific throughout fledgling women's basketball teams and gymnasiums towards the end of the 19th century, and these increased as more women were admitted to colleges. The middy blouse was established as leisure and sportswear by around 1910, and took on a patriotic air during the First World War when the sailor collar and colour scheme of red, white and blue signified a loyalty to the allied fighters. The sleek lines, dropped waist and hint of athleticism of the blouse later chimed perfectly with the modernity of 1920s fashions. The transition from sportswear to fashion is highlighted in a 1916 *Toronto World* advertisement which noted, 'The plain, practical regulation middy Blouse, like the brook, goes on forever, but starting with its simple lines as a base, Fashion has made hitherto undreamed of discoveries as to its possibilities.'[19] Middies are listed in an array of colours, rendered in 'washing silks' as well as utilitarian cottons. During this decade, the middy also became a college campus favourite, many companies launching their own 'collegiate' version.[20] Variations in fabric and trim allowed for seasonal changes, and the loose fitting shape ensured it was viable for early mass-manufacture.[21] The middy was advertised in fashionable publications like *Vogue* and *Town and Country*, and a 1924 patent for a convertible 'Two-In-One' middy assured wearers the garment could be worn loose for sports and leisure or cinched and belted, 'suitable even for formal occasions'.[22] The ultimate fashion accolade came in May 1925, when Edward Steichen photographed Ilka Chase, actress and daughter of *Vogue*'s editor-in-chief, Edna Woolman Chase, in a Lanvin polka dot dress with a large, white lace, scalloped collar reminiscent of the middy blouse.

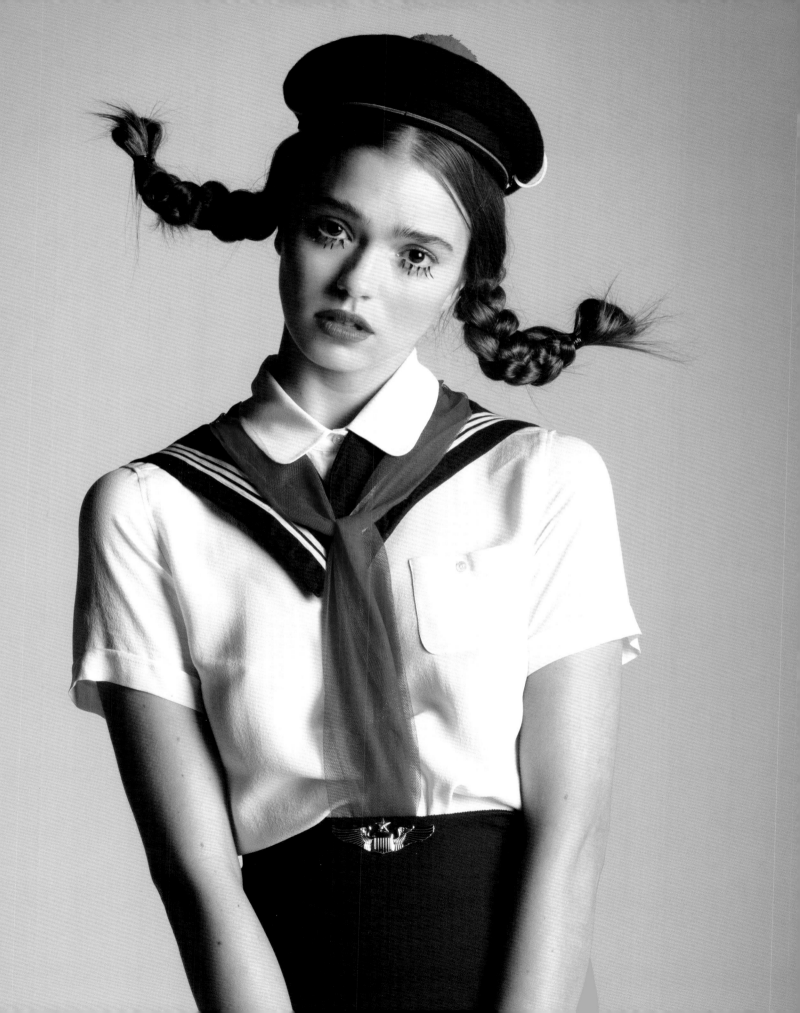

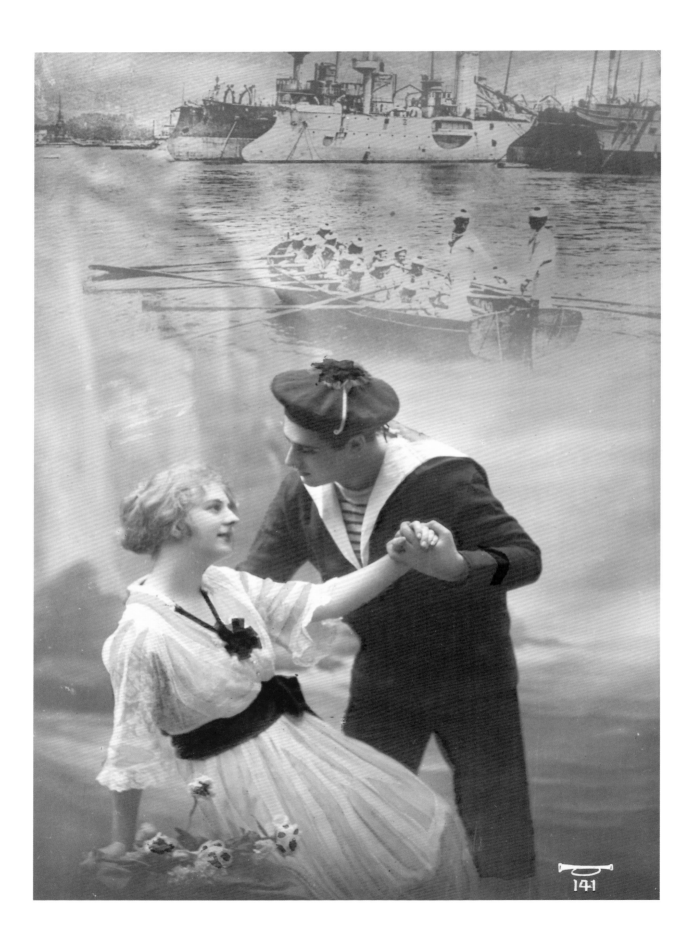

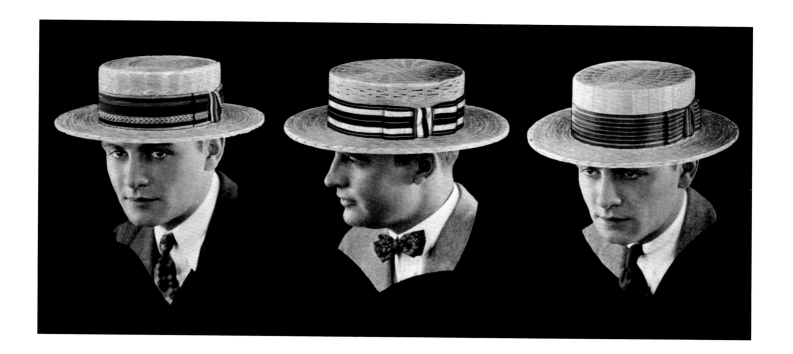

## THE BOATER HAT

The distinctive straw boater was first known as the sennet hat and was part of the sailor's summer uniform in Britain until 1921.[23] Sailor-style straw hats were being marketed to women by the late 19th century; music hall star Vesta Tilley sold a range on an American tour in 1894, where the *New York Press* exclaimed, 'sailor hats can be made becoming to most people, and there is a craze for them this season.'[24] Straw 'sailor hats', often with an upturned brim like the original sennet hats, were a popular item for women well into the 20th century, evident in a 1940 Schiaparelli design. This particular example is glossy and black, much like the original versions that were tarred to give extra protection from the elements. Worn by rowers from the 1870s, they were sold to civilian men by the early 20th century, given credence by *Vanity Fair* who included one in a 1915 article on summer clothes, 'Shopping for the Well-Dressed Man'.[25] It was also a straw boater hat – purchased at Galeries Lafayette and sparsely trimmed herself – that began Coco Chanel's career in millinery in the run up to her first boutique opening in 1910. The simplicity of the straw boater, the antithesis of the enormous confections of feathers, fruit and flowers that were in vogue at the time, would be the starting point of Chanel's fashion empire.

*Above: Straw boaters were the leisure headwear of choice for many men in the early 20th century. These models are by Georges Meyer & Cie., advertised as non-breakable and lightweight, c. 1925.*
*Opposite: The sailor as romantic hero, drawing on the centuries-old theme of the sailor's return in this French postcard from the First World War.*

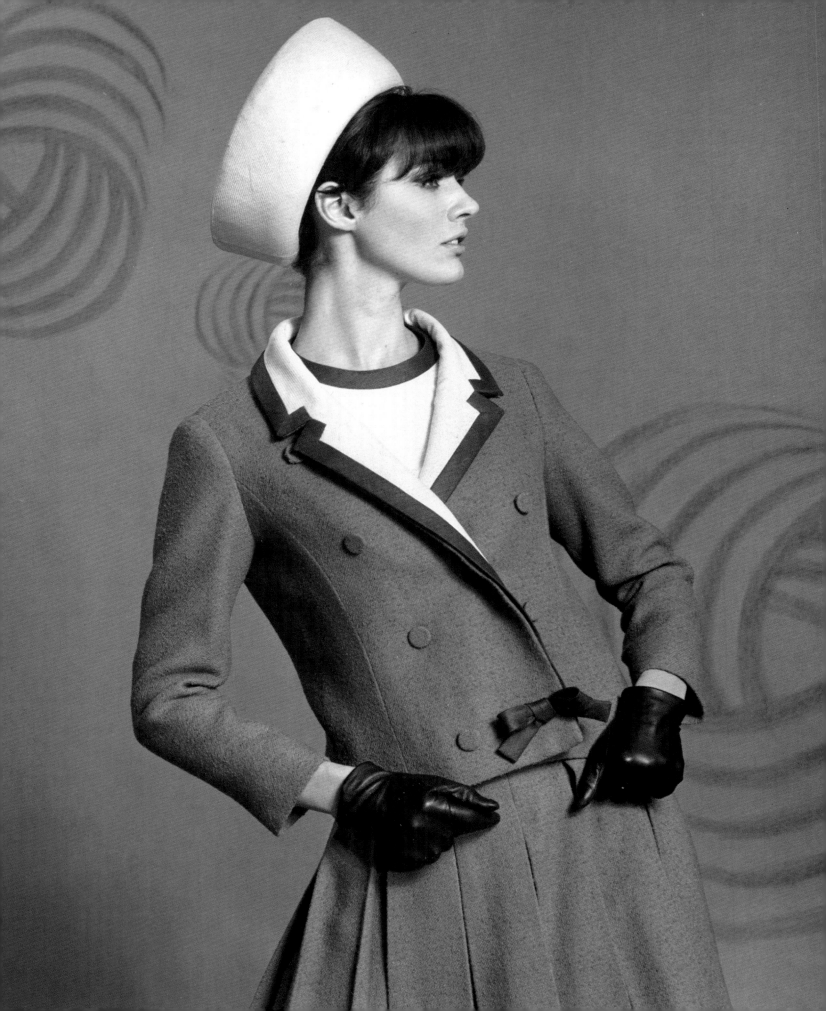

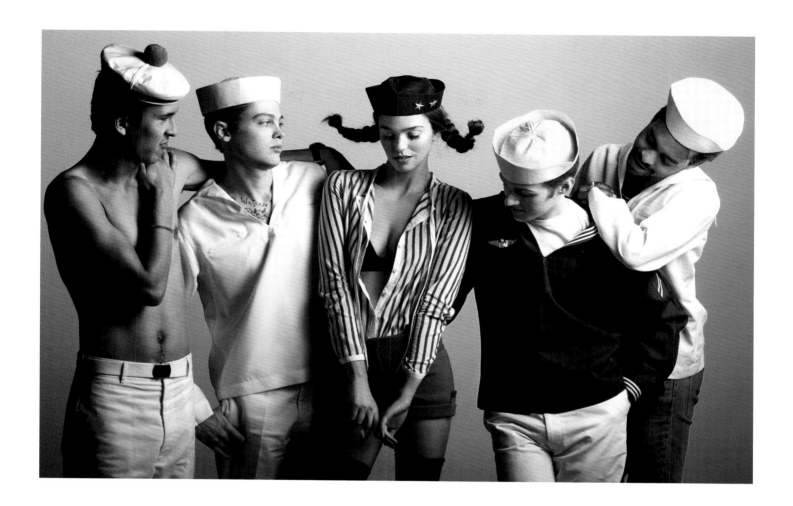

## THE AMERICAN SAILOR

Standardized uniform for American sailors was first introduced in 1817, but was only recorded in detail in 1841. It was largely based on items the Royal Navy were wearing prior to their official regulation. Around this time, stars were added to the striped piping to add a dash of national identity, succinctly linking the sailor with the country's flag. The Civil War in the 1860s was a major influence on uniform and standardization was adopted more thoroughly. As the collar became the key sailor signifier in Britain, the white 'dixie cup' hat became the marker of the seaman in America. A white canvas hat was introduced into US naval uniform regulations in 1886, replacing the former straw sennet hat of summer months.[26] This was exploited by the film industry and many of classic Hollywood's most bankable stars featured in sailor-inspired movies, from the fancy footwork of Fred Astaire and Ginger Rogers in *Follow the Fleet* (1936), to the all-American gusto of

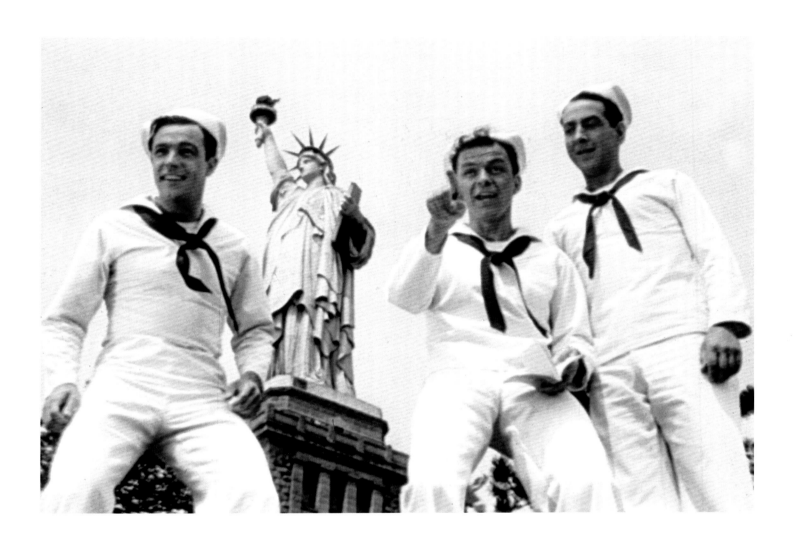

Above: *The all-American sailor on the silver screen. Gene Kelly, Frank Sinatra and Jules Munshin in* On the Town, *1949.* Opposite: *Crisp, fresh, summer sailor whites are referenced in this bell-bottom sailor dress with silk tie, c. 1954.*

Frank Sinatra and Gene Kelly in *On The Town* (1949). The hat was further embedded in public consciousness through the iconic image published in *Life* magazine of a sailor kissing a nurse in New York's Times Square during impromptu VJ Day celebrations at the end of the Second World War.

The dixie cup hat became a beloved aspect of American naval dress for both the public and personnel, and was written about in military magazines. In one example, a reader wrote asking for advice concerning uniform protocol regarding the hat.[27] The writer advised that 'no rakish angle' was to be adopted, yet American sailors frequently customized their hats to show an element of individuality, even though this practice was frowned upon by those in charge. The different ways of shaping the dixie cup hat are evident in *South Pacific* (1958), when the white hat is often the only identifying naval feature of men's dress that mixes tight white T-shirts, pale blue shirts and

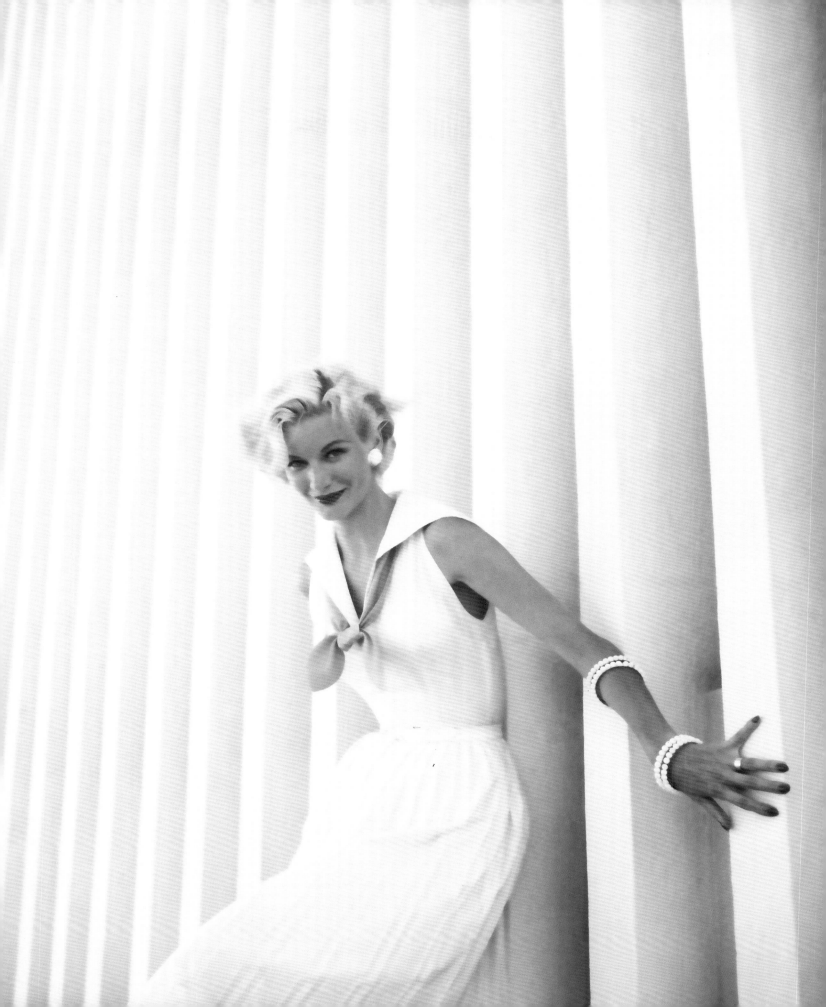

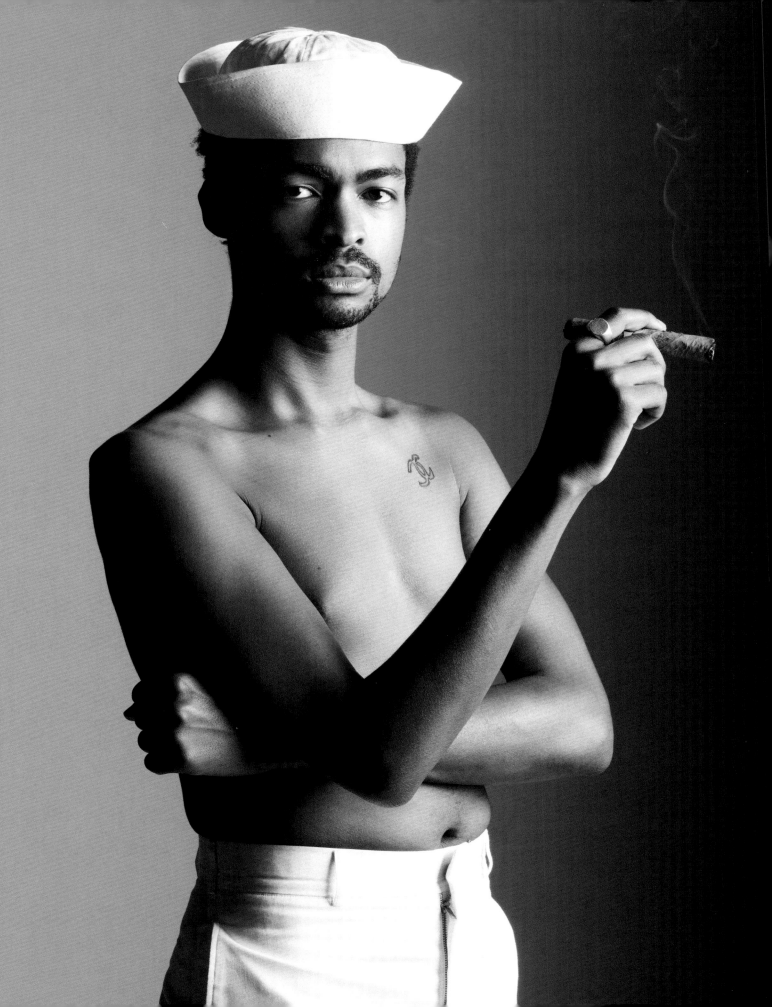

muscular bare chests. *South Pacific* found its way onto the catwalk for the Dior spring/summer 2011 show, when tropical prints and colours were combined with the dixie cup hat and other sailor motifs such as a pair of blue slouchy fly-front trousers. John Galliano took his applause post-show dressed as an officer, as the master of his ship. The dixie cup hat has become so identified with the sailor that it is often used as shorthand in fashion shoots to highlight a nautical theme, as is the case in much of the imagery for Jean Paul Gaultier's 'Le Male' perfume, in which the American dixie cup is often paired with a French striped marinière.

Despite – or because of – the imposed uniformity of life in the navy, opportunities would be taken to individualize clothing. In the 19th century, naval men from all countries were expected to sew and repair their own clothes (with occasional help from the ship's tailor), which allowed for some deviation from the regulations. Augmentations like silk piping at the seams or flashy hat ribbons were not unknown.[28] It was even said that some sailors fixed mirrored glass inside the crown of their sennet hats so they were able to check their appearance.[29] The customization of uniform was taken to its logical conclusion with the liberty cuffs of the US Navy. Dating from the 1890s, these embroidered patches were sewn with a hidden stitch inside the sleeves of the 'dress blues', ensuring they were concealed when on deck, but could be rolled up and exposed when on shore leave. Initially these designs on silk – often featuring dragons – originated in Asian ports, but from the 1950s patches were mass-produced. Many are collector's items today. Other popular designs featured mermaids, ships and wild animals, and Steve McQueen sports them in *The Sand Pebbles* (1966). The penalties for being caught with clandestine liberty cuffs were high: shore leave could be suspended and the sailor could be sent back to his ship. Undeterred by this, the practice lasted until the 1970s when civilian clothing began to be worn on land.[30] This desire to embellish is a universal theme; similar motifs of women, anchors or maps were also found decorating sailors' kit bags in the French Navy, especially throughout the first half of the 20th century.[31]

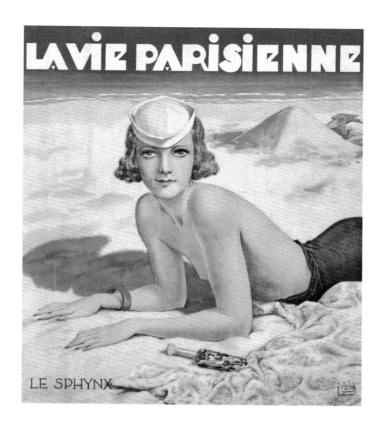

**Above:** *Saucy sailor chic on the cover of* La Vie Parisienne. *Illustrated by Georges Léonnec, 1934.* **Opposite:** *The sailor as sex symbol. 'Cruisin' for a Brusin' spread for* Jalouse *magazine, photographed by Matthew Frost, April 2011.*

**Following pages:** '*Sailor hats such as this are all the fashion just at present, and are seen everywhere ... the reason being probably that they are most practical as well as very smart and becoming, and are a welcome change from the very trying small shapes, of which, with their exaggerations and absurd height, the Parisian is beginning to grow a trifle tired.'* Vanity Fair, *August 1914. Sailor hats have endlessly reappeared in fashionable dress. The dixie cup hat is teamed with iconography of the 19th-century sailor by Olympia Le-Tan, spring/summer 2014 (left). The dixie cup makes another fashionable appearance, shown backstage at Dior, spring/summer 2011 (right).*

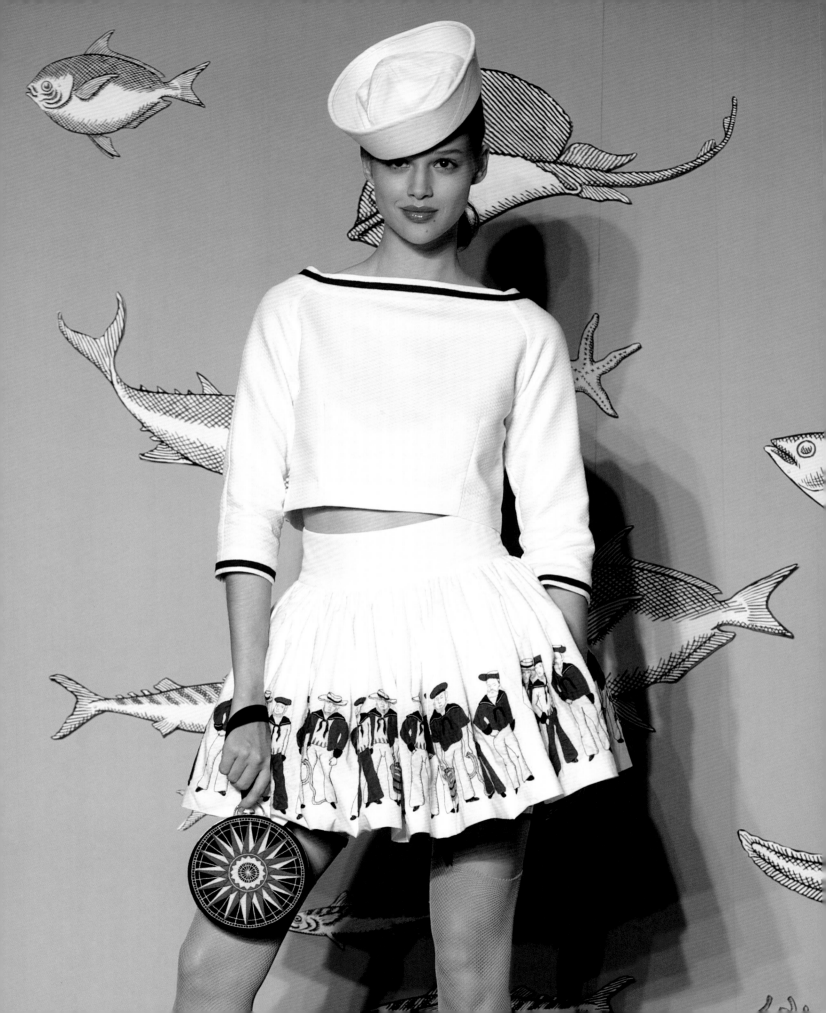

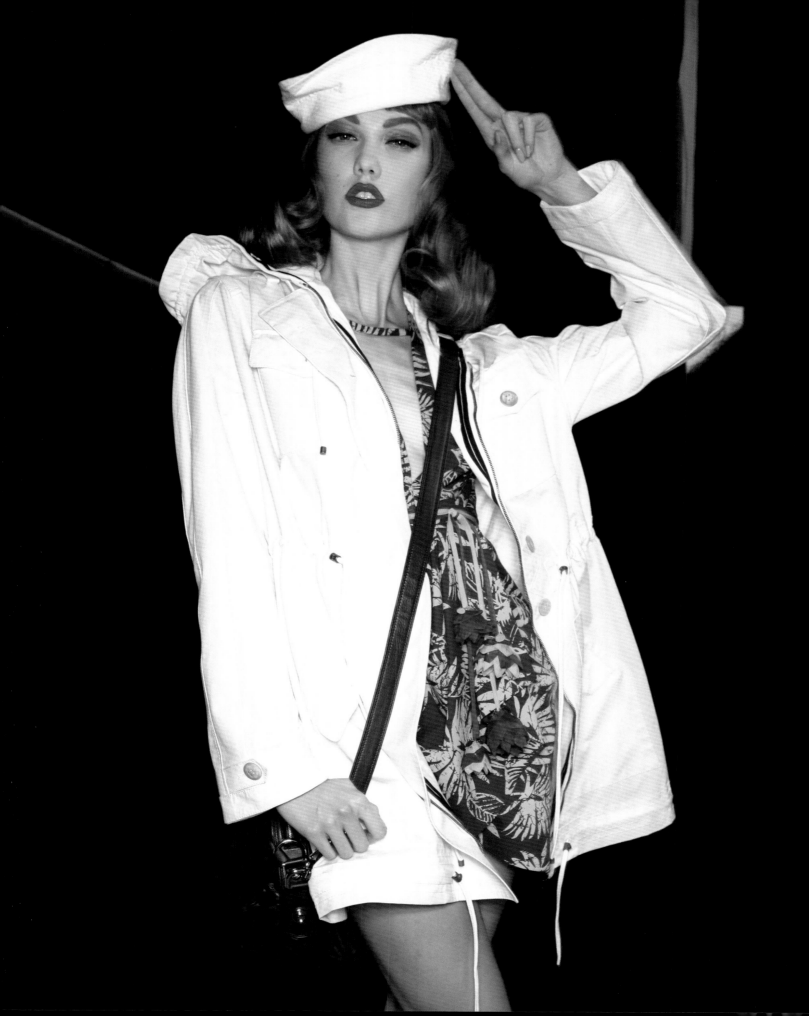

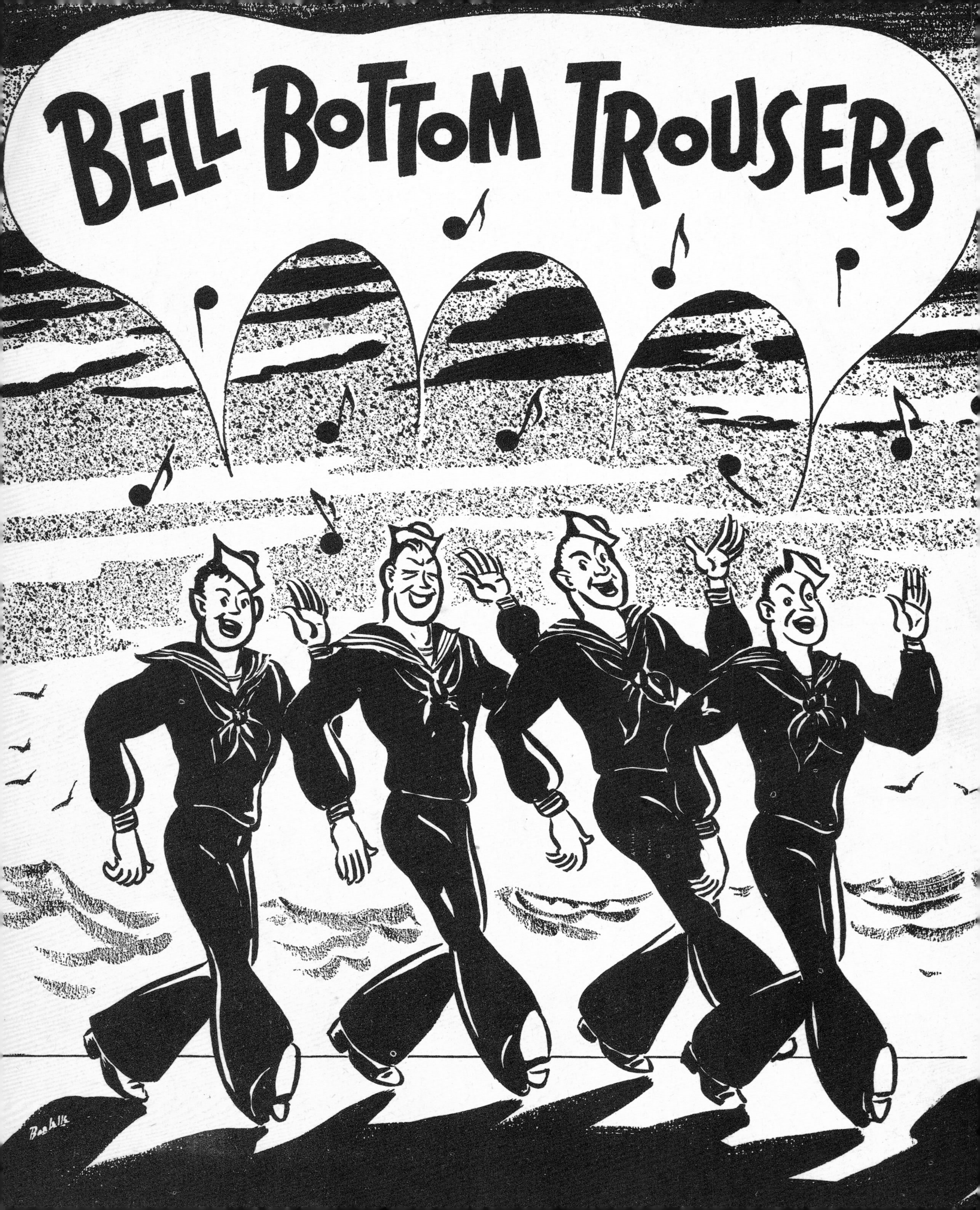
BELL BOTTOM TROUSERS

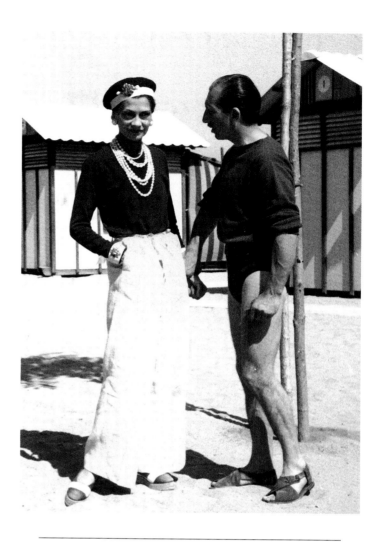

## BELL-BOTTOMS AND BEACH PYJAMAS

Throughout the 18th century, working seamen wore trousers while men of fashion wore breeches. This was a question of practicality, as working men needed more ease of movement, and it became a clear marker of class. The initial sailor trousers were fairly wide and stopped just above the ankle. In 1813, the first mention of bell-bottoms occurred when the US crew, under Commodore Stephen Decatur, appeared in New York 'dressed in glazed canvas hats with stiff brims decked with streamers of ribbon, blue jackets buttoned loosely over waistcoats, and blue trousers with bell bottoms'.[32] The term bell-bottoms stuck even though the 'flare' was not always extensive; the 1894 US regulations noted an increase of only one inch between the knee and the cuff.[33] But size was irrelevant as the distinctive wide trousers became indelibly linked with sailors in the popular imagination.

**Above:** *Coco Chanel in beach pyjamas resembling sailor pants, with her trademark pearls, on the beach at the Lido with Duke Laurino, 1930.*
**Opposite:** *The sheet music for 'Bell Bottom Trousers' by Moe Jaffe. This was a reworking of a folksong that found favour when it was composed during the Second World War in 1944.*

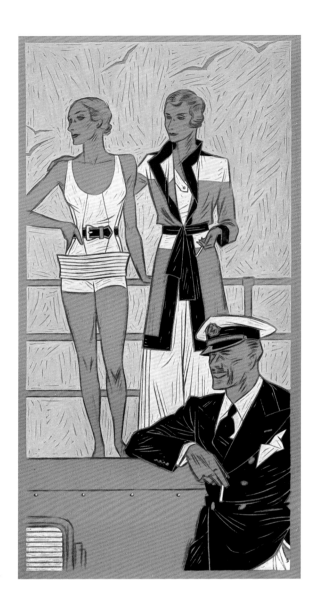

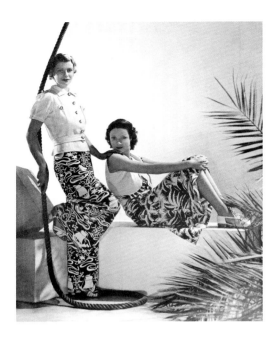

Above, left: *Advertisement for nautical-inspired sportswear by Jane Regny, illustrated by Ernst Dryden, 1931.* Above, right: *Couture beach dress and pyjamas with blue and white ship print by Worth, 1937.* Opposite: *The suggestive side of beachwear is the focus of the beach pyjamas featured in* Le Sourire *magazine, illustrated by Léon Bonnotte, 1931.*

Wide trousers first entered women's wardrobes courtesy of Coco Chanel. She donned beach pyjamas as early as 1918 and, throughout the following decade, wealthy women adopted pyjamas when holidaying by the sea. Chanel's early version were modelled on the line of male pyjamas, but the influence of the navy was soon apparent on designs such as a set she wore from 1929, which consisted of loose white trousers with a white double-breasted jacket, reminiscent of a modified pea coat or blazer. White, the colour of the sailor's summer uniform, easily transitioned into holiday wear for women at the coast. Later sportswear designers, such as Jane Regny, widened the legs and turned beach pyjamas into jumpsuits.[34] In 1925, *Vanity Fair* reported that extravagantly-patterned beach pyjamas were all the rage for men at Deauville in France and at the Lido, and Schiaparelli launched her own knitted version in 1928.[35] According to local news, the Riviera town Juan-les-Pins became known as Pyjamaland due to the popularity of this look.[36] The connection with sailor style persisted and, in 1931, British *Vogue* were advertising wide-legged 'Woollen Suits for the Beach' including 'Le Matelot', 'in navy blue and white stockingette' [*sic*].[37] Throughout the 1930s, the styles spread further and could be seen lining the beaches of Britain, although trousers for women remained somewhat taboo outside of the relaxed dress codes of the beach or the privacy of the home until later in the century.

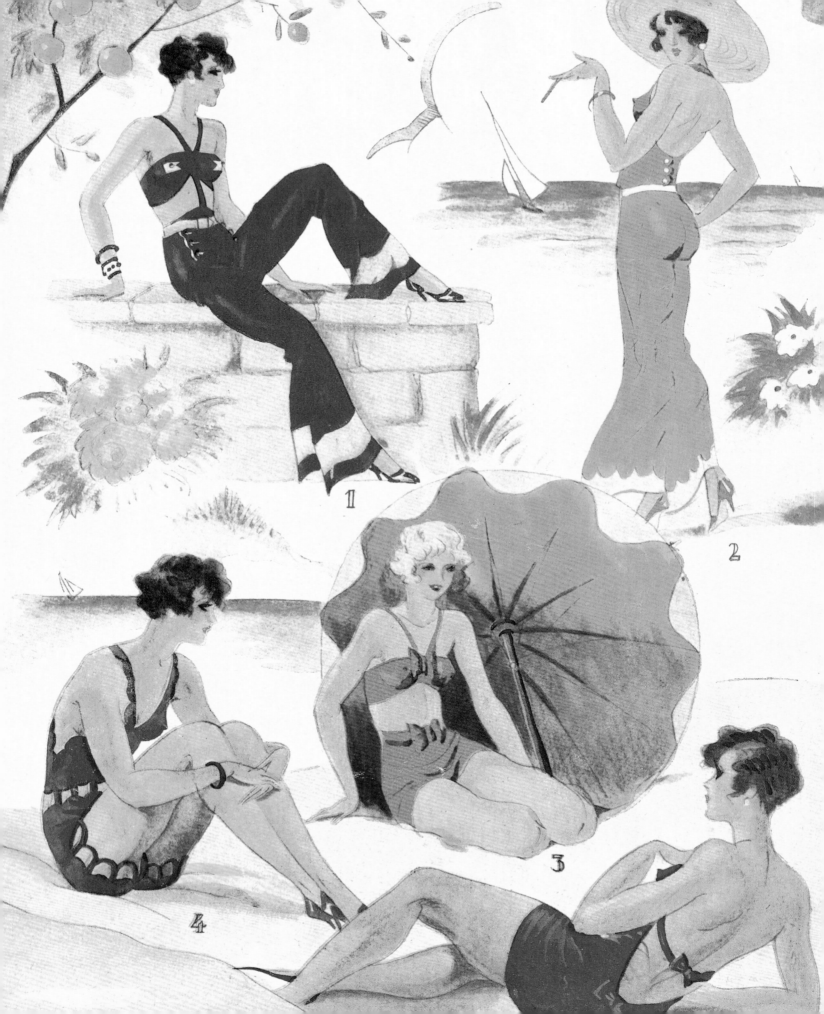

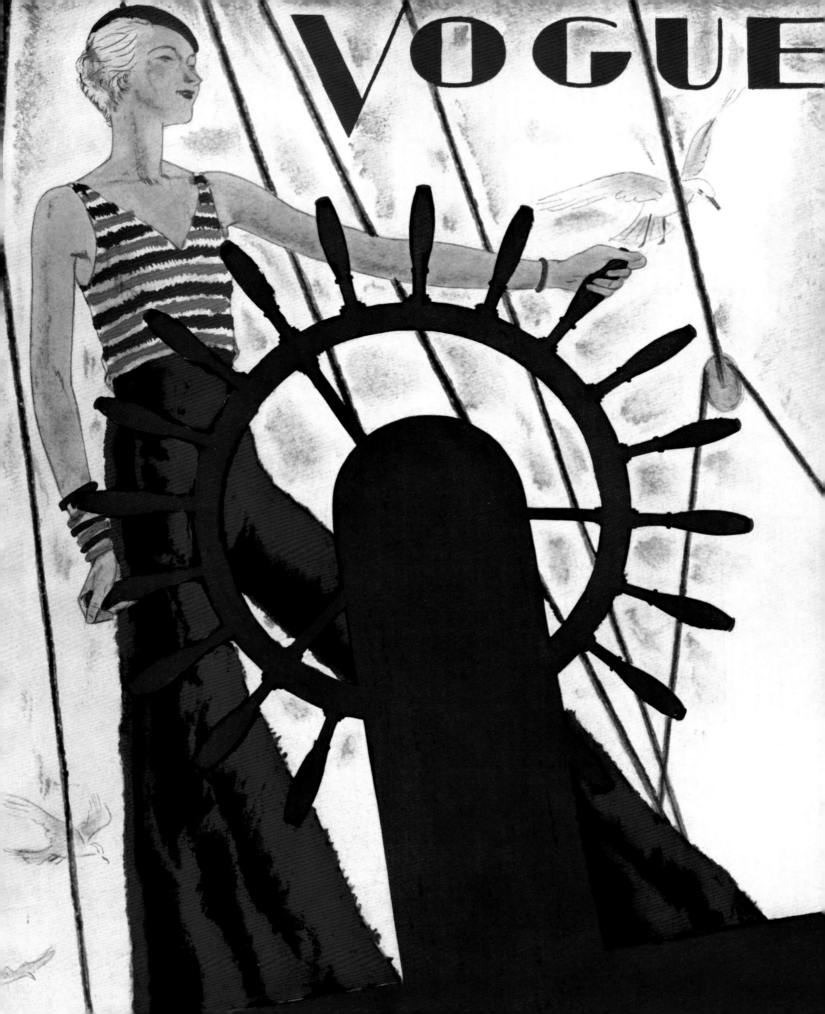

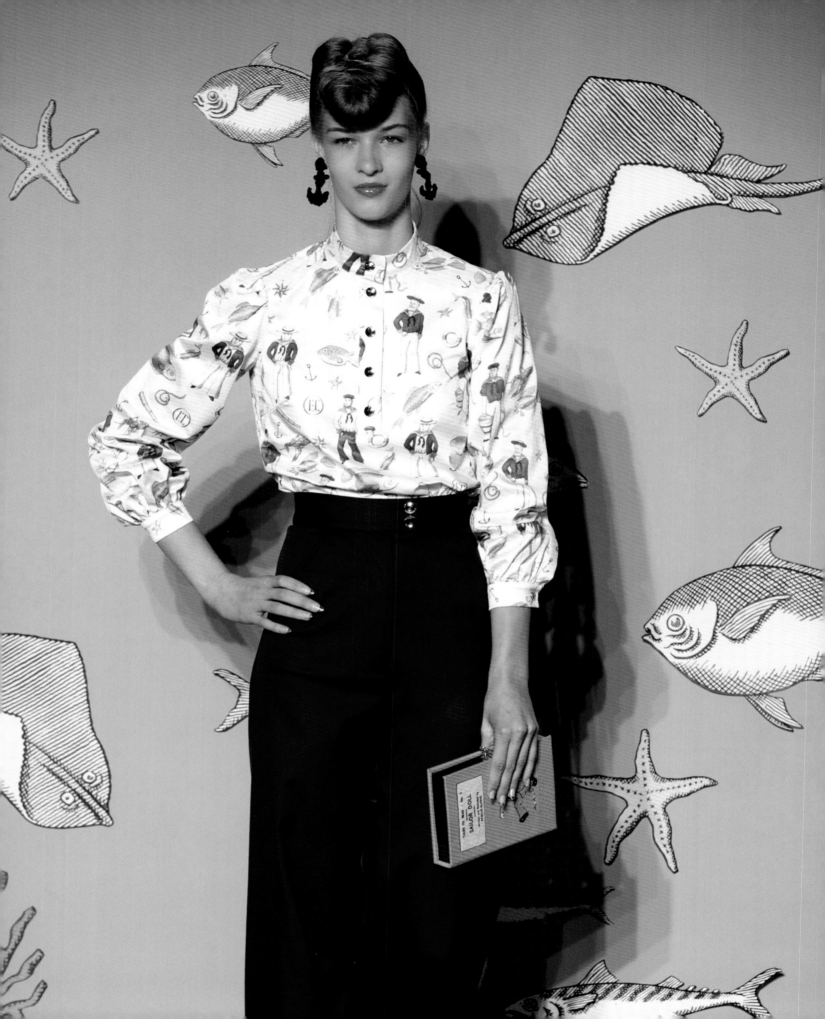

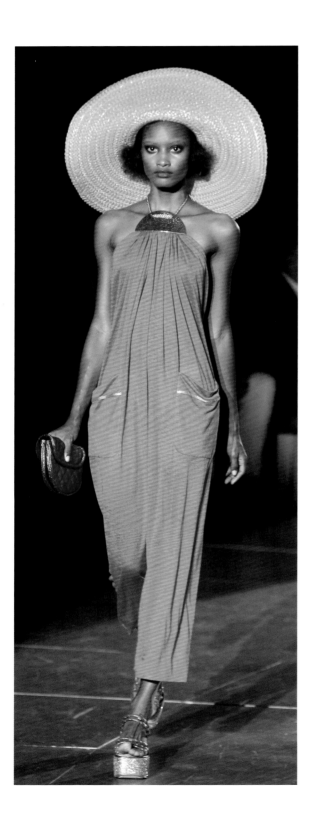

Bell-bottoms found favour again through military surplus outlets in the early 1960s. An article in *Esquire*, June 1966, noted that they were an important addition to a man's wardrobe in denim or cotton duck, or 'the real article, a pair of white-cotton regulation Navy bell-bottom pants'.[38] From early in the decade, students in London and across the States scoured army and navy surplus outlets for cheap clothing that was worn on the streets and campuses with a certain anti-establishment insouciance. This held a strong interest for iconoclastic designer Yves Saint Laurent, whose visit to Kaufman's Army & Navy surplus store on 42nd Street in New York sparked his 1966 collection that ultimately established the pea coat as a fashion classic. The collection also featured bell-bottoms, an element that British *Vogue* picked up on in July 1966 with the shoot 'Vogue's Sea View', featuring 'total nautical looks inspired by Saint Laurent'. Bell-bottom hipster trousers were photographed at Cannes on a society yacht.[39] Elsewhere in the issue, Jean Shrimpton was shot by David Bailey for an article titled 'Sea Change for Crepe', which included 'wide white sailor trousers' by Susan Small.[40] By 1973, flared pants were the dominant silhouette for both men's and women's trousers. British *Vogue* shoots began to resemble 1930s beach scenes, with wide, white, cotton trousers a regular feature. Flares were ubiquitous, epitomized in a shoot called, 'Deauville, Trouville out in the June Sunshinesville', photographed on a boardwalk and featuring London-based labels like Bus Stop and Mr Freedom.[41] The bell-bottom may have been ever-present but their nautical origins weren't forgotten.

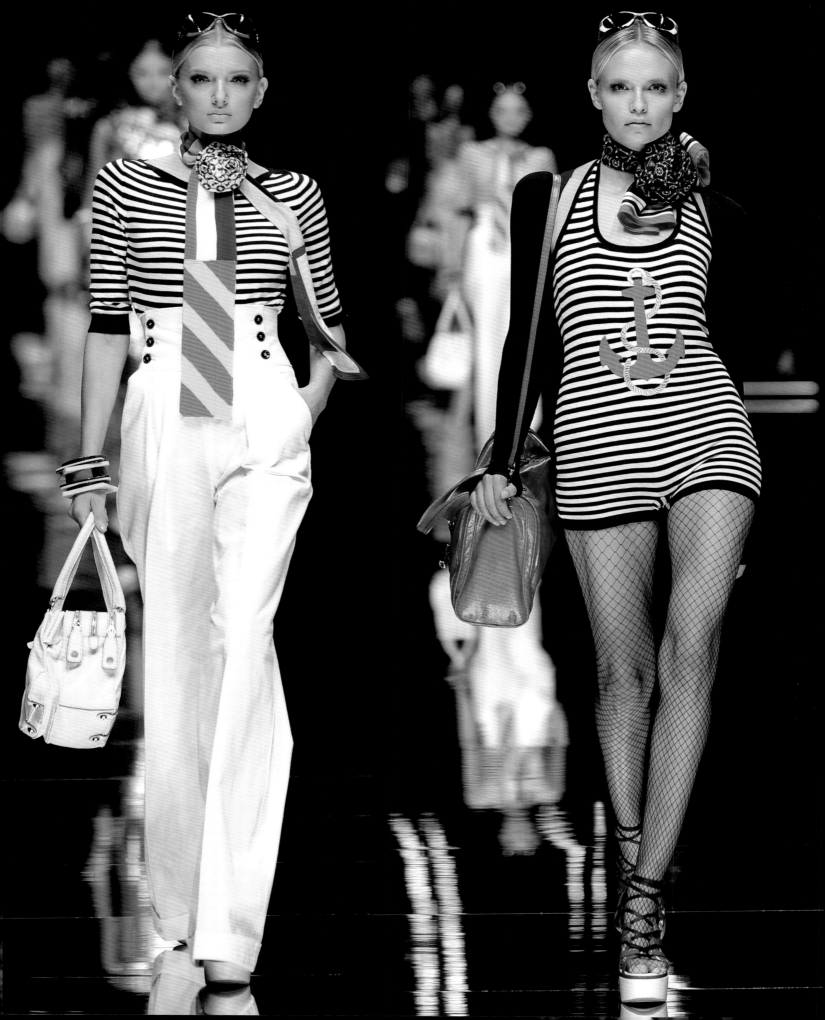

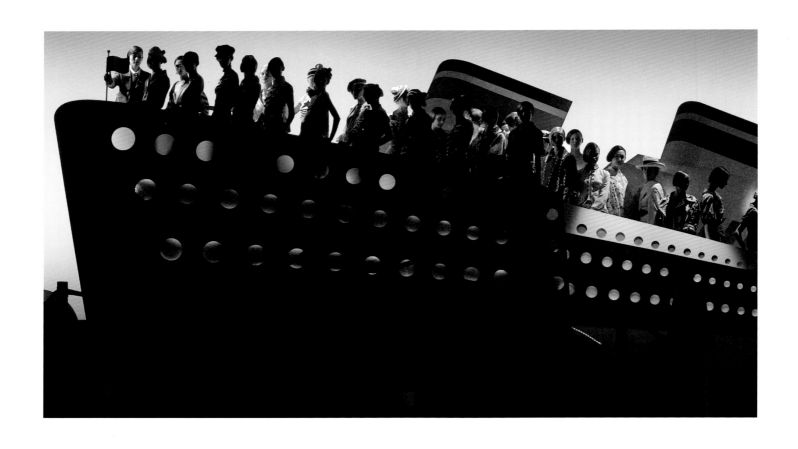

Sailor pants remain popular as an evening look in dark navy and equally as a summer resort favourite in sharp white. Givenchy by Riccardo Tisci revisited them in autumn/winter 2007, complete with high waistline and flared leg. For spring/summer 2009, D&G went into Riviera overdrive, with white, blue and striped flap-fly sailor pants in long or cropped lengths. Sailor trousers were rendered as their trademark bloomer shorts in a collection that even referenced Chanel's part in the history of nautical style with bouclé suits and beach pyjamas. Beach pyjamas have also been recreated in recent years by Marc Jacobs, whose reference point for spring/summer 2011 was distinctly 1970s-does-30s, with the requisite hint of disco and wide-brimmed sunhats. That season also saw wide palazzo-style pants produced by Thakoon and 3.1 Phillip Lim. Wide trousers have a timeless appeal that sees them equally popular whether interpreted as a chic classic or as playful holiday wear.

*Above: Shipshape style: this Kenzo catwalk presentation also featured cardboard seagulls and waves, spring/summer 2006. Opposite: Along with the ship presentation, the sailor was the key reference for Kenzo, spring/summer 2006.*

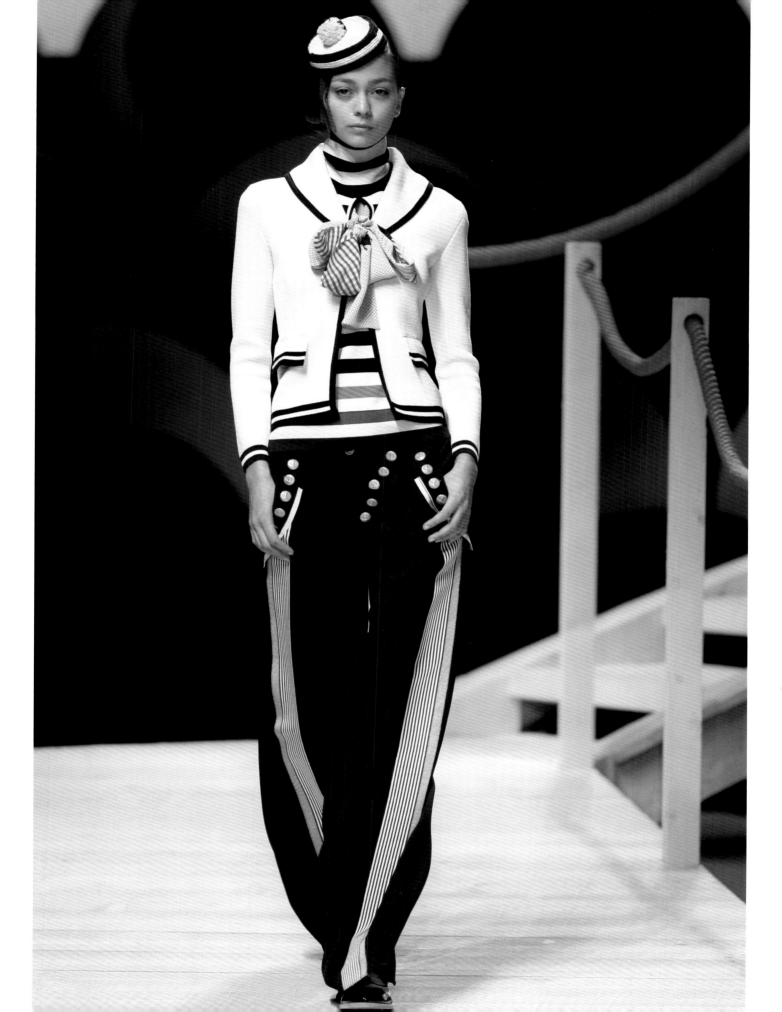

## MARITIME MASCULINITY AND THE BIRTH OF A GAY ICON

Due to the class stratification of the navy, the figure of the sailor came to epitomize a robust, working-class masculinity throughout the last decades of the 19th century. This chimed with the masculine ideal of 'muscular Christianity' that prevailed throughout this period. Physical, outdoor work and sport were increasingly esteemed, said to improve a sense of Christian morality, and were, according to the parson and author Professor Charles Kingsley, the 'antidote to the poison of effeminacy'.[42] This was emphasized in illustrated newspapers and journals by the frequent portrayal of seamen from behind; not only did this foster the association of the square collar with a standardized navy, but it also couldn't fail to emphasize the tightness of his trousers. In an age where urban middle-class men generally wore thigh-length coats or jackets, such as the frock coat, the morning coat and later the ubiquitous lounge suit, the comparative exposure of the sailor's posterior certainly stands out. These qualities were accentuated by his toned physique, exemplified by firm thighs and buttocks. Given that officer's uniforms could shape and mould the body to the desired form to achieve the illusion of sturdy muscularity, the sailor – with his demanding physical regime on board – was a quintessential ideal of manliness.

The emphasis on the virile physicality of the sailor and seafaring life fed into the increasing eroticization of the sailor throughout the 20th century and the birth of a gay icon.

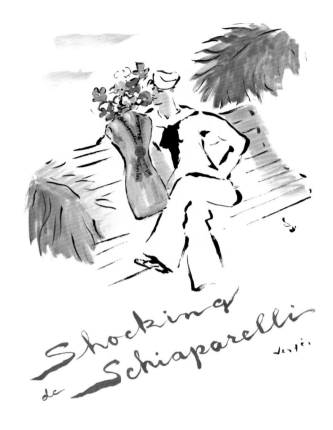

*Shocking de Schiaparelli*

Above: *The advertising for Schiaparelli's 'Shocking!' perfume often featured sailors, and the bottle itself was modelled on the hourglass shape of Mae West. Illustrated by Marcel Vertès, 1942.*
Opposite: *The romanticized sailor is a recurring feature of Pierre et Gilles' work.* Le marin, *Philippe Gaillon, 1985.*

The tightness of the uniform and specific design details were celebrated by British writer and raconteur Quentin Crisp, who emphasized that the 'crowning aphrodisiac feature was the fly-flap of their trousers'. He continued, 'more than one of my friends has swayed about in ecstasy describing the pleasures of undoing this quaint sartorial device.'[43] The unique fly-front of the sailor trousers, an anachronistic detail left over from earlier styles of breeches, essentially provides a frame for the genitals. Coupled with the snug fit around the posterior, they are perfectly designed for fetishizing and objectifying the male body.[44] Fantasies of homosexual life at sea were explored in Jean Genet's *Querelle de Brest*, first published in 1947 and turned into a film by Fassbinder in 1982, which has become a key referent for the sailor as gay icon. The photographers Pierre et Gilles draw on this lineage, playing with notions of masculinity, homoeroticism and kitsch, and sailors have been present in their images since their early work, including 1977's *Le marin*.[45] Alfred Courmes, the Surrealist artist known as 'The Angel of Bad Taste', also saw the homoerotic potential of the seaman when he repurposed another gay icon, Saint Sebastian, as a sailor in 1934, in a painting now owned by the Pompidou

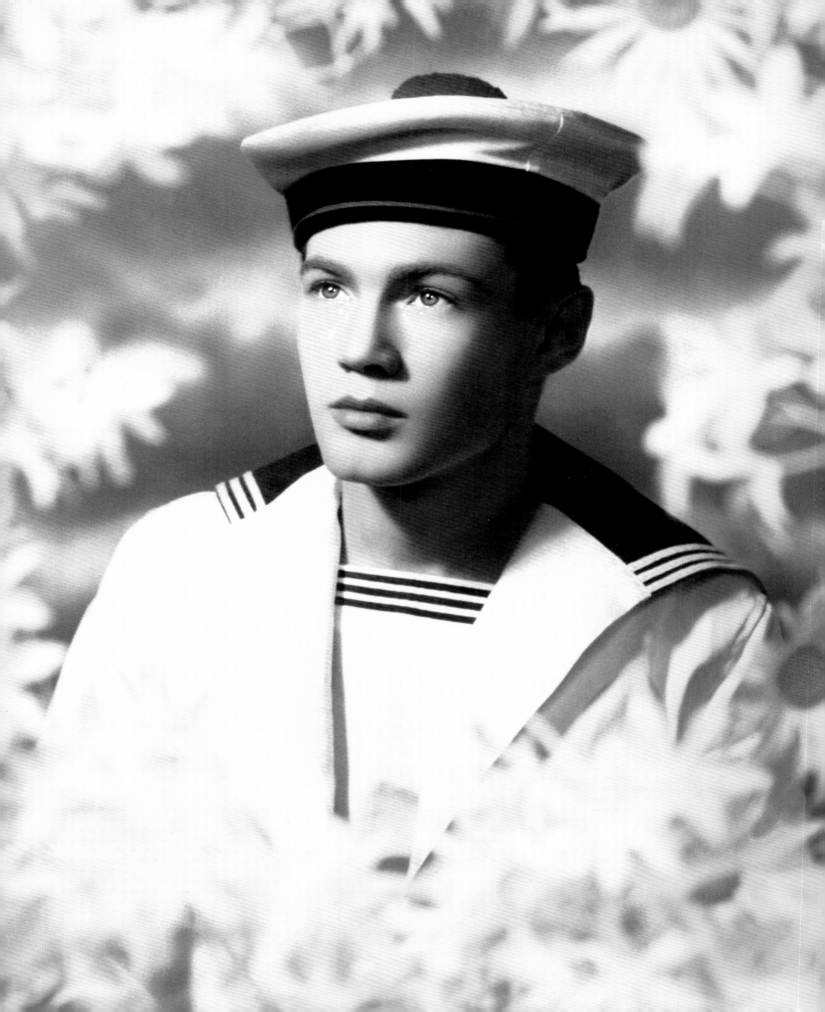

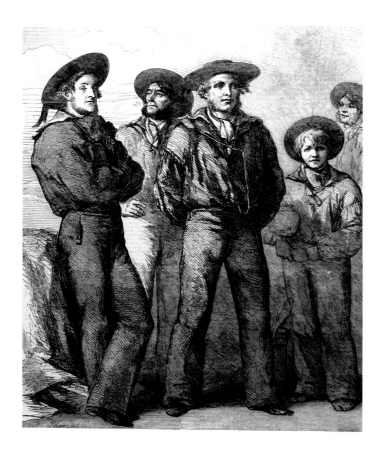

Above: *The virility of the sailor
and his physical qualities were
celebrated as the 19th century
drew on. His attributes were made
all the more apparent thanks to
the tightness of the trousers.*
'Man-of-War's Men' *printed in the*
Illustrated London News, *March
1854.* Opposite: *Brad Davis in*
Querelle. *Based on a story by Jean
Genet, the story celebrates the sailor
as homoerotic icon. Directed by
Rainer Werner Fassbinder, 1982.*

Centre (a theme revisited by Pierre et Gilles sixty years later).
The sexualization of sailor's bodies was exaggerated in the
homoerotic illustrations of George Quaintance for mid-century
physique magazines, and later in the rugged carnality of
Tom of Finland's artwork,[47] which has come to symbolize
the masculinization of gay identity since the 1970s. The
sailor was reinvented as a hypermasculine gay icon.[48]

The homosexual sailor was politicized in a campaign
shot by David LaChapelle for Italian brand Diesel in 1995.
Diesel are well known for engaging with controversial issues
in their advertising and, as part of the 'For Successful Living'
campaign, they superimposed an image of two male sailors
kissing onto an original photograph, *Victory!*, dating from the
end of the Second World War. With obvious reference to the
renowned VJ Day celebration kiss in Times Square, the Diesel
image adds a queer aesthetic to a contemporary issue. The
image was produced two years after the 'Don't Ask Don't Tell'
policy was introduced in the US, continuing the ban on openly
gay candidates from entering the military, and was seen as
a critique of this policy, which was finally repealed in 2010.

The homoerotic sailor is realized most succinctly in the
work of Jean Paul Gaultier. In 1990, he was shot by Pierre et
Gilles wearing a striped nautical top, continuing their tradition
of drawing on sailors to encapsulate an essence of nautical
kitsch. Their work adds a romantic air to the sailor, a move
away from the hypersexualized imagery and robust sexuality
of illustrators like Tom of Finland. In 1995, the launch of
Gaultier's fragrance 'Le Male' drew on the lineage of sailor
as muscular gay icon, and twins – a key element of Genet's
*Querelle de Brest* – were also referenced before the decade
was out.[49] The perfume itself is 'ultimately a play on age-
old masculine conventions', according to its creator, Francis
Kurkdjian, and the bottle replicates the sailor's muscular
torso.[50] Here it draws a parallel with Schiaparelli's 'Shocking!'
perfume of the 1930s whose advertising frequently used sailors
and whose bottle design was modelled on the hourglass figure
of Mae West.[51] Maritime iconography is a regular feature in
Gaultier collections, epitomized by a sailor ensemble made of
neoprene and spandex for the 'Pin-Up Boys' spring/summer
1996 collection. Gaultier incorporates elements of fetishwear
to present the sailor as an explicitly sexual object, and has
described the sailor as, 'a hypersexualized gay symbol, a
fantasy, an icon, a form of virility that could be ambiguous'.[52]

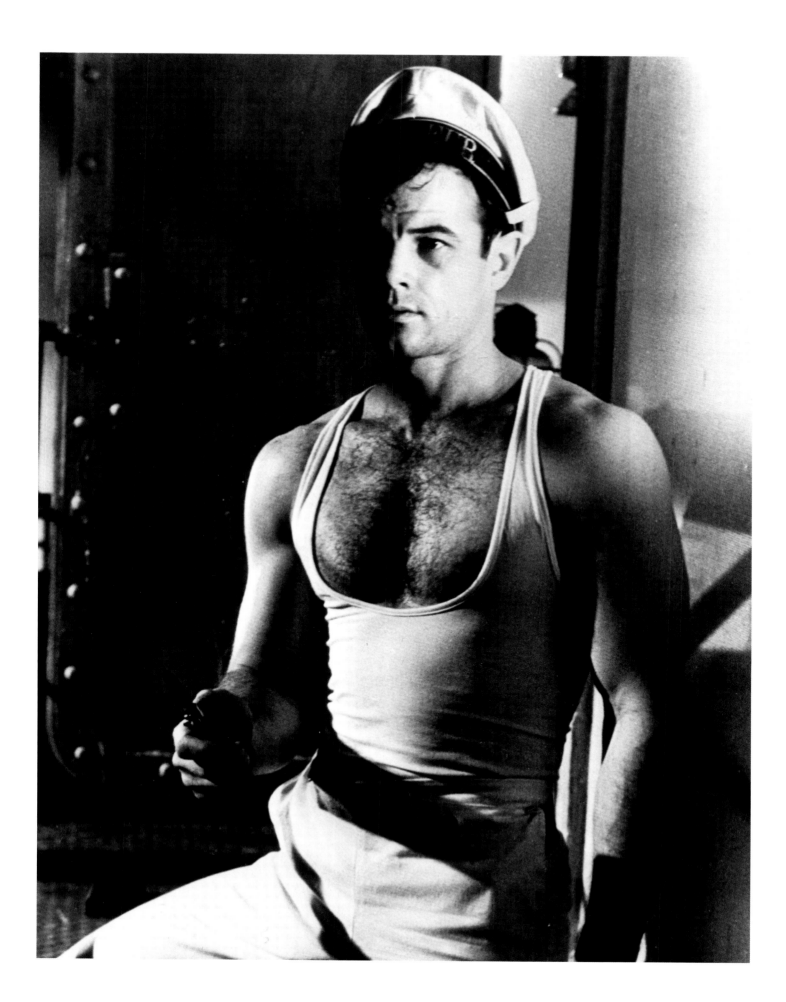

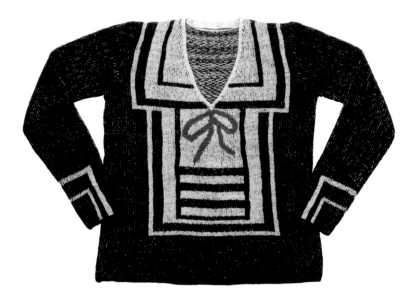

## THE SAILOR TODAY

The vogue for the middy blouse throughout the 1920s, coupled with an increased interest in both sports and beach leisurewear, impacted the early work of Elsa Schiaparelli. Her first success, in 1927, was a monochrome trompe l'oeil sweater featuring a bow knotted at the neck. This was not only one of the first instances that sweaters had been refigured in a high-fashion setting, but its popularity meant it remained one of her most copied designs. She continued with trompe l'oeil themes, and the following year created a sweater based on the French sailor's uniform featuring a striped top with a wide collar at the back.[53] Nautical motifs such as sailboats and fish adorned Schiaparelli's knit swimwear, and an even bolder design featured pierced hearts and snakes, replicating tattoos on a sailor's chest.[54] Quintessentially British design house Laura Ashley recreated the sailor dress as a marker of middle-class respectability in the 1980s, a look that Princess Diana made her own. This continued a connection with modesty and

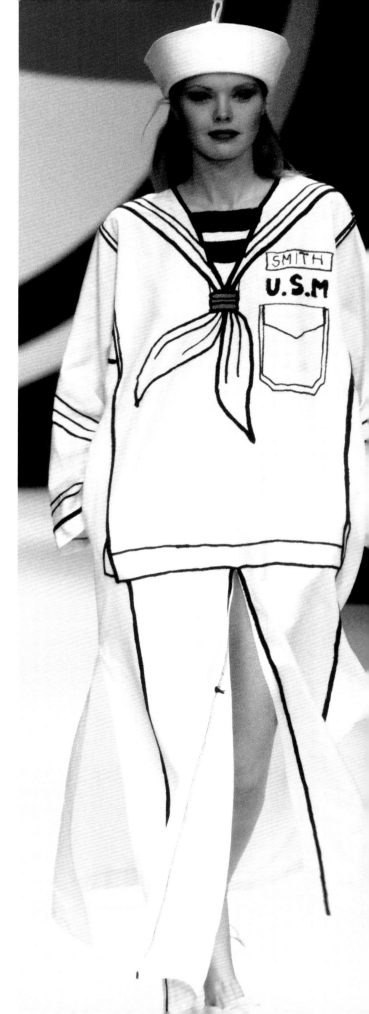

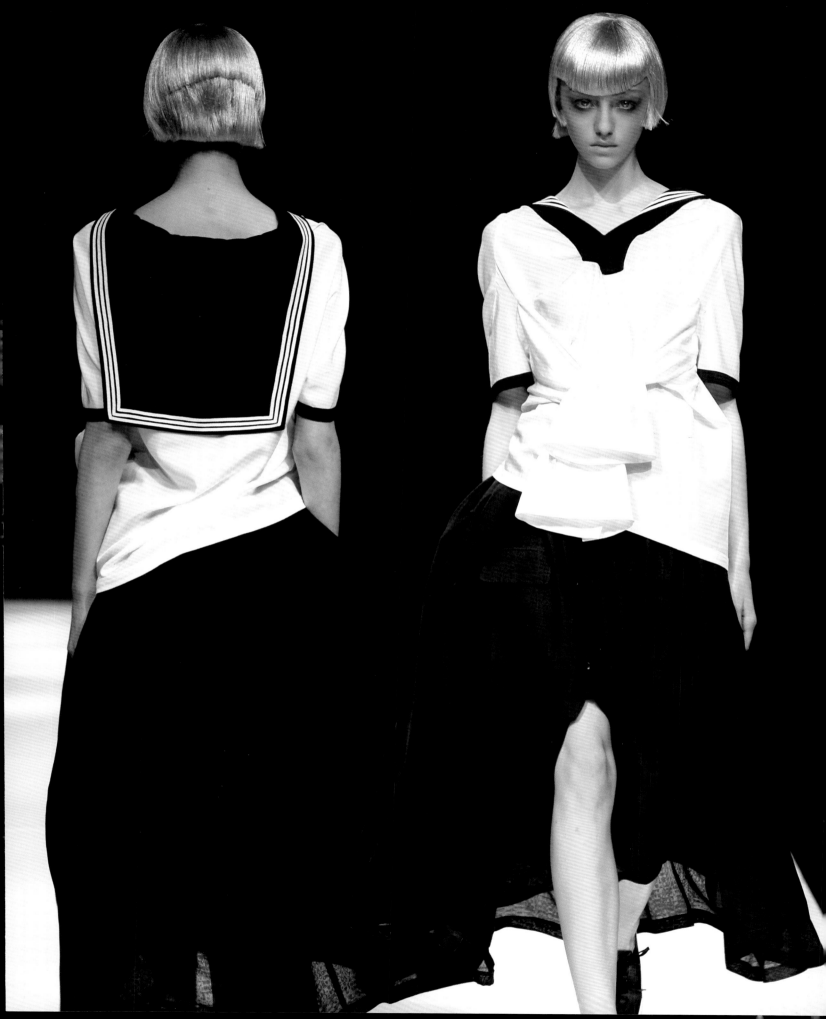

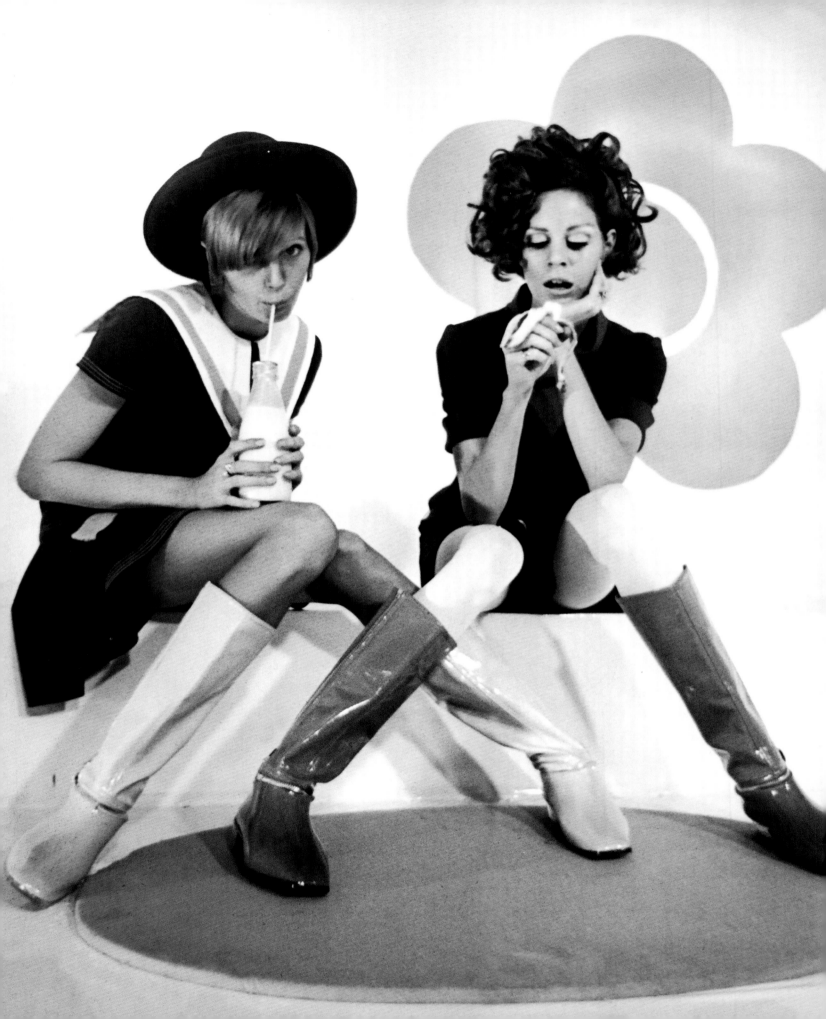

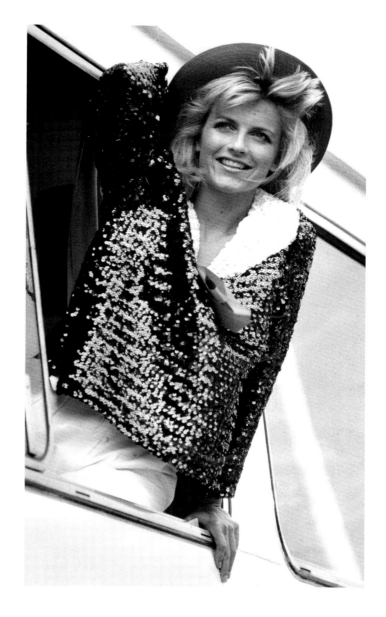

innocence that stretched back to the first days of the sailor suit being worn by children. Mary Quant also drew on the connections with childrenswear in the 1960s. With bright, bold collections offering freedom of movement, Quant's designs often appropriated children's clothing into womenswear. Returning to the trompe l'oeil theme, irreverent designer Jean-Charles de Castelbajac created an entire two-dimensional sailor suit in 1996, playing on the simplicity of the T-shirt. Yohji Yamamoto featured an oversize sailor collar for spring/summer 2007 in a collection that reconstructed many items of menswear as womenswear. A perennial symbol of seafaring life, the sailor suit has become an enduring icon to be reconfigured endlessly in fashionable dress, acting as a mirror to the tastes and desires of each generation.

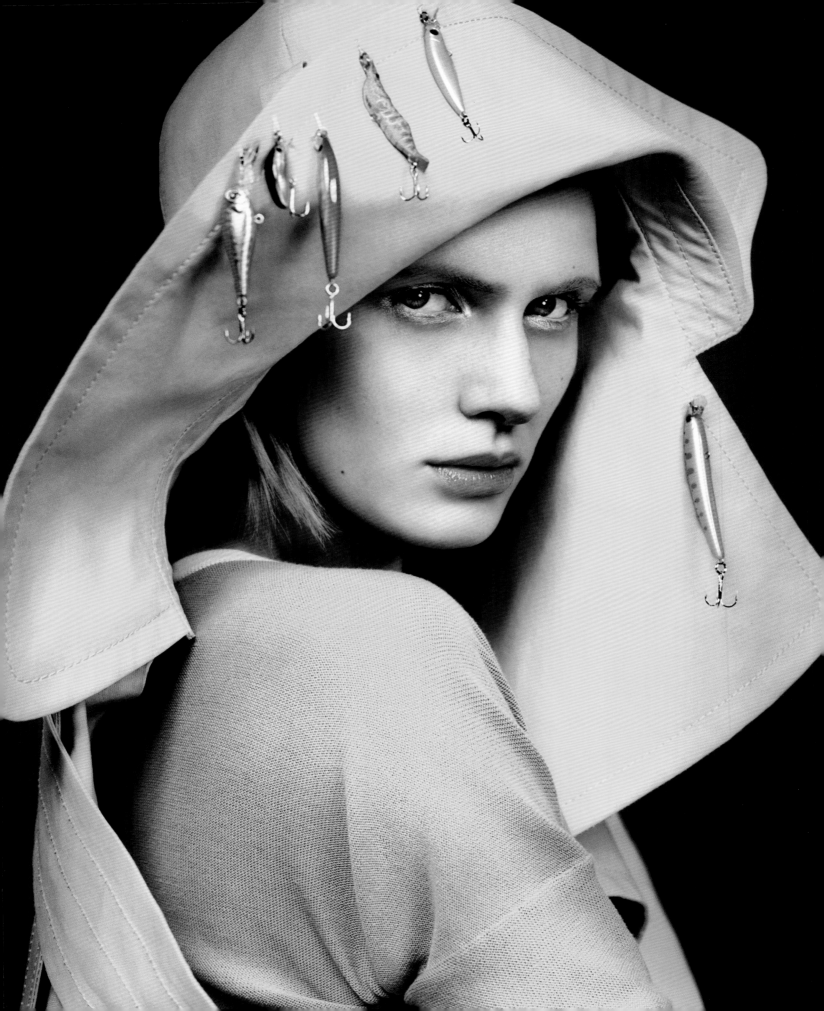

# CHAPTER 3

# D

## THE FISHERMAN

ue to the Fisherman's treacherous vocation, he demands a wardrobe that can offer protection from the elements. His occupational clothing formed the basis for chic classics, as avant-garde artists at the French coast embraced Riviera life. This style legacy is still with us today and the workwear of the fisherman has been transformed into haute couture by the likes of Chanel, Balenciaga and Dior.

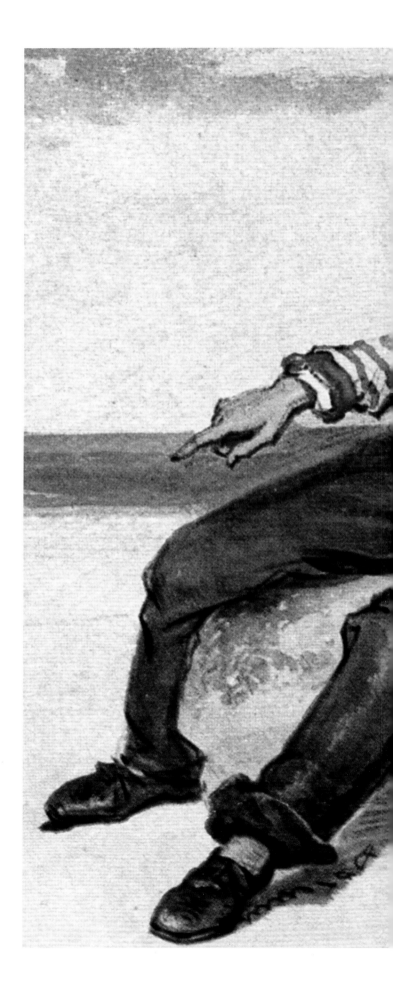

*How from the finny subject of the sea*
*These fishers tell the infirmities of men;*
*And from their watery empire recollect*
*All that may men approve or men detect!*
*Peace be at your labour, honest fishermen*

SHAKESPEARE, *PERICLES, PRINCE OF TYRE*, C. 1607[1]

Some of the garments we closely associate with chic, effortless style were once the most hardworking. The growth of tourism, spurred by bohemian visitors to the beach, helped to spread many styles that were developed outside of the fashion system, styles born from the necessities of working life. Fishing was a dangerous job. Men were at the mercy of the elements, leading to the oft-repeated caveat when fish prices were high, 'It's no fish ye're buying, it's men's lives.'[2] Fishermen's clothing had to be functional and offer protection from the elements and, in a bid to keep dry and warm, fishing communities developed their own distinctive clothing. Providing rich inspiration for fashion designers, many regional items, from Fair Isle knits to striped fishing tops, have crossed into the world of fashion. Unlike the navy, fishing was a world that involved women as well. While the men fished, women prepared and sold the catch, creating their own dress idiosyncrasies. As the beach became a space for fashionable display, it transformed from a place of work to a site of leisure, a seaside awash with suntans and stripes.

Page 86: *Sou'wester fishing style recreated with garments by Sonia Rykiel. Photographed by David Slijper for* Vogue Japan, *January 2008.*
Opposite: *The striped fishing top in its natural habitat. 'A Fisherman,' watercolour by William Derby, 1834.*

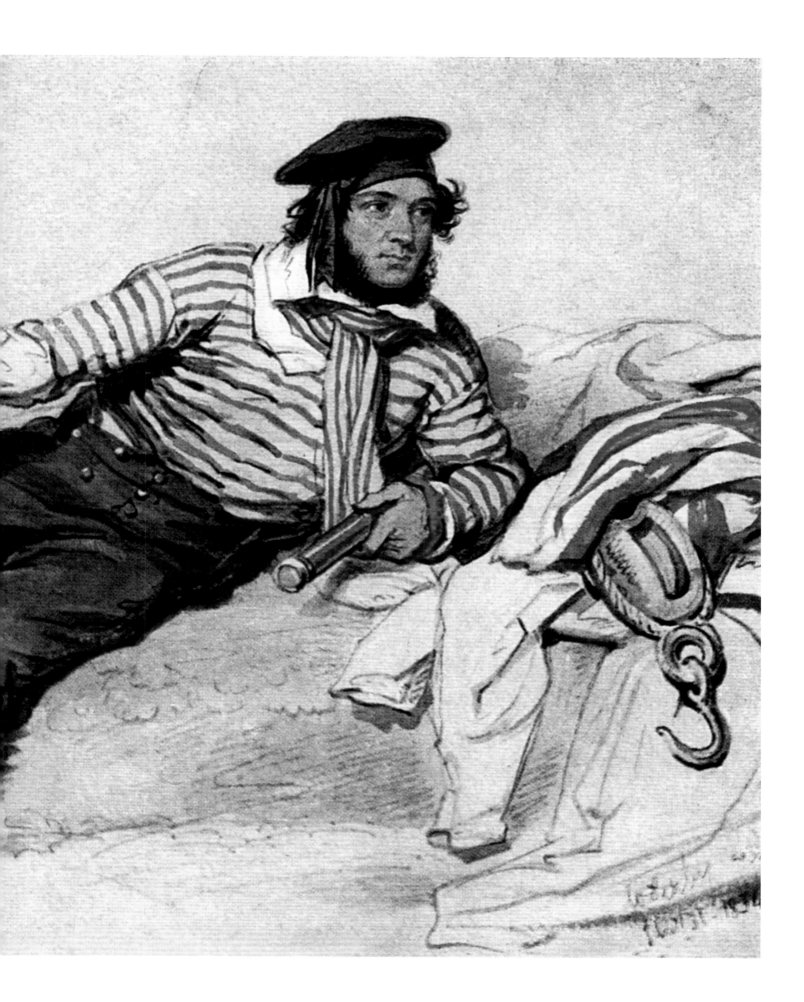

## ANATOMY OF A FASHION CLASSIC: STRIPES AND THE SEA

Stripes have a long association with the sea. From 17th-century Dutch whalers to early 18th-century mariners, artefacts showing the stripy side of seafaring life can be found in museums across Europe.[3] British and Italian fishermen are shown in striped tops in engravings, mezzotints and watercolours from the first half of the 19th century. Knitted hosiery and undergarments have been produced for centuries, often in white or ecru, as natural colours were thought to be more hygienic and were simpler to produce. Knitted striped hose had been in and out of favour since the 17th century, as breeches put men's legs on show, but this only extended to the upper reaches of society who could afford to keep abreast of fashion. Lord Nelson was wearing non-regulation blue and white striped stockings when he was wounded at Tenerife in 1797.[4] For fishermen, knitted undergarments were vital to conserve heat at sea. In 1816, a circular knitting machine, the *tricoteur*, was developed by a French-born British engineer, Marc Brunel (father of engineer Isambard Kingdom), which made knitting seamless striped stockinette (jersey) a more viable option.[5] As technology improved, knitted striped garments became available to a wider section of society and became a popular choice for sportswear. For mariners, they had the added advantage of visibility should a man fall overboard.

The association between stripes and the sea was strengthened with the adoption of the striped undershirt into French naval uniform in 1858. The first description of the knitted cotton jersey 'marinière' (officially called the '*tricot rayé*') was meticulous in its definition, listing twenty-one white stripes at twenty millimetres width (0.79 inches) and twenty or twenty-one blue stripes at ten millimetres (0.4 inches) for the body, with fifteen white stripes, and fourteen or fifteen blue stripes on the sleeves.[6] The twenty-one stripes were said to represent Napoleon's naval victories but, again, this is uniform myth. The striped undershirt, featuring a wide 'boat' neckline for ease of removal, was later incorporated into the Tsarist Russian Navy as the *telnyashka*, where it spread to other branches of the military during the Soviet era.[7] With the official adoption of the fisherman's striped top into French uniform it became indelibly linked with Gallic elegance, and by the late 19th century, stripes were a popular option for swimwear and promenade outfits.

## THE BRETON SWEATER

We may not consider woollen knits as a waterproof option today but, before technical clothing and rubberizing, tightly-knit sweaters with their natural oils were one of the best options for protection against the elements. Knitting has played an important role in fishing communities. In France, Brittany and neighbouring Normandy have long histories of knitting and of woollens: the Knitter's Guild in Rennes was organized as early as 1513.[8] Rouen and Nantes were some of the earliest centres of framework knitting in 17th-century France following William Lee's introduction of mechanical knitting. Used predominantly for hosiery such as silk and woollen stockings, it sat alongside hand-knit cottage industries in the region.[9] Nautical wear is closely associated with Brittany. Brest has been a crucial port since the 17th century, drawing mariners from the surrounding area. A number of businesses, the majority with ties to the area's historic textile trades, continue the tradition of supplying both fishermen's knits and the naval marinière.

Saint James was founded in Normandy in 1850 as a wool spinning and dyeing plant, whose skeins were sold in the

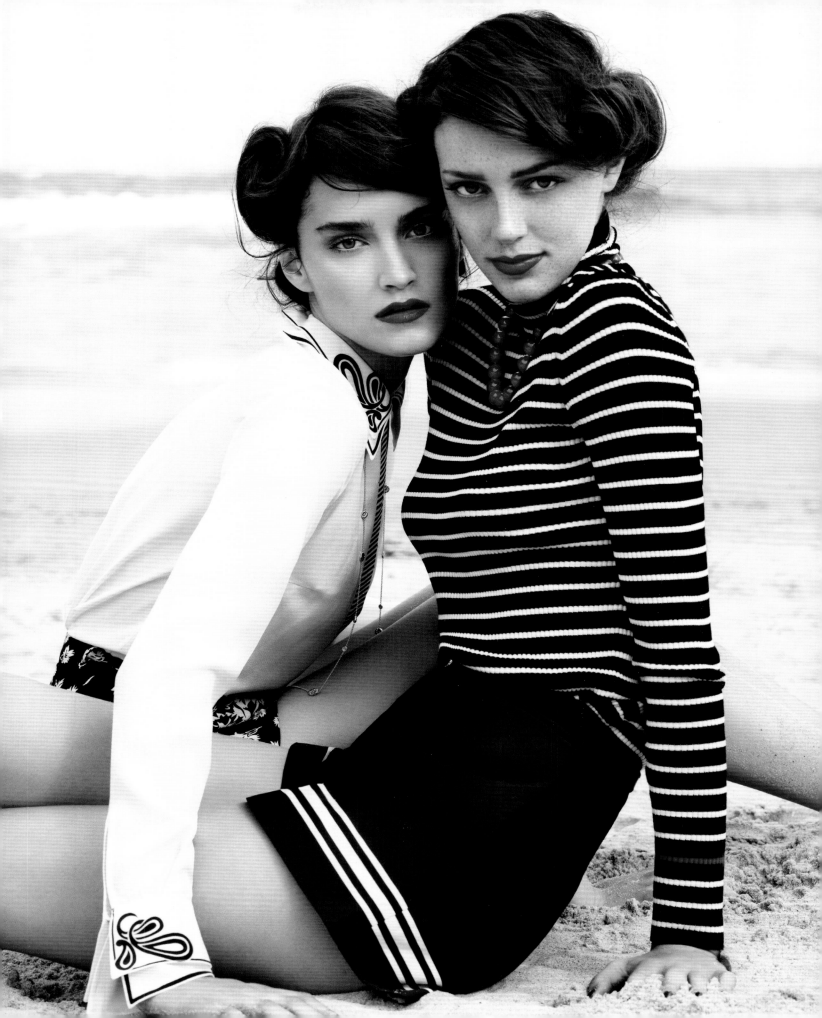

*'I've always loved the graphic and architectural aspect of stripes…. They go with everything, never go out of style and probably never will.'*

JEAN PAUL GAULTIER[10]

Below: *Stripes for the evening as well as the day: Lucien Lelong evening gown, illustrated by Jean-Baptiste Caumont, 1947.* Right: *Stripes continue to be a catwalk favourite. Symbolizing a mixture of seafaring life, leisure by the sea and French elegance, designers love to play with their varied meanings. D&G, spring/summer 2009.* Centre and far right: *Stripes are a vital part of the Gaultier brand, synonymous with a playful French identity that is constantly reinvented. For the 'Punk Cancan' couture collection, this was mixed with a distinctly British punk sensibility, naming some outfits after songs by the Sex Pistols and the Clash. 'Bateau-lavoir' gown (centre), Jean Paul Gaultier 'Punk Cancan' collection, haute couture spring/summer 2011. 'Lascar' dress (far right) from 'Les Indes galantes' collection, haute couture spring/summer 2000.*

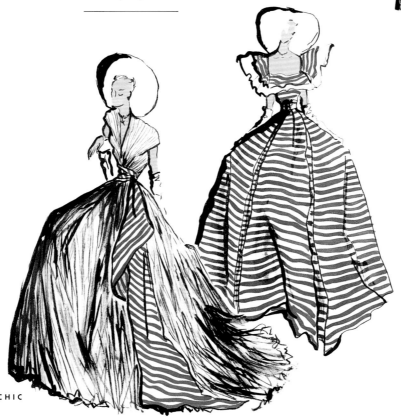

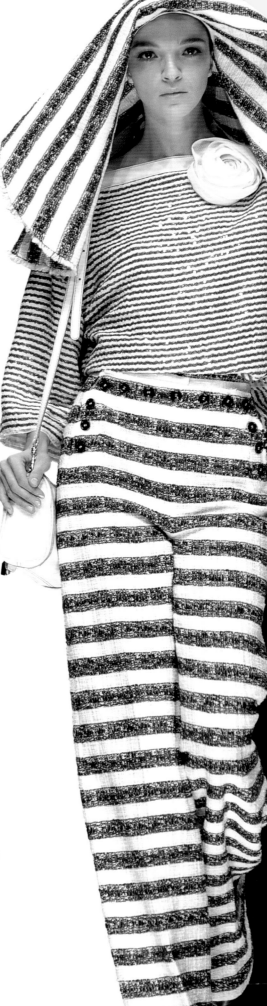

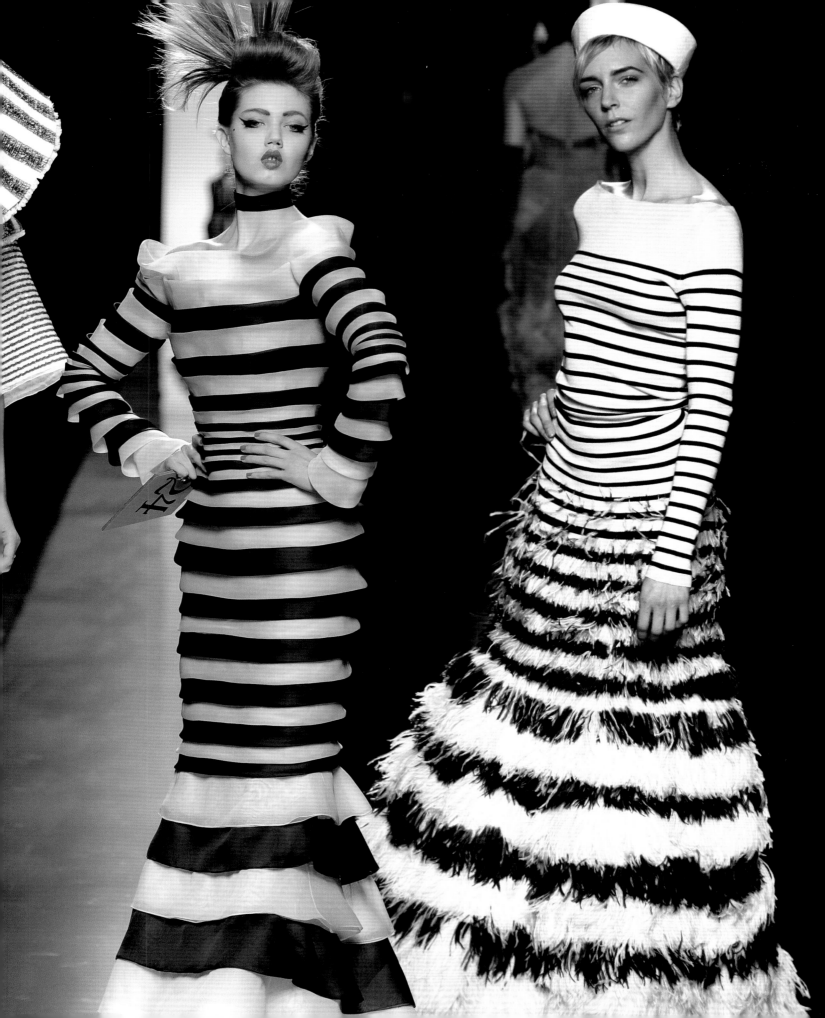

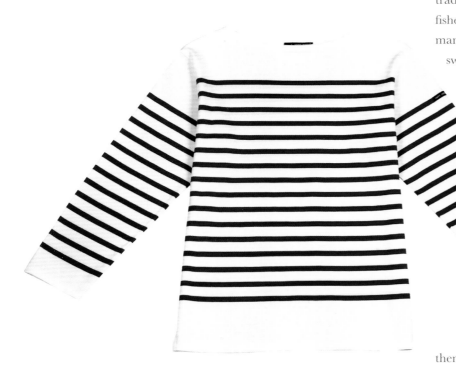

haberdasheries of Brittany for the hosiery and underwear trade, and were also used along the coast to knit the heavy fishermen's chandail sweater. A century later, they began to manufacture their own navy blue 'real Breton fisherman's sweater', with the distinctive side buttons at the shoulder, and they supply knitwear to the French army and navy from their factory, still located in Saint James. They branched out into other colours, and the ubiquitous stripes, and also produce jersey striped tops. The marketing for their 2012 capsule collection with Barneys New York featured the ultimate signifier of French identity: an Eiffel Tower sculpture adorned in blue and white stripes. Petit Bateau, known for its striped children's and adult wear, started as a hosiery factory in the textile centre of Troyes in 1893, specializing in underwear for children. They have subsequently developed into a nautical-themed lifestyle brand. Meanwhile, Armor-Lux, originating in Quimper in 1938, produces both the fisherman's sweater and striped marinières. They have also expanded into a lifestyle range, including homewares featuring sea creatures and rustic scenes of life in Brittany, where they remain based. A year later, in 1939, Orcival was founded in Paris. Previous outfitters to the French Navy, they expanded beyond their traditional markets of fishermen and sailors in the 1970s and continue manufacturing their marinières in France today.

Above: *The classic* marinière. *Saint James 'Naval II' jersey boat-neck striped top.* **Opposite, left:** *Karl Lagerfeld updates Chanel's original fishing chandail sweater. He also noted similarities between the classic Chanel design and a jacket worn by a Singaporean fisherman in a photograph from 1880. Chanel 2014 cruise collection, presented in Singapore.* **Opposite, right:** *Gabrielle Chanel in front of the store in Deauville, 1913. Chanel wears the fishing chandail sweater first created that year.*

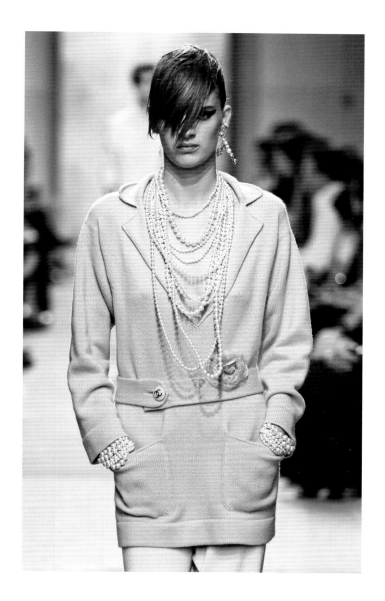

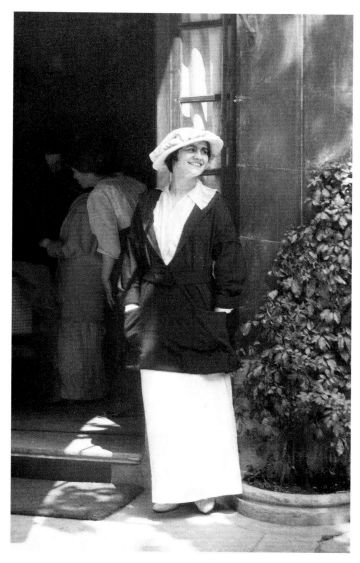

## COASTAL COUTURE

By the beginning of the 20th century, sportswear was starting to make its mark on fashionable women's wardrobes. The walking outfits and cycling-friendly tailoring of the last decades of the 19th century was morphing into a new appreciation of activewear, which would reach its zenith in the interbellum heyday of physical fitness. In the 1920s, the couturier Jean Patou allocated an area of his Paris store for sporting apparel and dressed notable sports stars such as the tennis player Suzanne Lenglen. He also had salons at the resorts of Deauville and Biarritz.[11] Tennis player Jane Regny tapped into the sports market with her designs and, a few years later

in 1927, Schiaparelli opened her Parisian store, Pour Le Sport.[12] With this emphasis on utility, it is understandable that occupational clothing – whose *raison d'être* was functionality – would also be subsumed into high fashion.

In 1913, Coco Chanel opened her first clothing boutique in the resort of Deauville on the Normandy coast (her first shop, opened three years earlier in Paris, was dedicated to hats). One of her first items was inspired by the smocks and chandails (sweaters) of Normandy fishermen.[13] Fashioned in knitted jersey, a fabric previously used only for sportswear and underwear, it pulled on over the head, rather than doing up at the front like a blouse, and had deep pockets, a belt, and a square sailor collar at the back. The simplicity of the item chimed with the times – wealthy women were becoming less

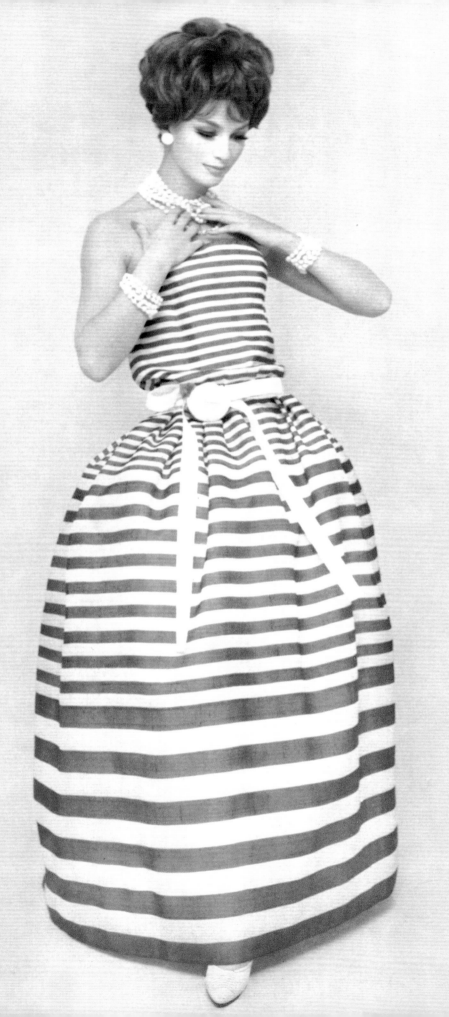

Left: *Couture stripes: Christian Dior evening gown, 1961.* Opposite: A bold-striped Balmain dress, modelled on the embankment of the River Seine in Paris. Photographed by Genevieve Naylor, 1946.

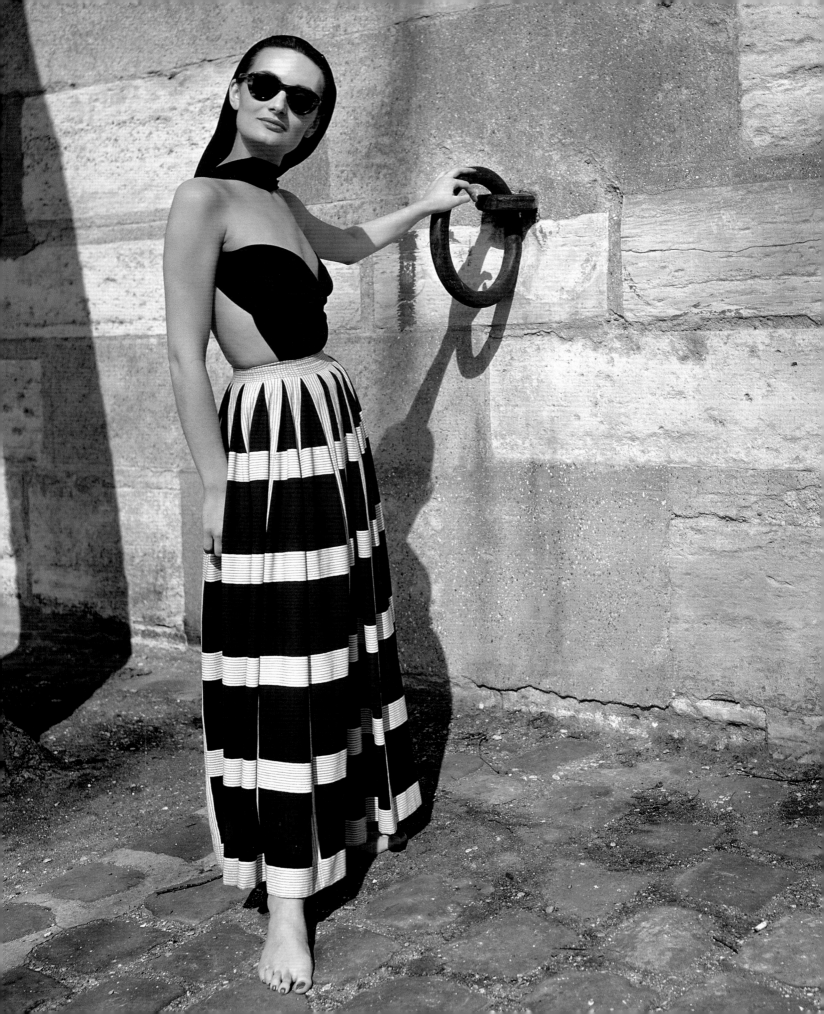

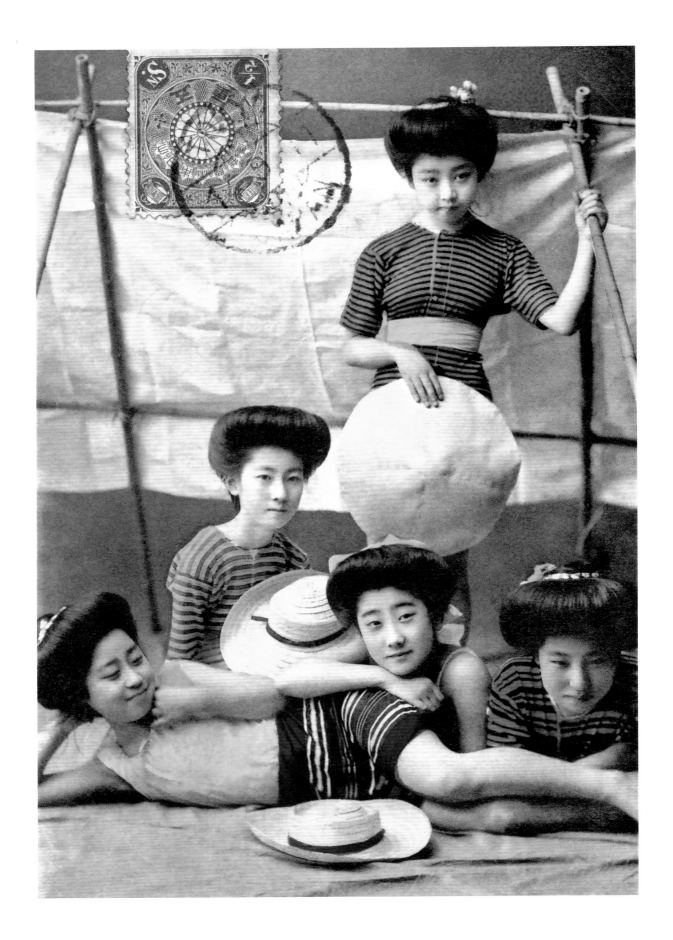

reliant on maids to help them dress – and its ensuing popularity saw it featured in fashion publications, as well as on the sands of Deauville, over the coming years.

In 1916, Chanel's chandail made a whole page spread in British and American *Vogue*, albeit with more luxe trimmings: 'Being a true chandail it is drawn over the head, opening in the front in a shallow V which is finished with a deep sailor collar of grey fur.'[14] The following year, *Les Elégances Parisiennes* feted a new fashion fabric – jersey – illustrated by Chanel's smock-like designs, while British *Vogue* christened Chanel the 'Jersey House'. Chanel was not the only designer at the time to be working with jersey, but her use was extensive and she was praised for her ability to utilize its properties to create something entirely modern. For working people, historically a sharp distinction had been drawn between work clothes and those reserved for Sunday best. Chanel subverted this divide, and future designs saw her incorporate items such as stonemasons' neckerchiefs, dockworkers' T-shirts and mechanics' dungarees into her collections.[15] Her synthesizing of men's workwear into women's fashion paired occupational-inspired clothing with the fancy trappings of high society.

Chanel owed much of her success to the seaside resorts and outdoor pursuits of the French coast, as opposed to the confines of Paris. Deauville remained prosperous throughout the First World War as the moneyed elite fled the capital. In 1915, Chanel opened a couture house in Biarritz, another fashionable spot that, until the 1850s, had been a fishing village and, from 1917, her designs were seen at notable American resorts such as Palm Beach and Newport.[16] The transition from fishing to fashionable playground was not uncommon from the mid-19th century onwards, as picturesque coastlines across Europe began to be dominated by the seasonal visits of the wealthy classes. The allure of the traditional and 'authentic' way of life of fishing communities had long been a draw for the artistic or bohemian temperament, albeit through their own romantic proto-tourist gaze,[17] and, during the interwar period, an emerging group of international writers and artists – whom we would today term tastemakers – began to holiday along the southern stretch of the French coast known as the Riviera.

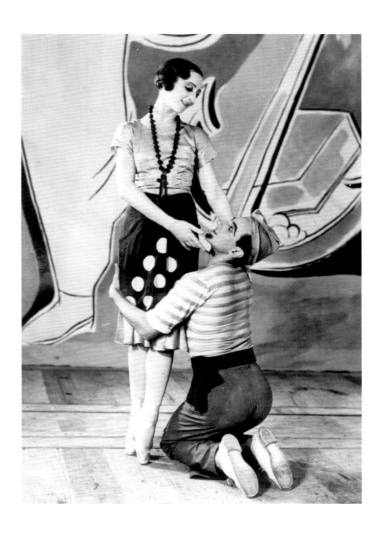

Above: *Alexandra Danilova as the Young Girl and Leon Woizikovski as the First Sailor in the Ballets Russes production of* Les Matelots, *c. 1925/6.* Opposite: *Geisha and Maiko (Geisha-in-training) in striped swimwear fashions of the day. Late Meiji era, c. 1910.*

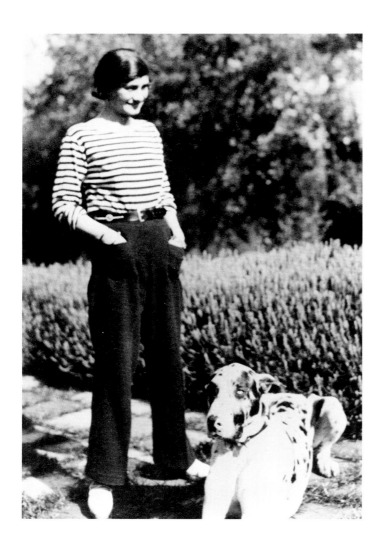

Above: *Chanel dons a striped top at her Riviera home, La Pausa, 1930.* Opposite: *'Hold on to Your Hat' illustration by Sat, featuring the changing wartime silhouette, including the narrower 'barrel-line' silhouette and stripes.* La Baionnette, *27 June 1918.*

# RIVIERA CHIC:
## THE BIRTH OF A STYLE STAPLE

In 1887, the writer and poet Stéphen Liégeard coined the term Côte d'Azur to refer to this particular stretch of coast.[18] A few years later, the pointillist artist Paul Signac set up home in the then fishing village of Saint Tropez. Encouraging fellow artists to visit him, it became known as the first artist's retreat on the Riviera, a tradition that continued along this section of the Mediterranean as creative personalities gradually overtook the aristocracy in social influence.

Chanel opened another resort-based boutique in 1923, in the former fishing village of Cannes. As with many of her designs, Chanel took sartorial cues from the Duke of Westminster and, after her first trip on board his yacht the *Flying Cloud*, she is said to have said that navy and white are the only possible colours.[19] This was also the year that the American artist Gerald Murphy took a trip to Marseille to get supplies for his boat, returning with striped marinière tops for himself and his guests and kick-starting a trend that continues to this day.[20] Gerald and Sara Murphy first visited the Cap d'Antibes the previous year as guests of Cole Porter. They

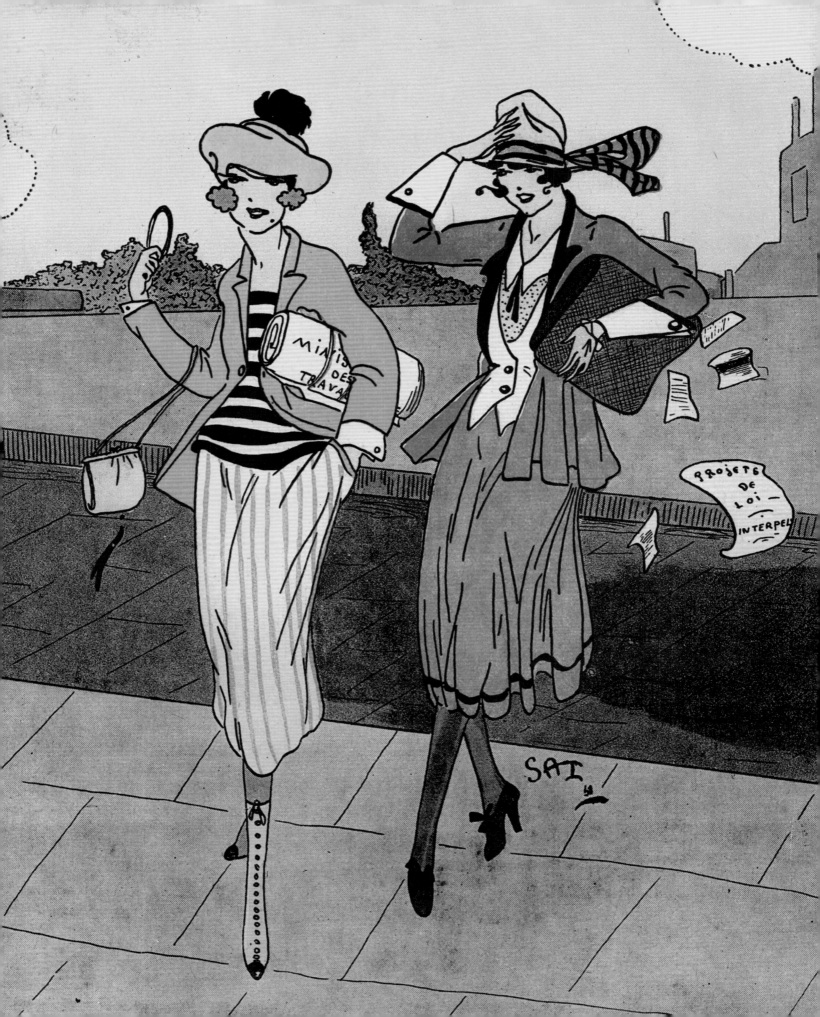

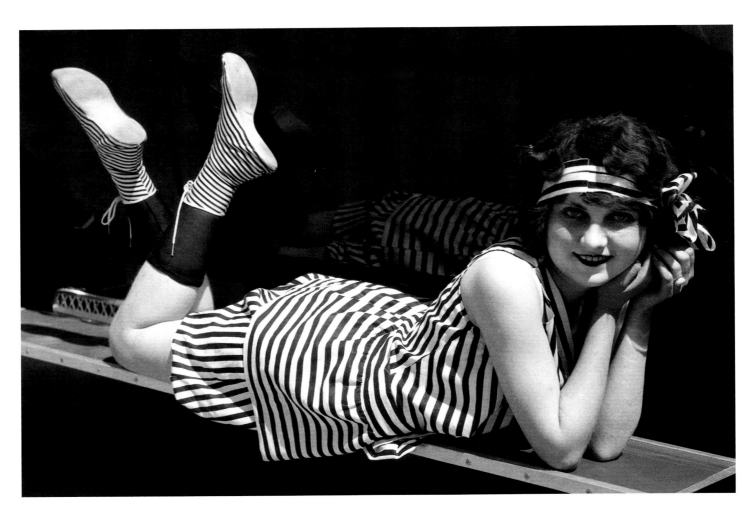

liked it so much they returned, creating a summer 'season' and welcoming various shining lights of the modernist movement into their 'Villa America', including Man Ray, Dorothy Parker, Stravinsky, Ernest Hemingway, Picasso, and Zelda and F. Scott Fitzgerald, who dedicated his novel *Tender is the Night* to the couple. The novel chronicles the Riviera as it shifted from creative colony to an overcrowded holiday spot, and the sartorial influence is noted as one character reminisces about 'the sailor trunks and sweaters they had bought in a Nice backstreet – garments that afterward ran through a vogue in silk among the Paris couturiers.'[21]

The Murphys had a finely attuned aesthetic sense and both Gerald and Sara were admired for their dress. Sara's obsession with tanning and wearing pearls to the beach predated Chanel, and Gerald – frequently seen sporting a fisherman's cap – had won the 'best dressed' award while at Yale.[22] The popularity of the striped top spread quickly, and was often paired with rope-soled espadrilles that had been worn by peasants in the French-

*Above: Stripes were cemented as a popular beachside style throughout the 19th century. 'Kentucky belle' Miss Mary Catherine Dear models the latest striped beachwear fashions at Ocean Park resort, California, 1923. Opposite: Stripes as a chic, casual classic. Saint James top photographed by Guy Aroch for* The Ritz-Carlton Magazine, *October 2009.*

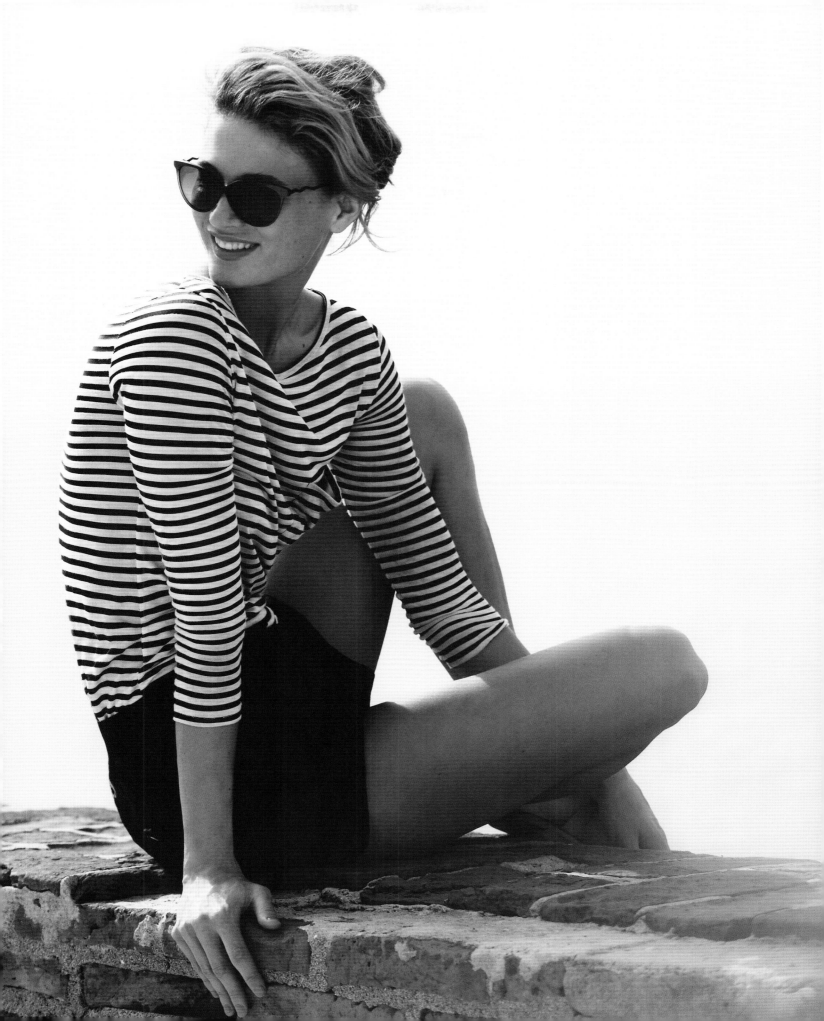

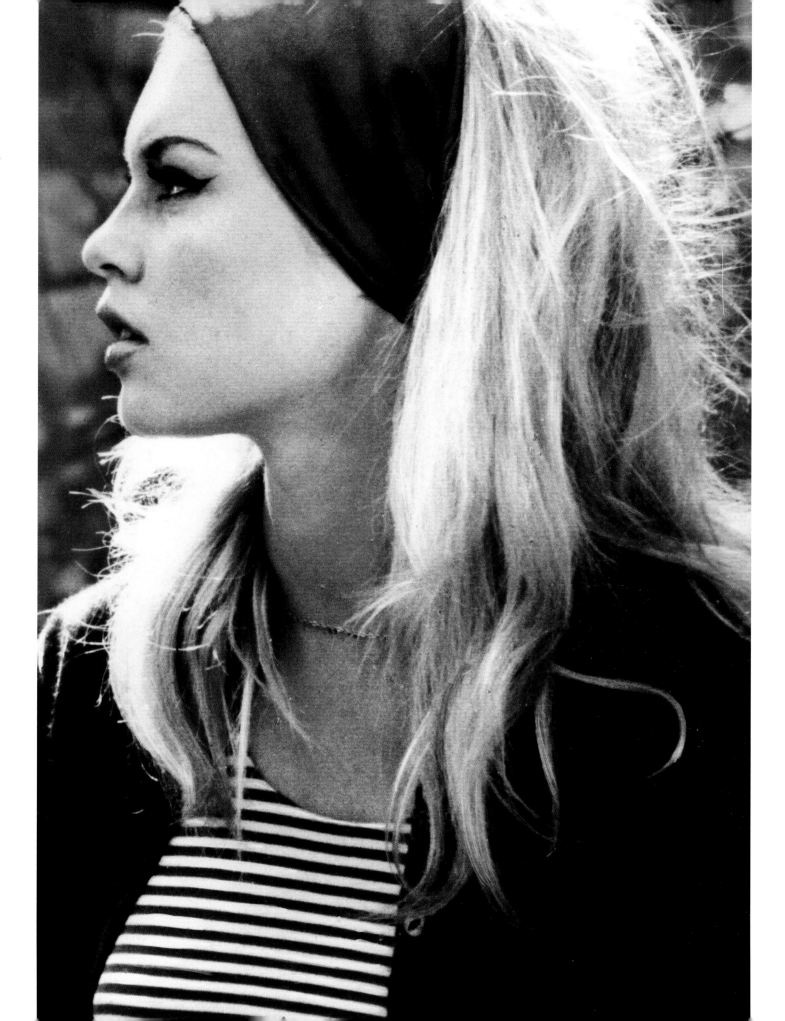

Spanish border region for centuries. Immediately, this look became something of a unisex leisure uniform.[23]

A perennial favourite among the Riviera set, writers and artists were instrumental in popularizing the striped fishing top. Ernest Hemingway had become a fan in 1927 when honeymooning with his second wife in the Mediterranean fishing village of Le Grau-du-Roi.[24] Possibly influenced by his time with the Murphys, and undoubtedly swayed by his own love of fishing, it was immortalized in *The Garden of Eden*, published posthumously, in which the couple are described as the first people in town to wear fisherman's shirts, bought from the local marine supplies store.[25] The Murphys and their coterie were innovators both in terms of clothing styles and holiday spots. In late 1922, the 'Blue Train', as it became known, started its journeys from Calais via Paris to the Mediterranean coast, initially a first class-only service, soon to be advertised in magazines such as *Vogue*. The train was immortalized in a 1924 Ballets Russes production, *Le Train Bleu*, a Cocteau-penned operetta that gently mocked beach society, and for which Chanel created sporty costumes and Picasso designed the programme. Seafaring life was the subject of another Ballets Russes production later in the decade, *Les Matelots* (1925), which even incorporated sea shanties into the score.[26] Enamoured with beach life, by the end of the decade Chanel had bought land at Roquebrune to build her own Riviera home, La Pausa.

Opposite: *Stripes and sex appeal: Brigitte Bardot in* Le Mepris, *directed by Jean-Luc Godard, 1963.*

If the 1920s were the decade when the striped top crossed from workwear to stylish casual dress, the 1930s saw it cemented as a fashion classic. As with most trends, the initial uptake by a fashionable few leads to mass-market adoption. So it is telling that a 1931 British *Vogue* article characterizes the dress of the husband of future fashion editor Diana Vreeland as 'gay and unconventional' when he is photographed wearing a striped matelot top on holiday in Tunisia. The following year, it is given full credence on a French *Vogue* cover featuring an illustration of a Chanel-like figure clad in stripes at the Riviera.[27] The Duke of Windsor, in the style spotlight both pre- and post-abdication, was photographed afloat in a striped top in the thirties, again helping to enshrine the place of French stripes in a fashionable lifestyle. *Esquire* enthused about a horizontal-striped cotton Basque shirt that was all the rage on the Riviera in 1937.[28] By the 1950s, Jaeger were advertising in *Vogue* using René Gruau illustrations of unisex striped sweaters, and Hollywood gave stripes a helping hand through James Dean, Audrey Hepburn and Kim Novak. In a pleasing cycle of nautical chic, the striped top worn by Hepburn on the set of *War and Peace* in 1955 was made by American luxury goods company Mark Cross, owned by the Murphy family and whose then-president was Gerald Murphy. The company now trade on this heritage, with leather bags named 'Villa America', 'Antibes' and 'Hemingway'. In France, meanwhile, Brigitte Bardot was doing more than her fair share of popularizing

Below: *Training officers and cadets on a French ship on the Thames. Sailors wear the* tricot rayé *jersey marinière top, August 1935.*
Opposite: *Stripes and the French pompom sailor hat on the catwalk at Kenzo, spring/summer 2006.*

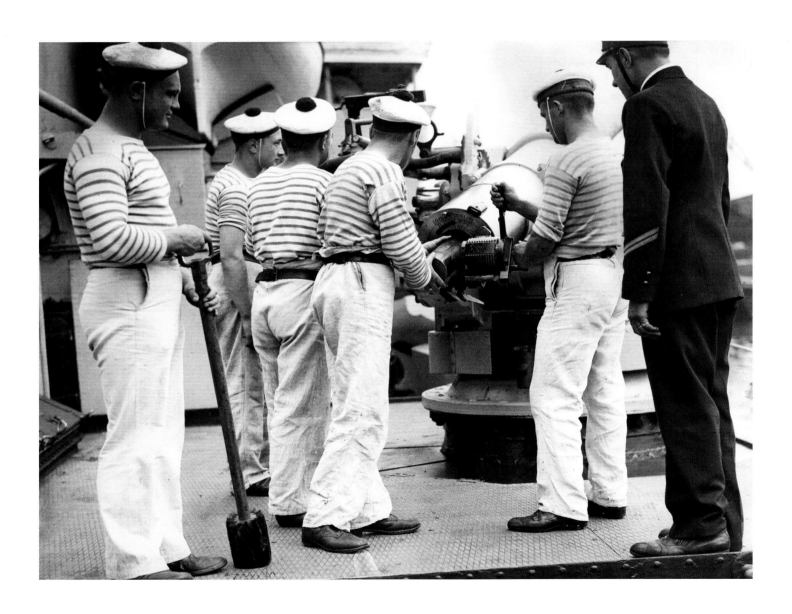

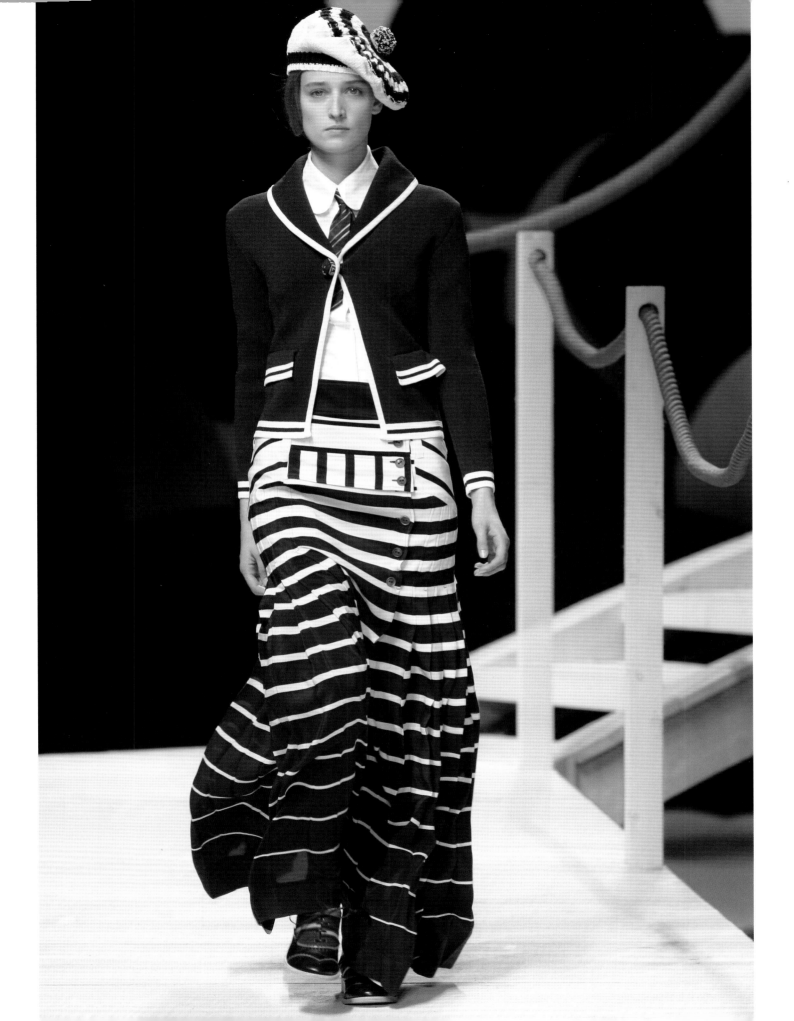

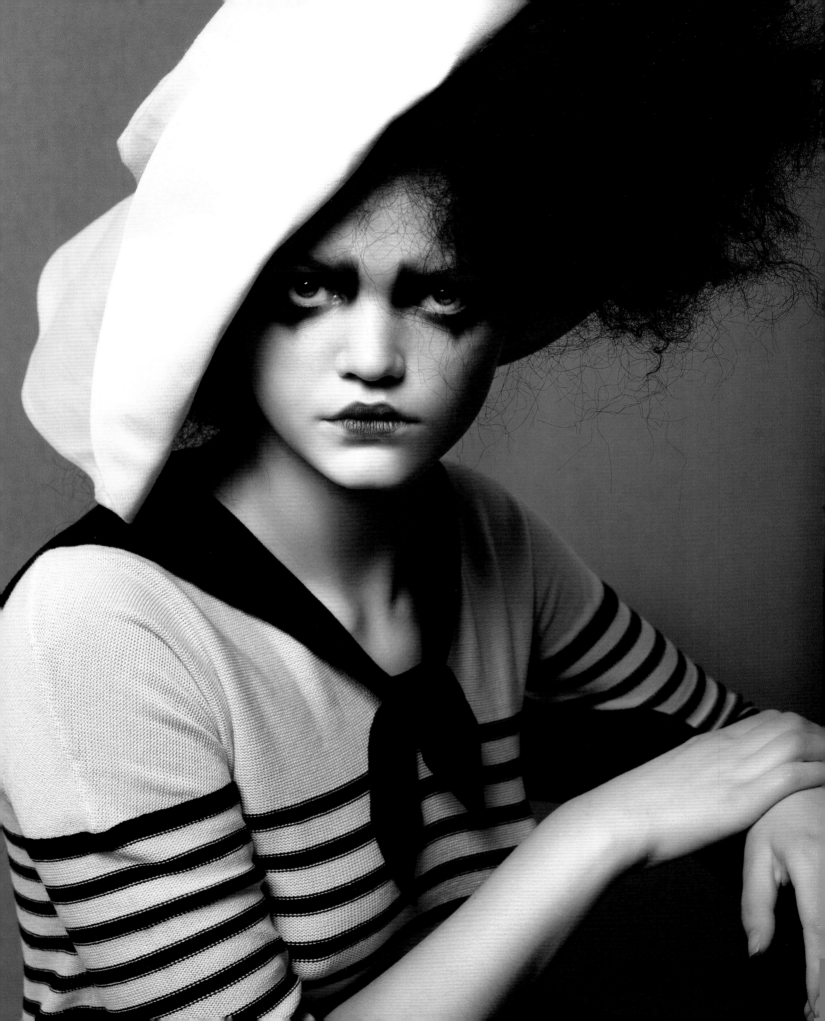

the national style. Picasso immortalized the jersey in his composition *Night Fishing at Antibes* (1939), but became synonymous with the style during the seven years he worked in Vallauris on the Côte d'Azur, his preference for the clothing of working men possibly indicative of his affiliation with Communism. In 1930, the artist Francis Picabia and his partner Germaine Everling were pictured sporting matching striped tops at their Riviera home,[29] while Jackson Pollock wears a blue and white striped fisherman's shirt in the last photograph taken of him before his death in 1956. He is pictured with his long-term mistress, Ruth Kligman, and the pair reportedly had many of these tops, again highlighting their unisex appeal.[30]

This association with the art world meant that, towards the end of the 1950s, stripes were garnering a vaguely countercultural air, picked up by Tinsel Town in a number of 'beatnik' movies. Although Audrey Hepburn is clad in black, it is notable that one of the male dancers wears stripes for her 'beatnik' dance in *Funny Face* (1957). In 1960, Jean Seberg in *Breathless* showed the world that nothing epitomized French chic like boat-neck stripes and, later in the decade, Andy Warhol and Edie Sedgwick lent it an air of Manhattan cool. Joan Baez sported one at the Newport Jazz Festival in 1968, while Anna Karina also contributed *Nouvelle Vague*, Left Bank elegance. This subversive air wasn't limited to postwar counterculture: striped blue and white shirts had also been worn by *Les Apaches*,

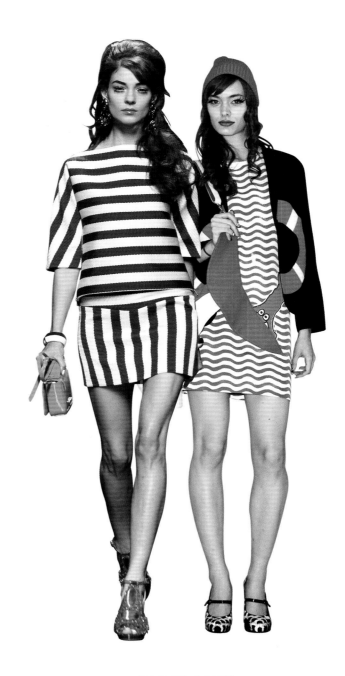

Above, left: *Boat-neck stripes on the catwalk at Moschino, in a collection that also referenced bold graphics and shift dresses of the 1960s, spring/ summer 2013.* Above, right: *Stripes double as waves in the 'Cod Save the Sea' collection by The Rodnik Band, spring/summer 2012.* Opposite: *Sonia Rykiel nautical designs feature in 'Imaginarium' shoot for* Leonardo *magazine, Moscow, photographed by Andrey Yakovlev and directed by Lili Aleeva, 2010.*

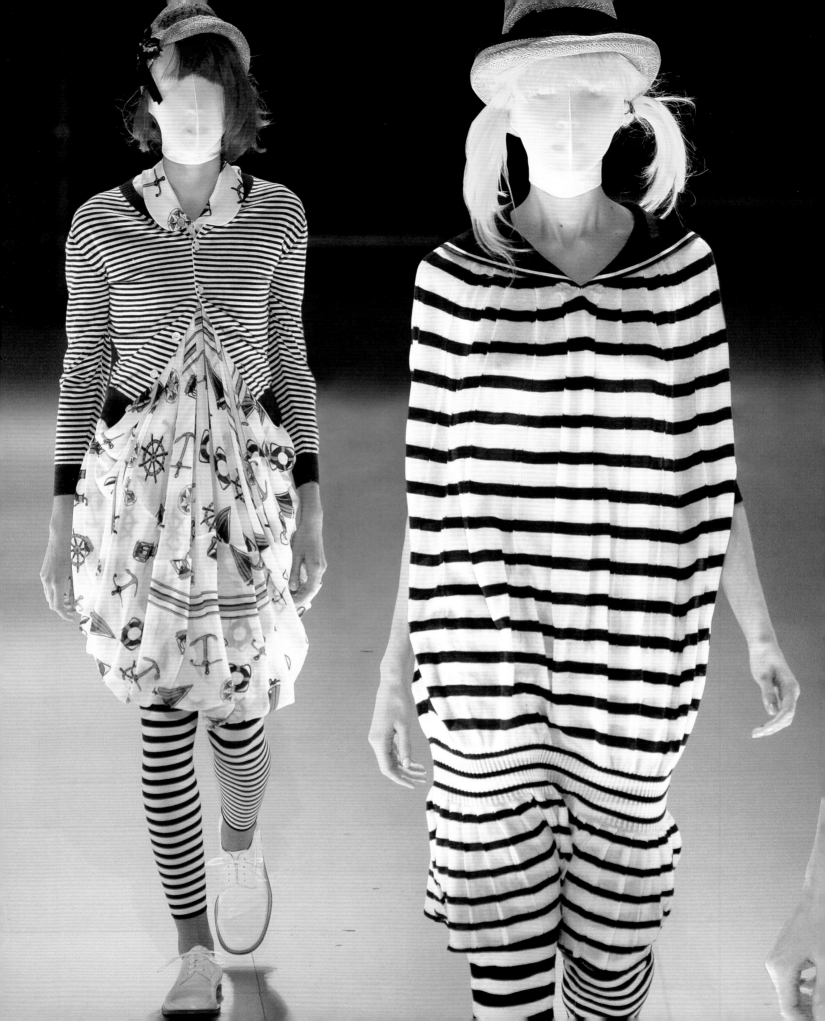

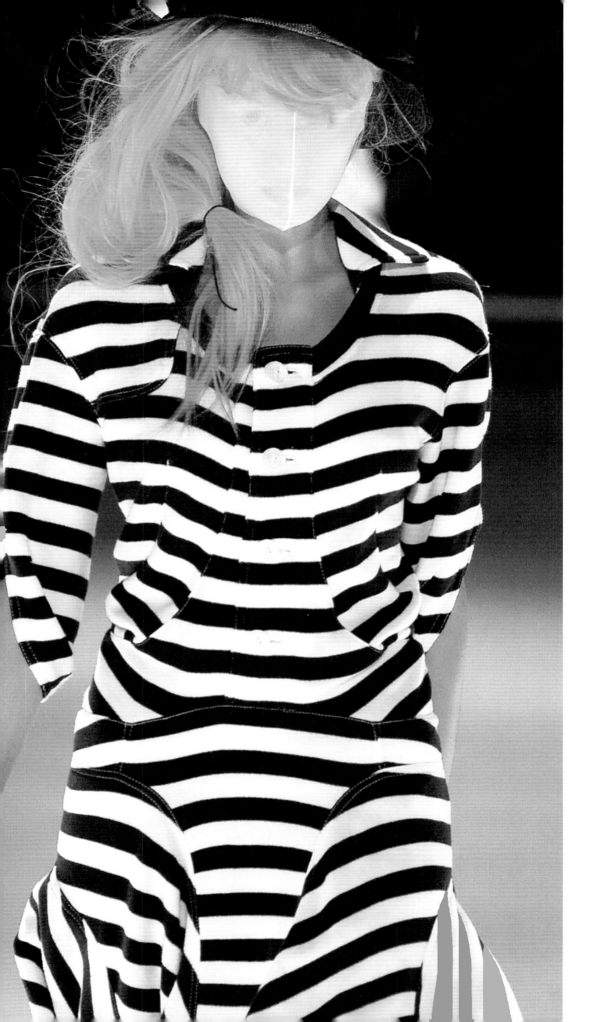

*Junya Watanabe added an Op Art element to stripes, combined with nautical motifs such as anchors and ship's wheels, in this collection that referenced Edwardian swimwear with a contemporary, sporty feel for spring/summer 2011.*

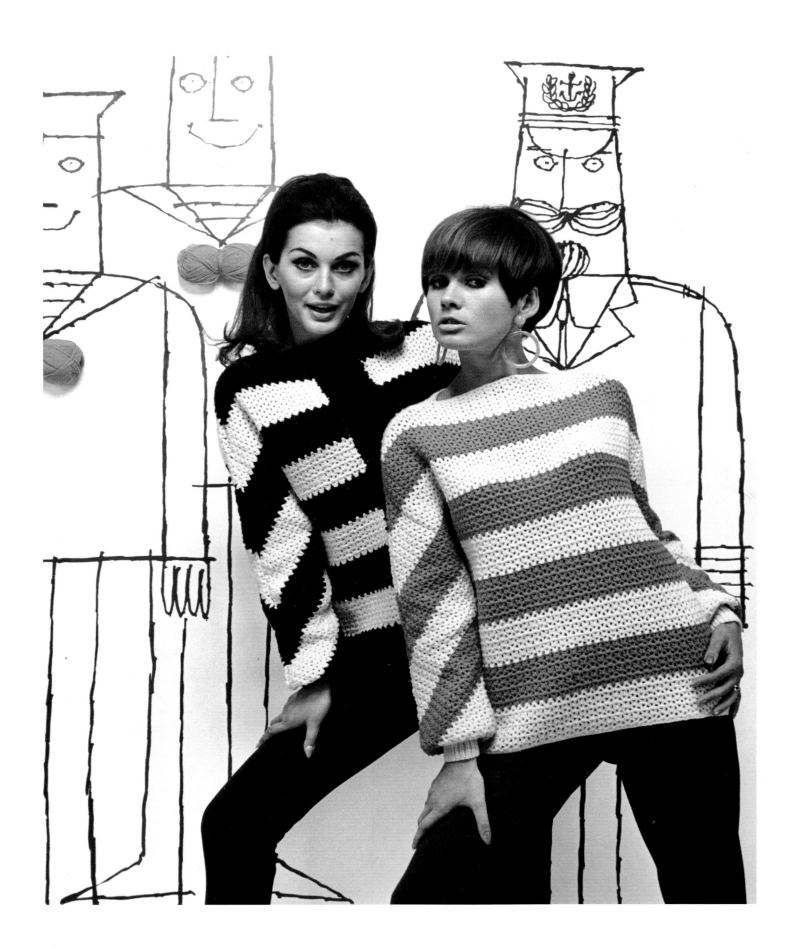

a group of sartorially-obsessed gangsters in early 20th-century Paris.[31] These street gangs inspired a series of fancy dress balls, and Gerald Murphy was so entranced with their style he risked his safety to acquire certain pieces.[32] In later years, worn by everyone from Patti Smith to the Ramones, Kurt Cobain and Kate Middleton, the striped top is somewhat unique in that it is both a marker of effortless classic French chic but can still hint at countercultural associations, one of the only fashion staples that can look both bourgeois and bohemian.

Stripes were a fashion favourite of the 1960s. In his January 1966 couture collection, the same collection that popularized the pea coat and sailor trousers, Yves Saint Laurent rendered smocks and dresses in sequin nautical stripes. His interest in nautical motifs stretched back to his debut collection in 1962 and, while his collections were high fashion, he injected his own take on Left Bank style. The same year, William Klein's fashion satire *Qui êtes vous, Polly Maggoo?* used exaggerated stripes that chimed not only with the Op Art of the decade (that an article in *Vogue* linked directly to the dazzle camouflage of the First World War[33]), but also illustrated how firmly entrenched stripes had become in the notion of French style. The same decade Sonia Rykiel created her first knitwear designs – the 'poor boy' sweaters – and stripes soon became indelibly woven into her brand identity. Jean Paul Gaultier regularly reinvents the nautical stripe, and often appears in his signature matelot top. His 1990 portrait by Pierre et Gilles, featuring him in a striped top with the Eiffel tower in the background, successfully incorporates the maritime into an image constructed to be both quintessentially French and unequivocally camp.

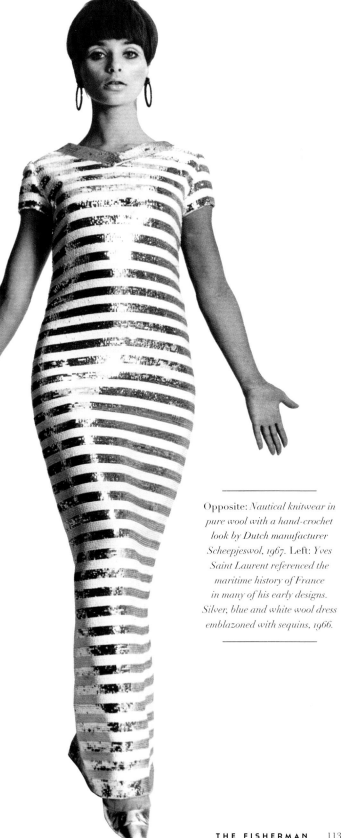

Opposite: *Nautical knitwear in pure wool with a hand-crochet look by Dutch manufacturer Scheepjeswol, 1967.* Left: *Yves Saint Laurent referenced the maritime history of France in many of his early designs. Silver, blue and white wool dress emblazoned with sequins, 1966.*

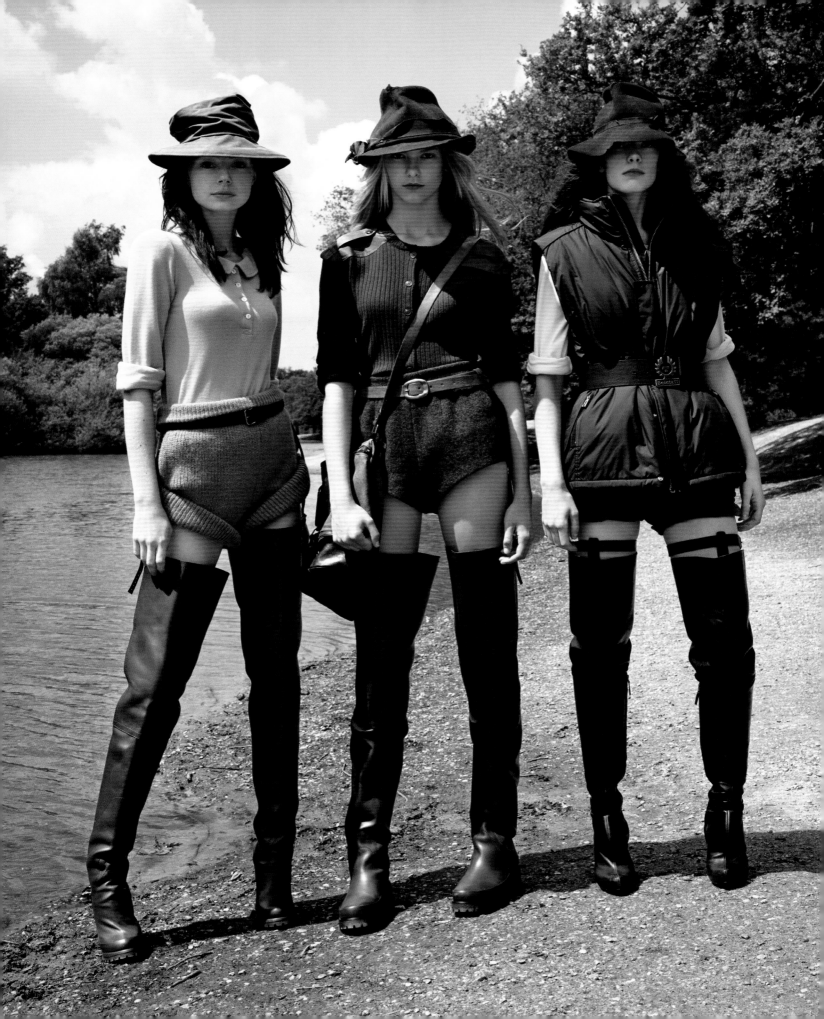

Opposite: *Fishing fashion in a spread titled 'Thigh Society' that extolled the virtues of the wader: 'Both Miuccia Prada and Hussein Chalayan raided the tackle shop to create boots that are whimsical and luxurious, but tough and practical too.' Photographed by Chris Brooks for* Love *magazine, June 2009.*

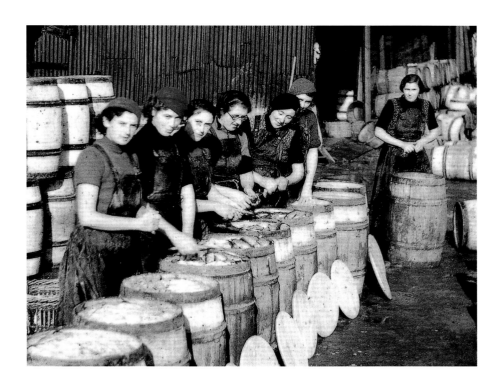

## STAYING DRY WITH STYLE: WATERPROOFS

Above: *For around a century from 1860, the Scottish fisher lassies were a distinctive sight around the coast of Britain. Women from Newhaven or Aberdeen in Scotland would follow the herring fleet down the east coast, where they joined local girls in gutting, packing and salting the catch. They were instrumental in spreading the designs of regional fishing knits. Here, fisher girls in Lowestoft wear knitwear with thick leather aprons as protection from the gruelling work, 1930s.*

Waterproofing became something of a holy grail for fishing communities. Distinctive thigh-high fishing waders, as recreated on the catwalk by Prada in autumn/winter 2009, can be traced back at least to the 17th century, through an illustration of the Fishmonger's Company at the Lord Mayor's Day pageant in 1616.[34] In the years preceding rubber, goose fat or melted cod liver were mixed with lard and applied to leather sea boots to add weatherfast properties, albeit somewhat pungent ones.[35] Early tarpaulin (tar-impregnated canvas) was used until the early 19th century, when it was replaced by boiled linseed oil, often mixed with pipe clay to form 'oilskins' when brushed over linen or cotton.[36] By the middle of the century, oilskin overalls and sou'wester hats were worn, named for strong winds or storms hailing from the southwest. From the 1880s, the distinctive yellow colour was in use, visible if lost overboard, and, in 1877, Norwegian mariner Helly Hanson and his wife began producing a waxed linseed oilskin that proved so popular they were soon exporting it worldwide. Later that century, Barbour were founded in South Shields, UK, providing

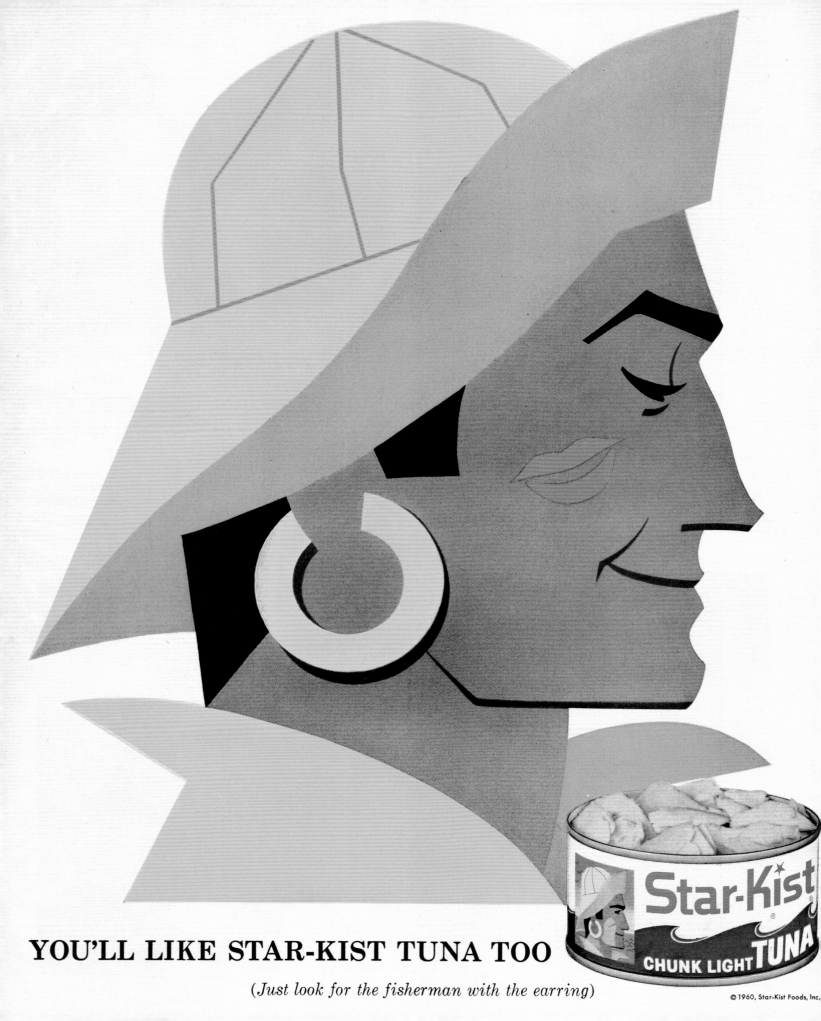

**YOU'LL LIKE STAR-KIST TUNA TOO**

*(Just look for the fisherman with the earring)*

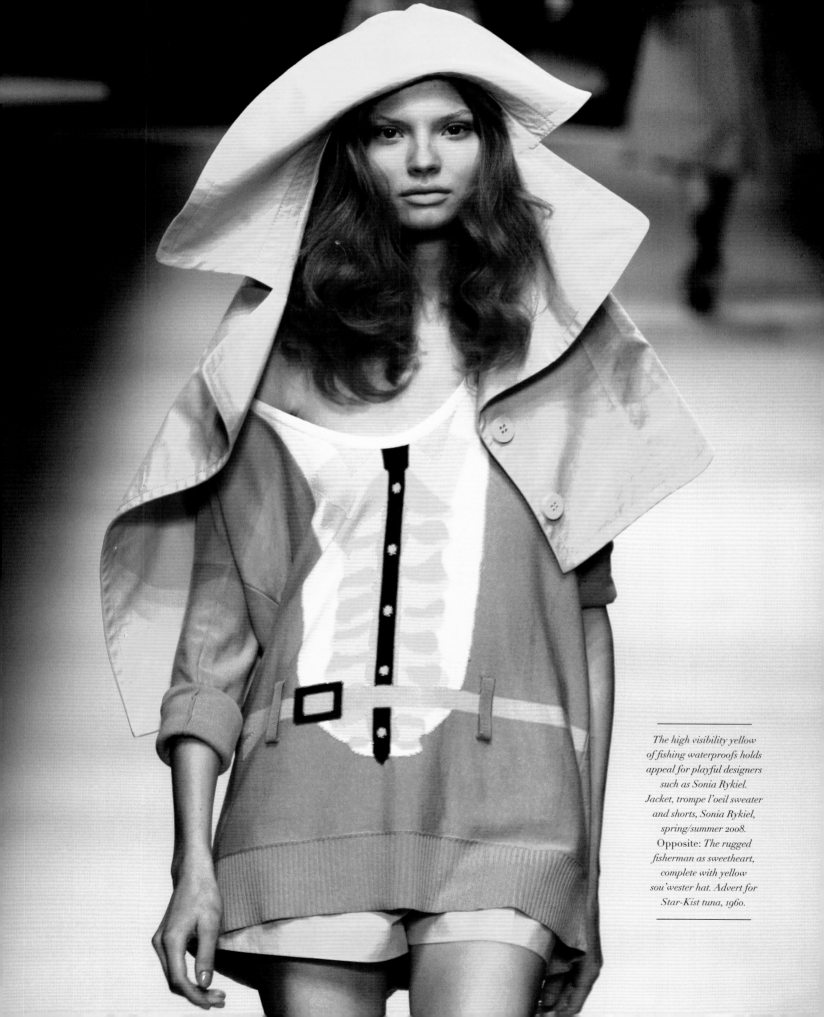

The high visibility yellow
of fishing waterproofs holds
appeal for playful designers
such as Sonia Rykiel.
Jacket, trompe l'oeil sweater
and shorts, Sonia Rykiel,
spring/summer 2008.
Opposite: The rugged
fisherman as sweetheart,
complete with yellow
sou'wester hat. Advert for
Star-Kist tuna, 1960.

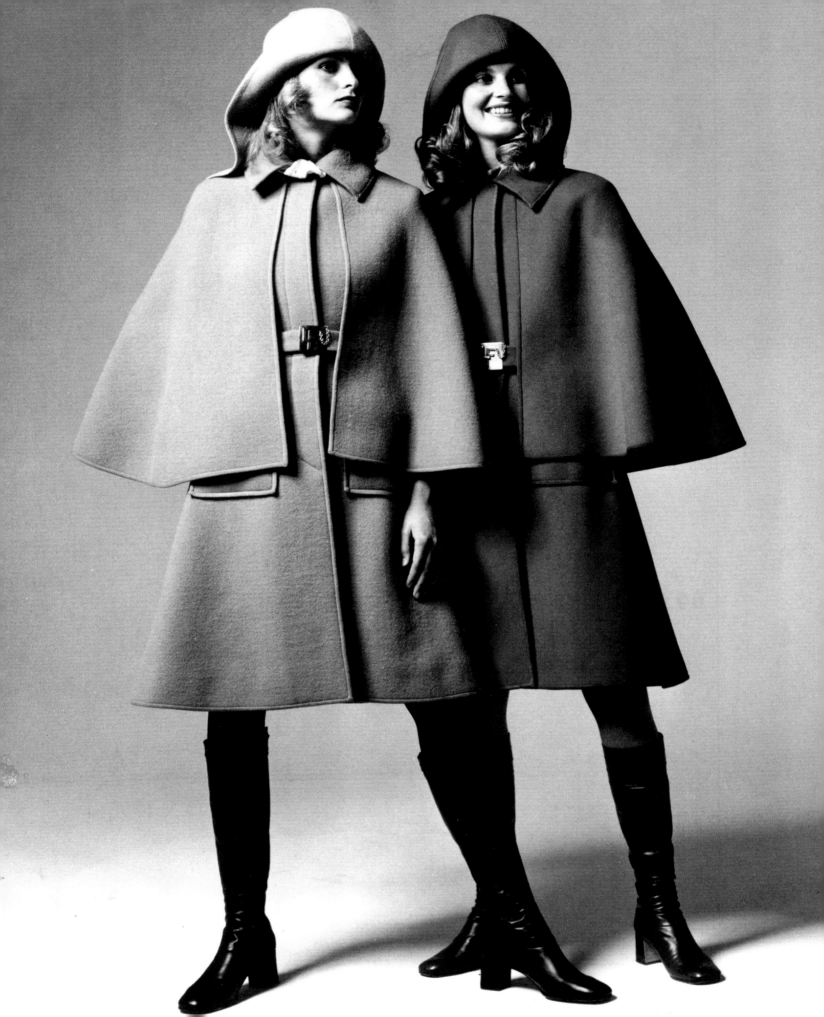

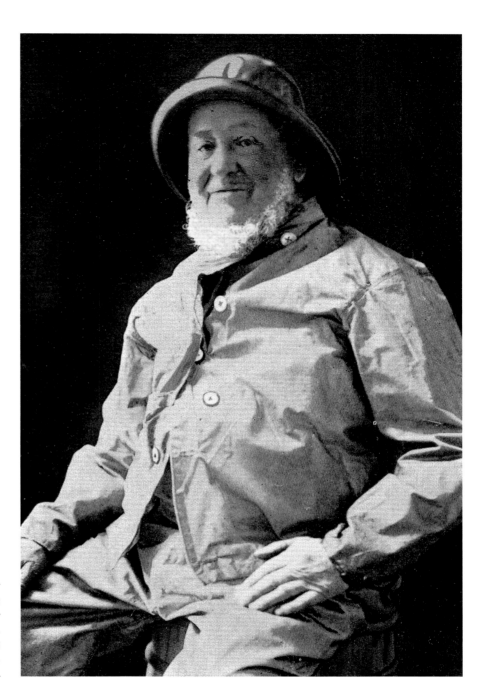

waxed waterproof clothing for the merchant navy and fishing, yachting and boating, as well as the country pursuits the brand is associated with today. Sou'wester-style hats were fashionable during the cloche craze of the 1920s. In 1929, British *Vogue* noted, 'Agnes continues to make the "fisherman's hat" with great success.' Sou'wester models by Jean Patou also featured.[37] The drive for innovation in waterproofs crossed into high fashion in 1949, as Balenciaga developed Cracknyl, a high-shine, lacquered fabric to be used for raincoats and skiwear.

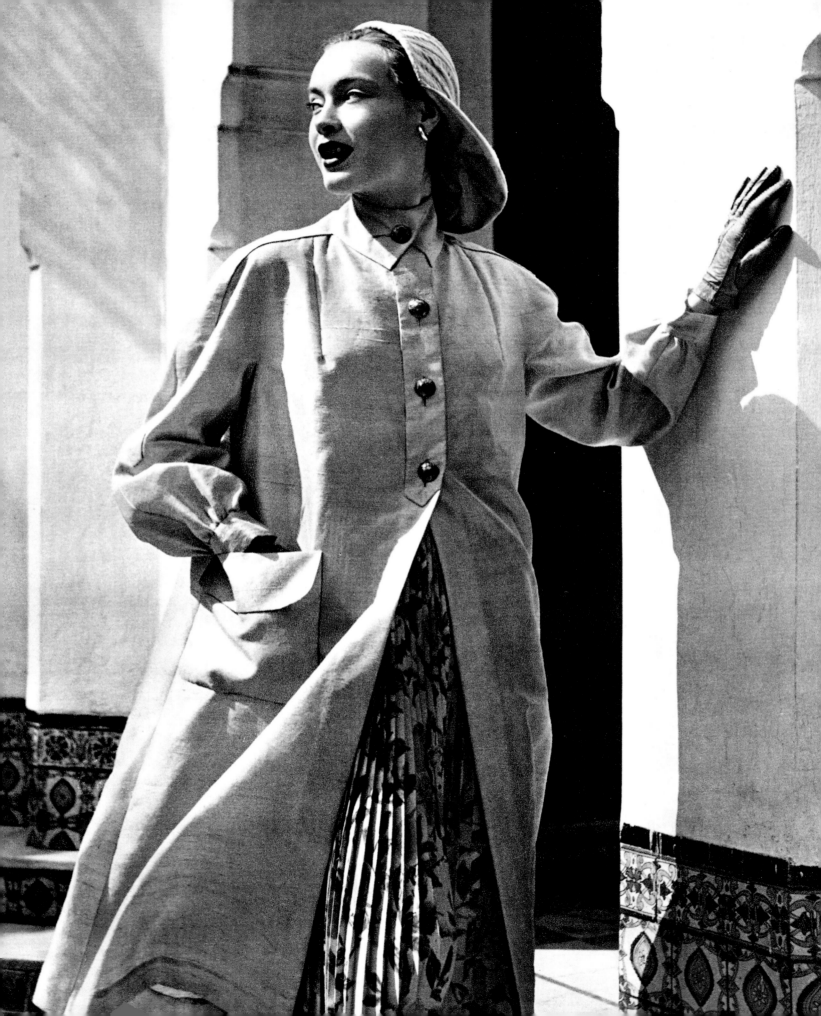

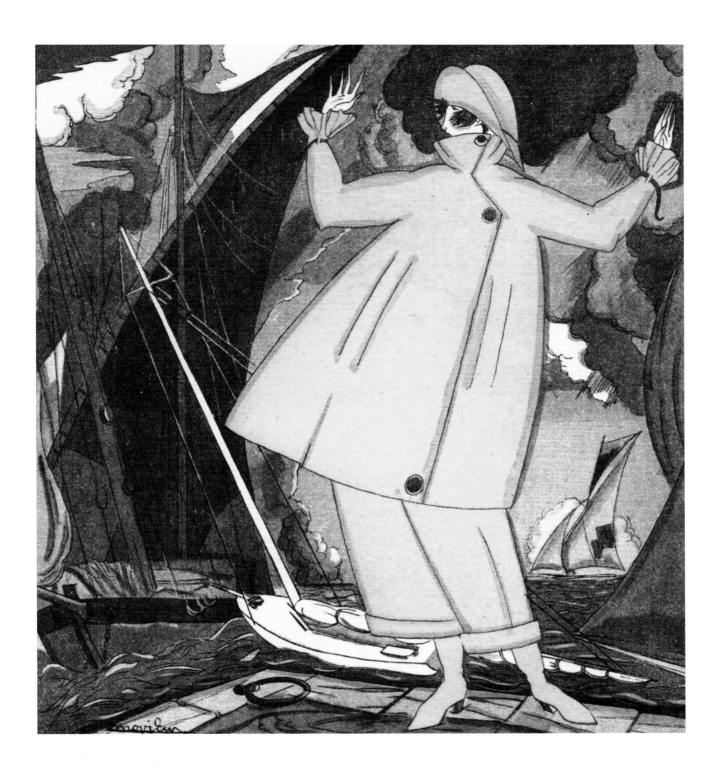

Above: *Yellow waterproofs as a yachting costume, illustrated in* Gazette du Bon Ton, *July 1920.* Opposite: *Marine-style couture coat and hat by Schiaparelli. Photographed by Philippe Pottier, 1952.*

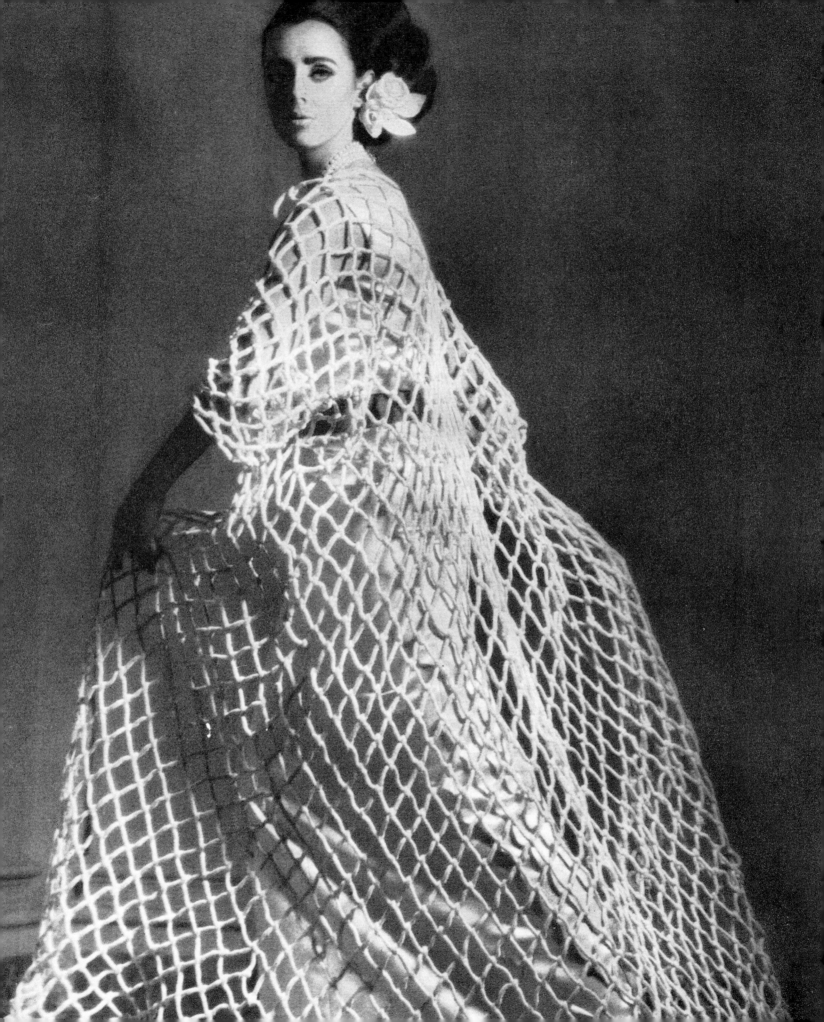

## FASHION, FISHING & KNITTING

Before developments in waterproofing, wool knitwear was the staple material for fishermen looking for a degree of protection from the weather. Although knitting was one of the first textile industries to be partially mechanized, the majority of fishermen's knits were made by hand. The Channel Islands' rich knitting history dates back to hosiery in the 16th century, and Jersey has lent its name to a knit fabric – made popular by Chanel – and a knitted pullover.[38] Guernsey may have been modified to become the 'gansey' sweater found in many fishing ports around Britain and the Channel, worn under fishing smocks for additional warmth. Alternatively, the name may be a corruption of 'yarnsy', meaning 'made from yarn.'[39] The gansey dates from the end of the 18th century, but grew in popularity from the 1850s onwards and is traditionally dark blue, made from tightly-knitted worsted or wool that retained its natural oils to offer an element of water and wind resistance. High-necked and tight-sleeved, they are knitted in the round to provide seamless protection. As gansey knitting spread, distinctive patterning began to develop across the chest. The patterns varied from region to region, which led to belief that villages, and even families, had their own personal designs.

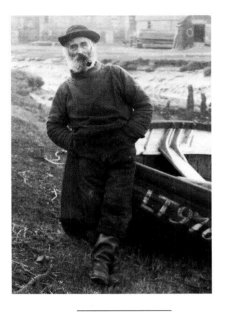

Above: *Southwold fisherman with a pipe, smock and boots, c. 1900.*
Below: *In homage to Coco Chanel's love of the sport, Karl Lagerfeld created a Chanel fishing kit as an accessory for the 2008 autumn/winter ready-to-wear collection.* Opposite: *Balenciaga's childhood was spent on the Basque coast of Spain, and the sea informed many of his designs. Balenciaga fishnet dress, photographed by Tom Kublin for American* Harper's Bazaar, *November 1964.*

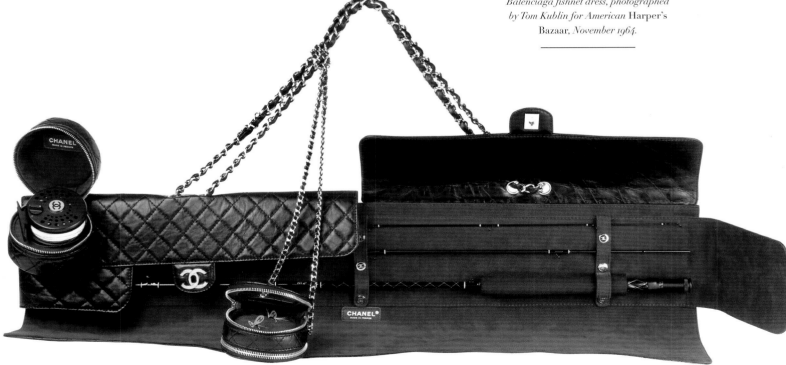

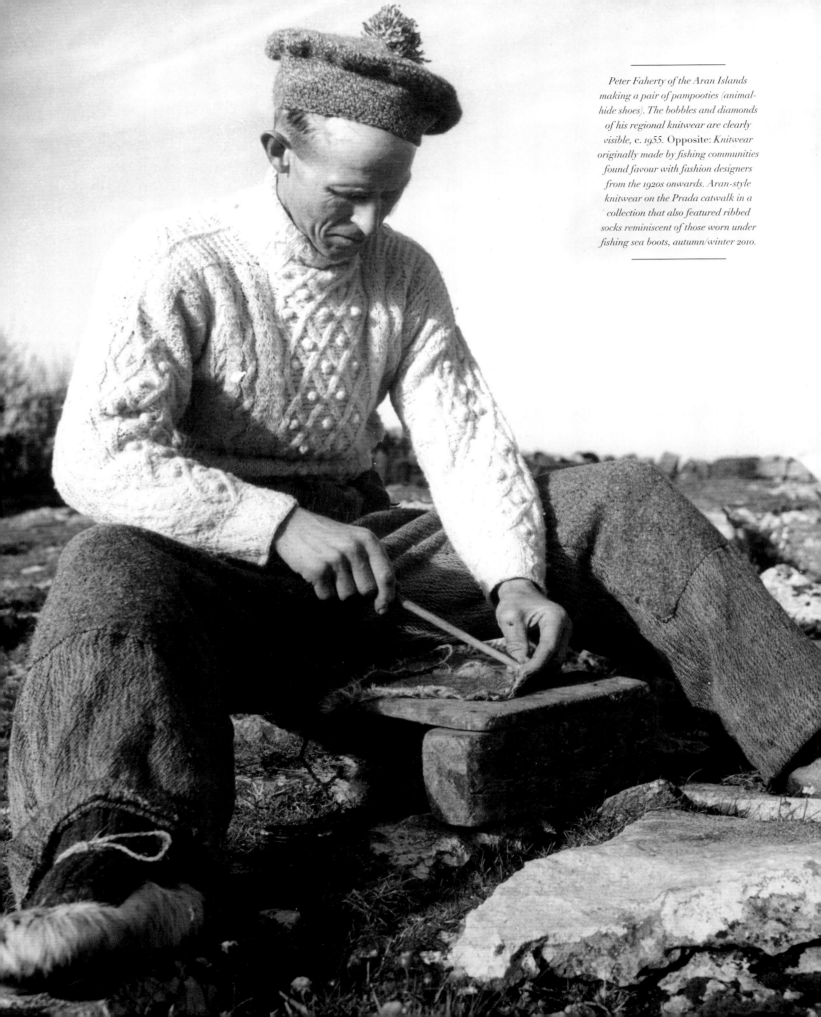

Peter Faherty of the Aran Islands making a pair of pampooties (animal-hide shoes). The bobbles and diamonds of his regional knitwear are clearly visible, c. 1955. Opposite: Knitwear originally made by fishing communities found favour with fashion designers from the 1920s onwards. Aran-style knitwear on the Prada catwalk in a collection that also featured ribbed socks reminiscent of those worn under fishing sea boots, autumn/winter 2010.

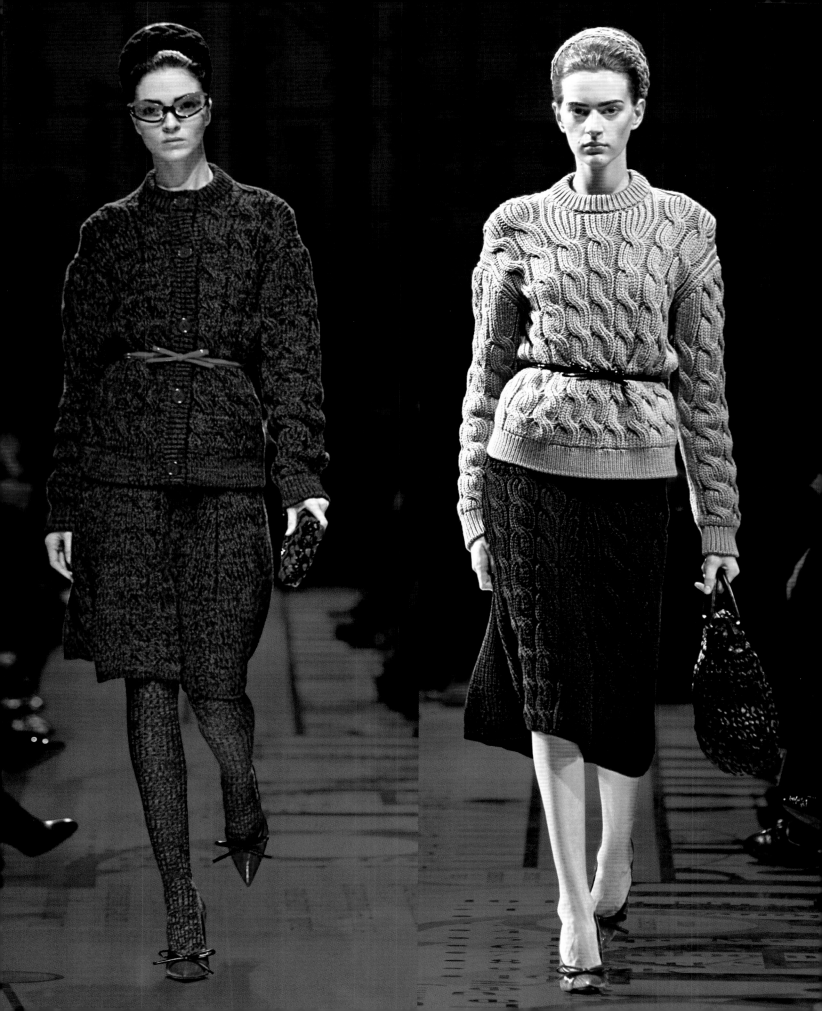

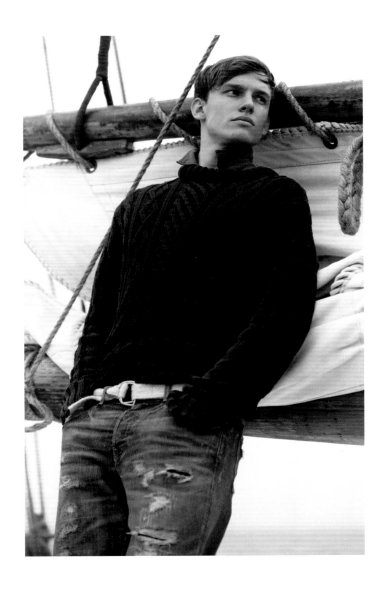

Above: *Cable knitwear by Gant Rugger, spring/summer 2012.*
Opposite: *Aran-stitch sweater for the Hand Knitting Wool Council autumn presentation held at the Café Royal, London, in 1958.*

The reality may be that these 'regional' styles were set by early researchers recording them for posterity.[40] The patterning can be traced to elements of the fisherman's life: cable represents rope, diamonds the fishing net mesh, while elements such as anchors and waves are also depicted.[41] The newest gansey would be saved for Sunday best. There was a surprising trend for them in womenswear at the end of the 19th century, spearheaded by the Princess of Wales in 1878 and, shortly after, they were also adopted into naval uniform.[42] Hand-knit sweaters came into vogue again in the early 1980s, sparked by Perry Ellis's catwalk versions. The subsequent availability of his knitting kits enabled home creation.[43] Traditional regional ganseys are still hand finished on Guernsey by Le Tricoteur, while Flamborough Marine produces fully hand-knitted ganseys in Yorkshire.

Throughout the 19th century, knitting was a way for many women to support their families. By the mid-19th century, on Fair Isle, part of the northern Scottish Shetland Islands, the stockings, caps and scarves initially created to keep fishermen warm were being traded from the island. The distinctive patterning of Fair Isle knits is said to have come from Spain, via seamen stranded after the breakup of the Spanish Armada in 1588. This is probably sartorial legend but, as Fair Isle was on the trading route between the Mediterranean and Scandinavia, it contains an element of truth regarding design influences.[44] Particular sheep breeds and natural dyes local to the landscape have also contributed to the distinctive look of Fair Isle knits.

Developed as sweaters during the First World War, Fair Isle knits enjoyed their first fashion moment in the 1920s when the Prince of Wales was given one and adopted them as part of his golfing attire. The Prince was well known for popularizing British styles on a global scale, leading *Men's Wear* to rhapsodize in 1924, 'the average young man in America is more interested in the clothes of the Prince of Wales than in the clothes of any other individual on earth.'[45] Scottish knits took the world by storm. Brooks Brothers had introduced plain Shetland knits to America in 1904, expanding the range in 1938 as they continued to be a hit on college campuses. Hand-knit items continue to be produced on Fair Isle today and carry their own trademark 'Star Motif'. They are regularly reinterpreted on the catwalk: Ralph Lauren included them in his first collection,[46] and, for autumn/winter 2012, teamed them with checks and herringbone in an homage to British country

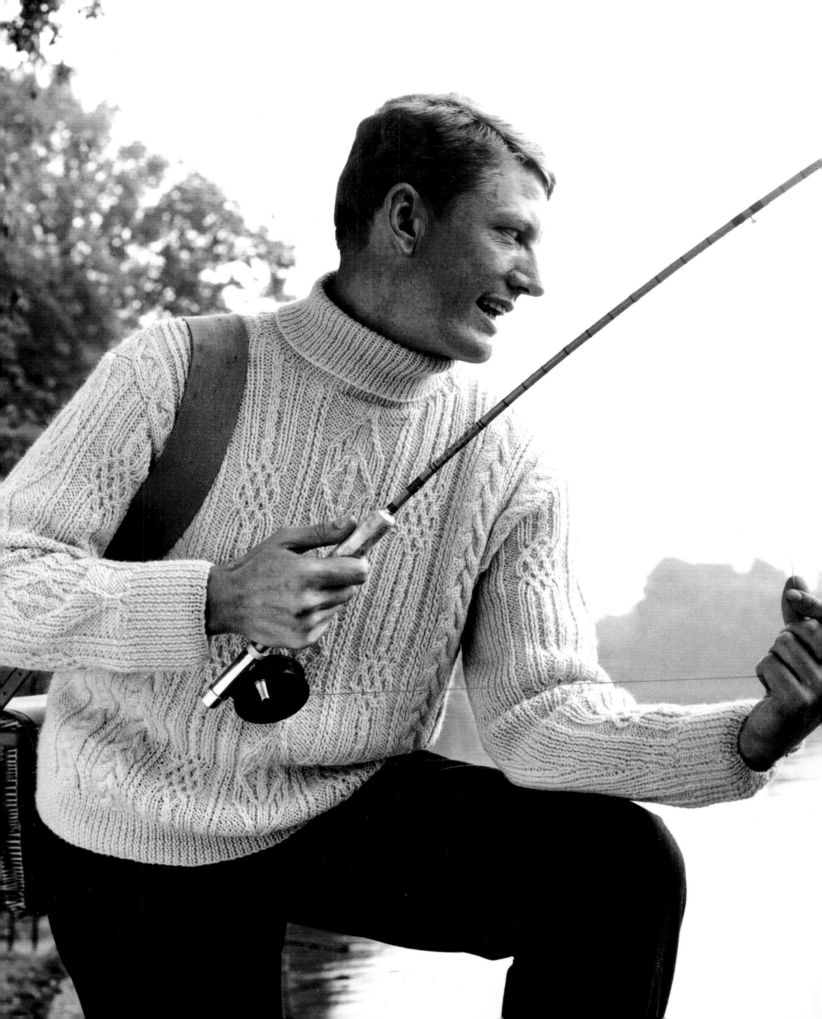

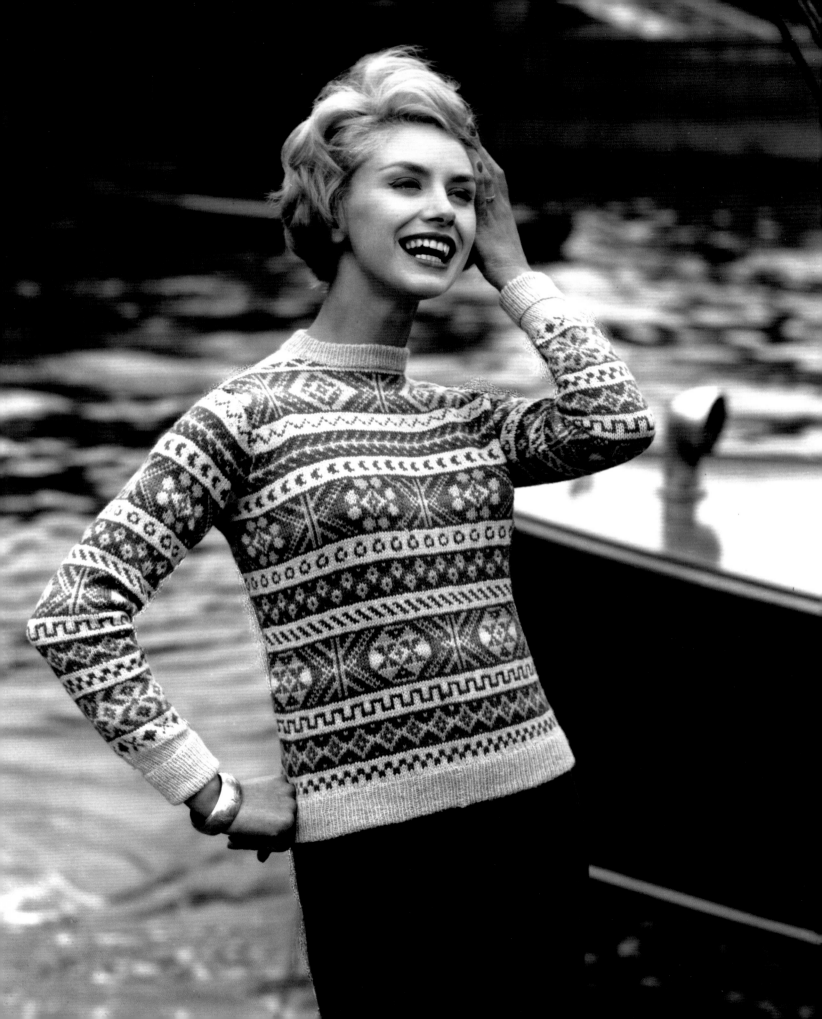

dressing. Another fan was Coco Chanel, who became an unlikely but avid salmon fisher during her visits to Scotland with the Duke of Westminster from the mid-1920s, which had an immediate impact on her work. The Duke acquired a tweed mill to guarantee Chanel exclusive product, and she also used Fair Isle designs in her collections.[47] Building on this lineage, for 2008's autumn/winter ready-to-wear collection Karl Lagerfeld for Chanel designed a fishing kit complete with quilted leather and double 'C' logo. The youngest of all the fishermen's knits hails from the Aran Islands, west of Ireland, where the characteristic undyed colour is used to create cable and diamond patterns with bobbles. In 1891, a government board was established to stimulate the local economy, encouraging people to produce garments for sale, and offering training in complex knit patterns. The styles took off in the early 20th century and, by the 1930s, the tourist market was booming, helped by a campaign by the owner of Art Needlework Industries in Oxford.[48] A Vogue Knitting pattern was published in 1956, and the style was further popularized by Irish folk group the Clancy Brothers in the early 1960s, as the homemade feel of Aran knitwear made it a big hit during the folk music revival.[49] The motifs of Aran knits have subsequently been reworked by designers. Jean Paul Gaultier's 'Le Charme coincé de la Bourgeoisie' autumn/winter 1985 collection included an Aran knit dress complete with his trademark conical bra. For autumn/winter 2010, Miuccia Prada devised a series of oversize cable knits as dresses, skirts, sweaters and cardigans, coupled with ribbed knee-high socks. The colour palette, ranging from sky blue to speckled reds and browns, updated traditional Arans, and the cable pattern was repeated as a print motif on dresses and jackets.

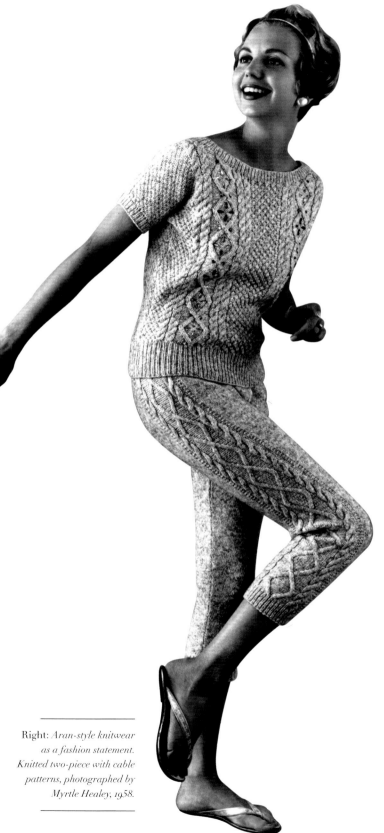

Right: *Aran-style knitwear as a fashion statement. Knitted two-piece with cable patterns, photographed by Myrtle Healey, 1958.*

## FISHERMAN'S FRIEND: THE PENNY LOAFER

An unexpected item that left the shores of Europe to find success on Ivy League campuses is the penny loafer. First made by hand by Norwegian fishermen during the off-season, the fishing slipper was taken to the States by Americans who had been travelling in Europe. According to a 1951 interview in the *Lewiston Daily Sun*, Maine, it was *Esquire* who picked up on the shoes, teaming up with the clothiers Rogers Peet. The shoe company G.H. Bass & Co. was approached to make the 'Weejun', as *Esquire* had named them, referencing their Norse roots. Introduced in 1936, they were heavily promoted by *Esquire* with advertisements playing up their peasant origins and also their adoption at fashionable Palm Beach.[50] The Bass Weejun became a firm college campus favourite for both sexes.

*Opposite: Jacques Fath ensemble illustrated by Roger Descombes, published in a feature titled 'Mer' in* L'Officiel de la Mode et de la Couture *magazine, 1947.*

## FASHIONABLE FISHWIVES

Unlike the navy, fishing was an industry often involving the whole family. While men went to sea, their wives gutted the catch and mended nets, and also knitted insulating layers for the menfolk. They, and often their children, could catch shrimps and dig for cockles, mussels, oysters and worms for bait. For these communities, fishing was a way of life and the demands of the catch dictated the year's activities.[51] Women were also tasked with selling the catch, which meant they worked the markets and essentially ran the financial side of the business. As with fishermen, the women developed distinctive dress styles that reflected the necessities of their occupation. The striped petticoats worn by fishwives from Scotland to Brittany and the Basque coast made them popular subjects for picture-postcard souvenirs for urban visitors keen to romanticize their pre-industrial way of life. The black, pleated skirts of Dior's 1947 New Look were inspired by fishwives from the fish markets of Marseille: skirts dubbed 'the essence of femininity' by *Harper's Bazaar*.[52] The outer layers of many skirts were pinned up to form a pocket and therefore reveal the lower layers. This stylistic device has passed into fashionable dress several times, notably in a 1947 Cristóbal Balenciaga design.

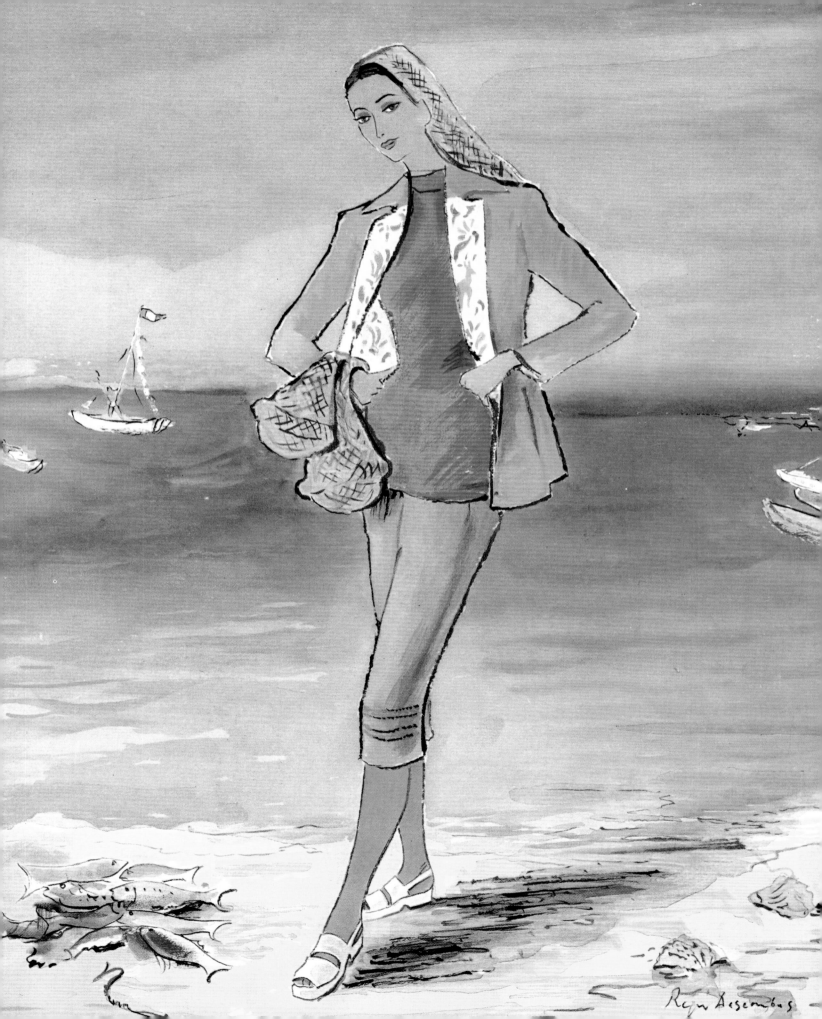

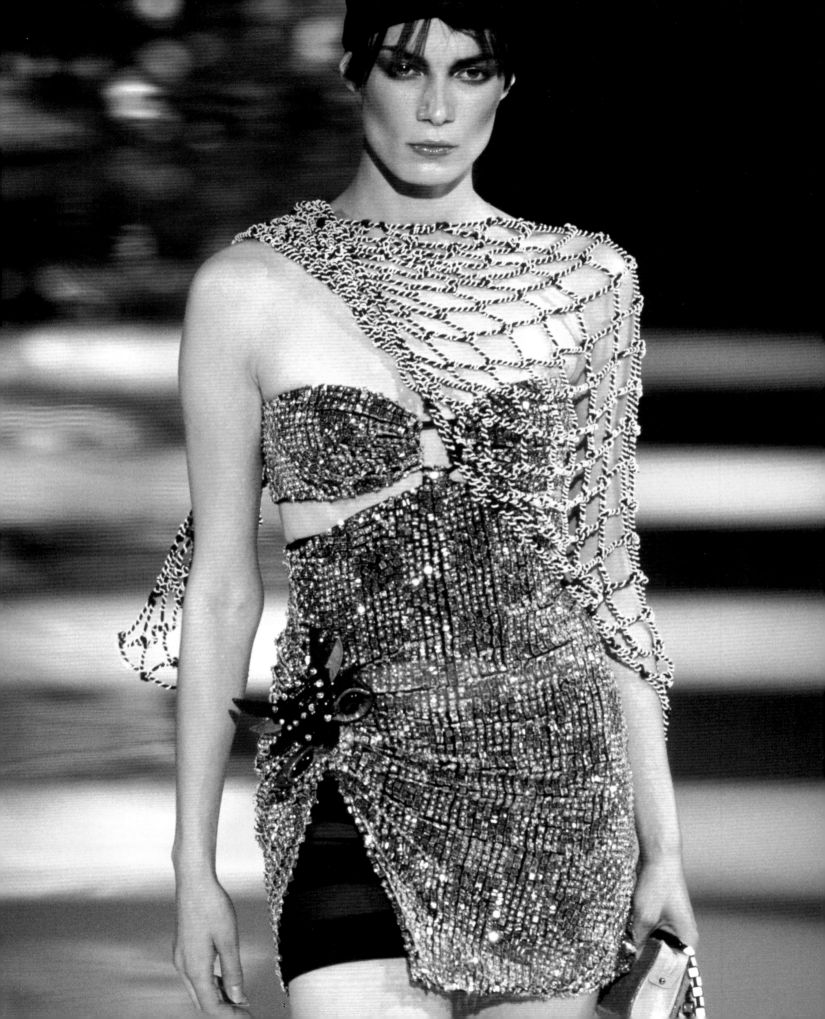

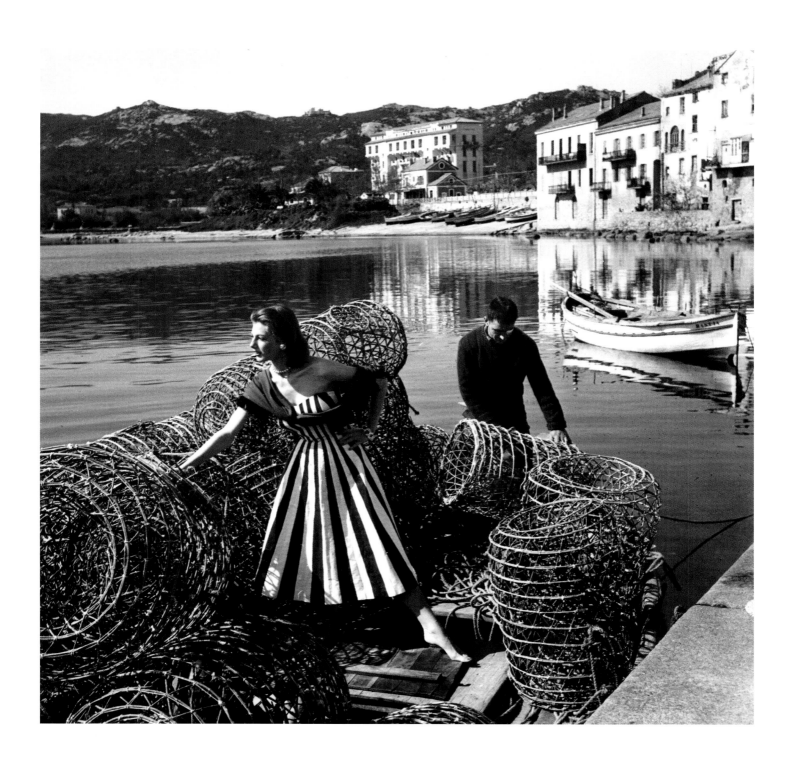

Above: *The full, striped skirts mimic the petticoats of fishwives. Haute couture summer collections photographed in Corsica by Georges Dambier, 1954.*
Opposite: *Fishing fashions: swimming cap-style hat and net shawl over sequinned one-piece, complete with large jewelled crab. Armani, spring/summer 2004.*

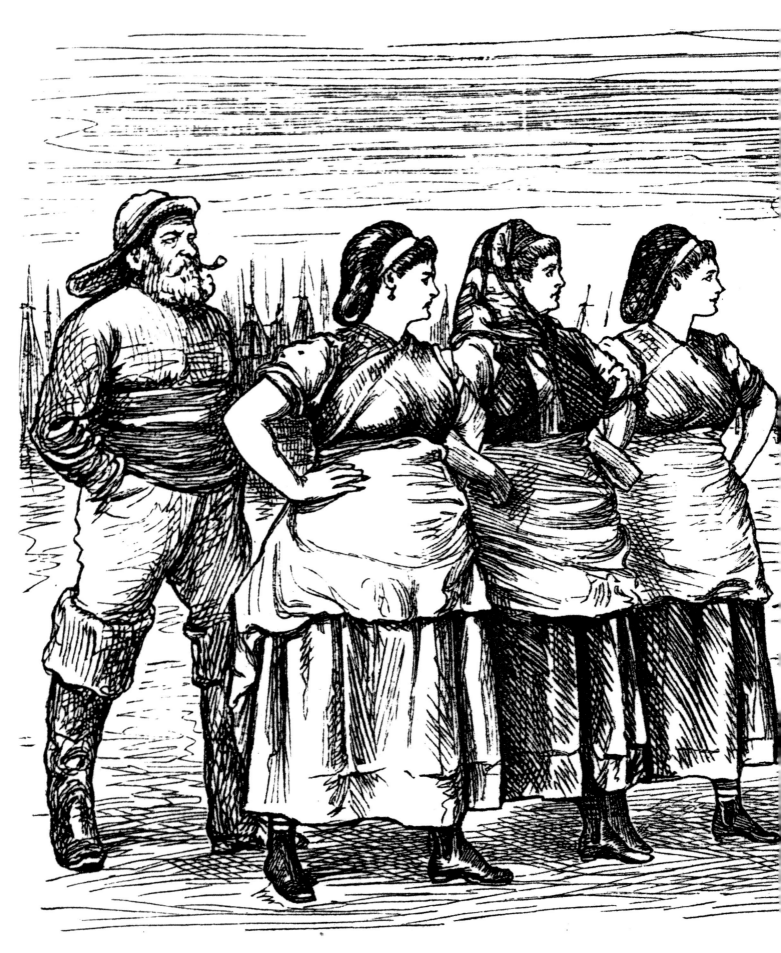

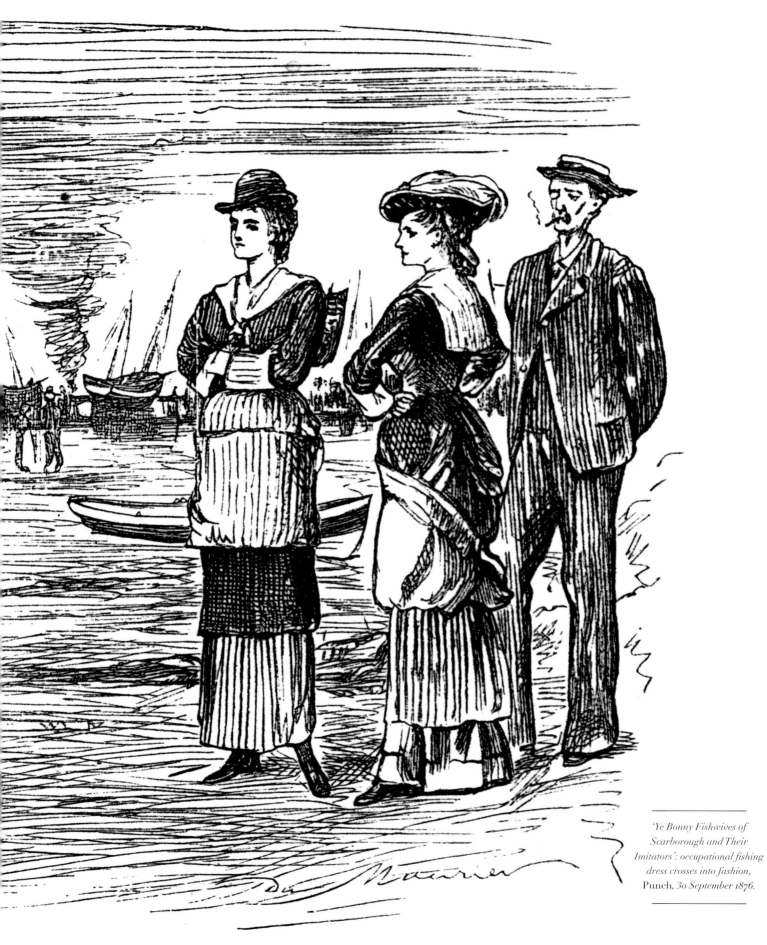

*'Ye Bonny Fishwives of Scarborough and Their Imitators': occupational fishing dress crosses into fashion,* Punch, *30 September 1876.*

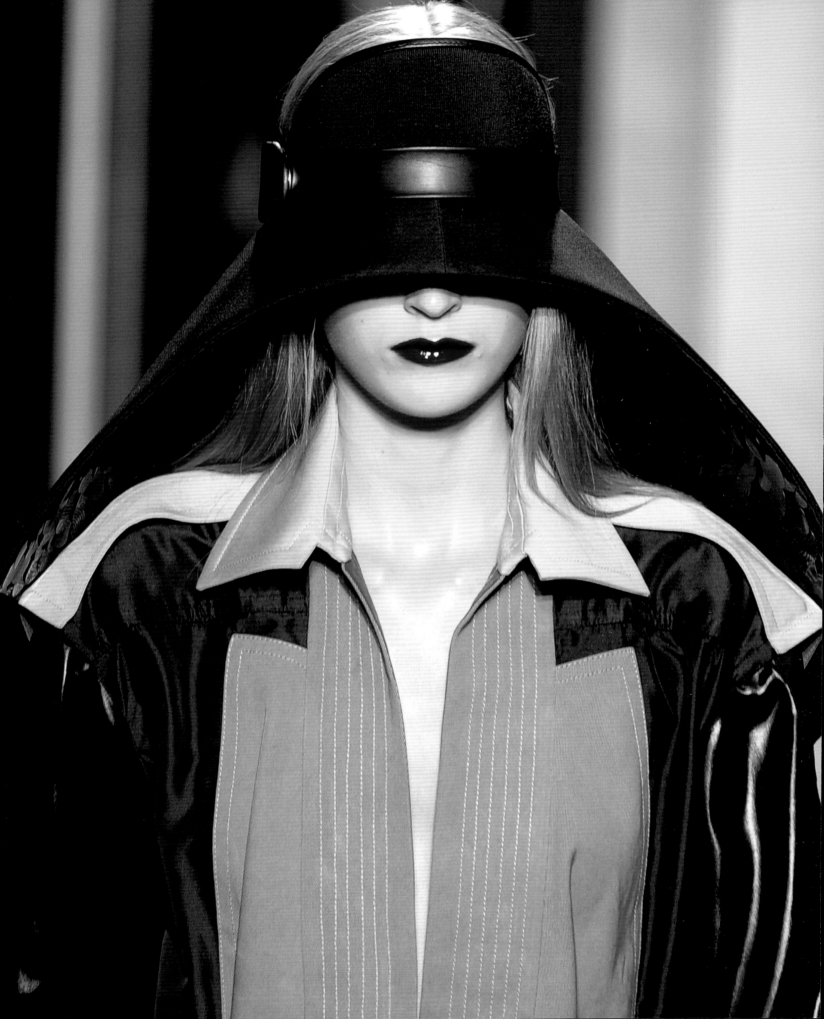

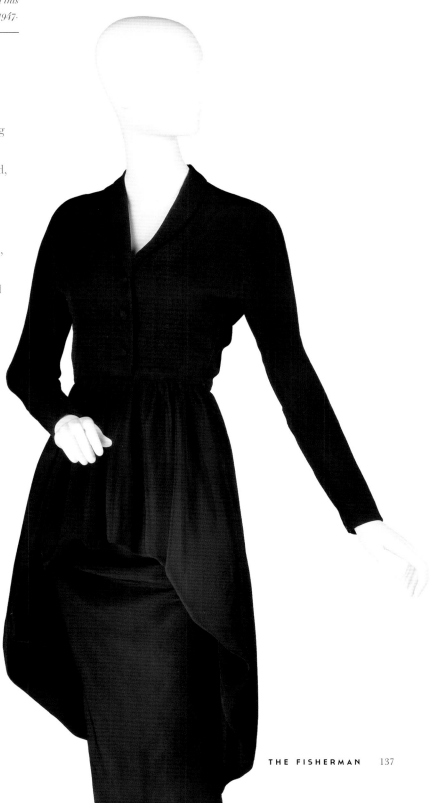

Born at the end of the 19th century in a busy Basque
fishing village, Balenciaga was familiar with fishwives' folding
and tucking of skirts, a practice adopted along the Spanish
coast, as well as around Britain. His father was a seaman and,
for a while, the local mayor, and these early influences had
a long-term impact on his work. He began his career as a
tailoring apprentice in the nearby town of San Sebastián, a
coastal resort popular with the Spanish royal family. In 1917,
he set up his own business and, by the outbreak of civil war
in 1936, when he left Spain for Paris, he had also established
stores in Madrid and Barcelona.[53] Bettina Ballard, fashion
editor of American *Vogue*, was introduced to Balenciaga's
best San Sebastián client at a fish market. Ballard recalled
'a raw-voiced fishwife with her skirts tucked up as she
skidded around the slippery wet floors selling her fish'.
'She orders all of my best models,' Balenciaga assured
her, 'she's the richest woman in town out of season.'[54]

Throughout his work, Balenciaga drew on the lure of
the sea. The early 1950s saw marine-inspired designs, from
white cotton piqué fishing-style smocks to middy blouses
styled over narrow skirts.[55] As Chanel had done, Balenciaga
repurposed the work clothes of fishermen for a fashionable
audience. Nicolas Ghesquière explored these influences
while at the helm of the design house. For spring/summer
2012, he revisited the nautical themes in Cristóbal's
designs, including the clothing of Basque fishermen.
The finale featured oversize brimmed hats, reworking
a 1967 design inspired by the sòu'wester. The dress of
fishermen and women continues to provide sartorial
inspiration as the clothing of working people
is romanticized and reconfigured as high fashion.

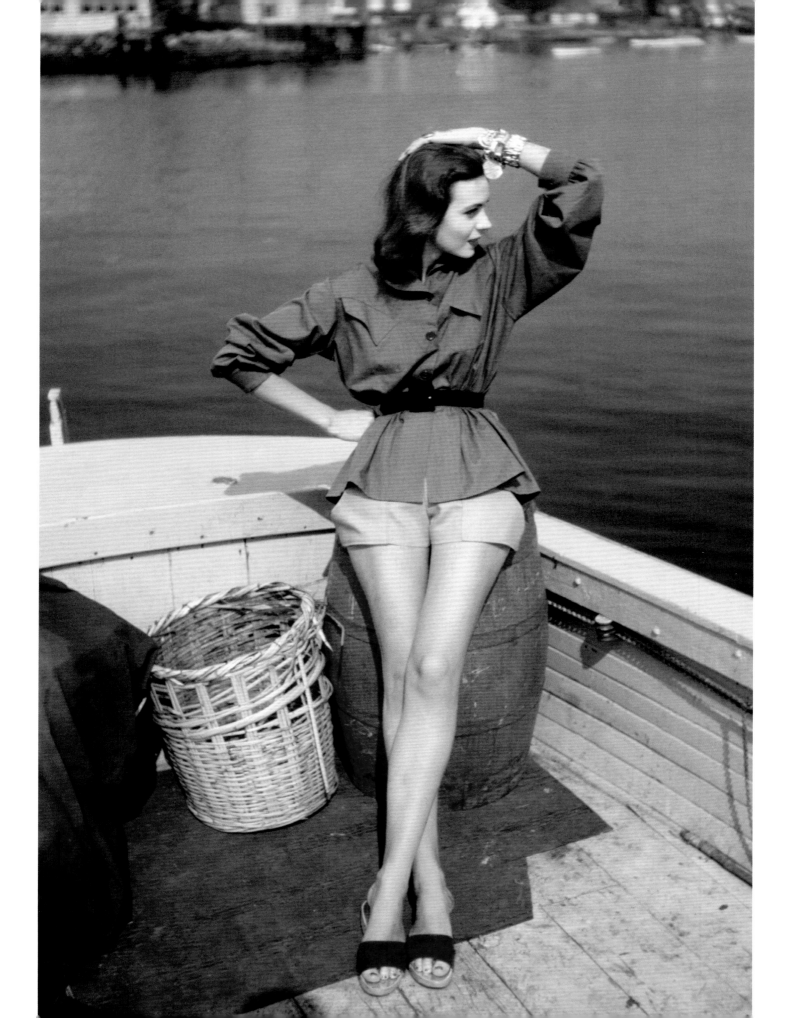

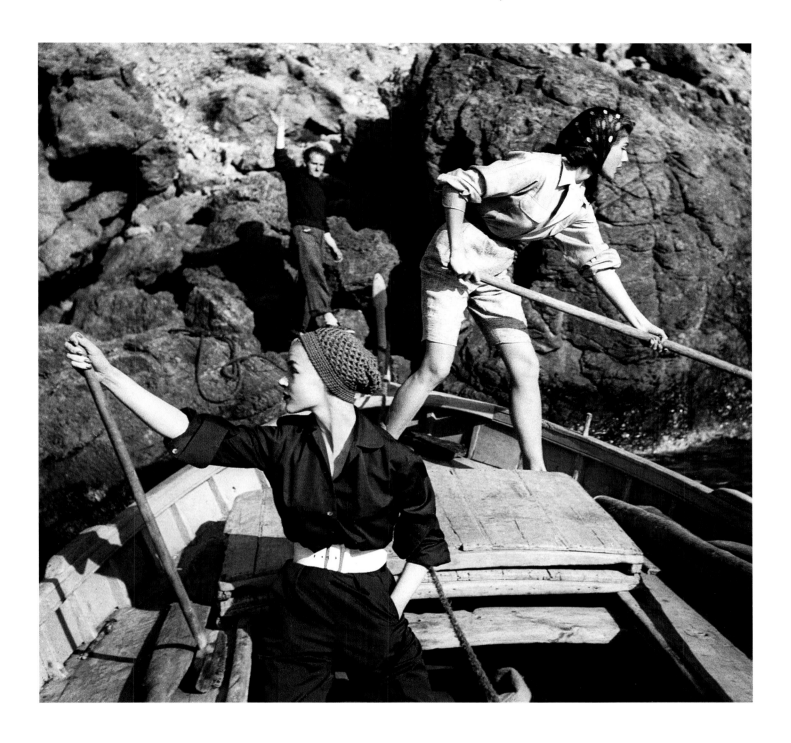

Above: *Fishergirl fashion, originally shot for* Nouveau Fémina *magazine, photographed in Corsica by Georges Dambier, 1954.* Opposite: *Model on a fishing boat wearing suit and shirt by American sportswear designer Carolyn Schnurer with shoes by David Evins, also known as 'The King of Pumps'. Photographed by Clifford Coffin, 1951.*

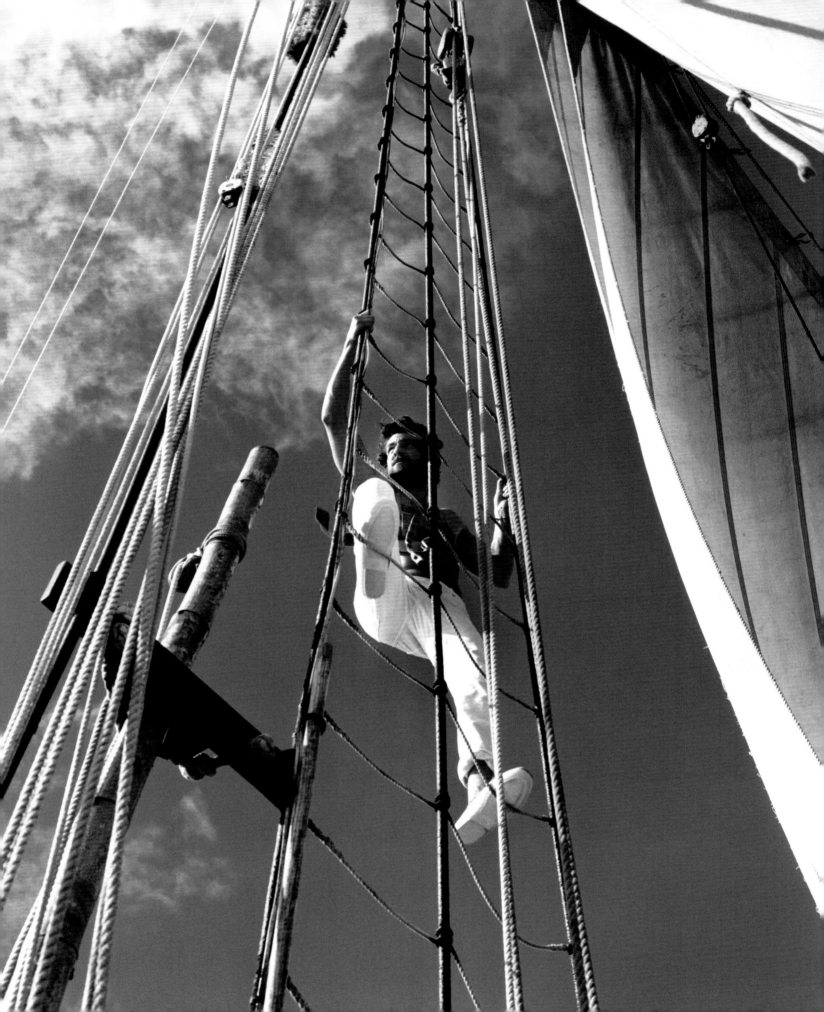

# CHAPTER 4

# THE SPORTSMAN

*uxury, leisure and lifestyle come together in the figure of the Sportsman, whether a millionaire yachter from America's Gilded Age or the embodiment of the privileged preppy style of the Ivy League campus. The associated pared-down, sporting elegance of this lifestyle has become an essential element of aspirational east coast Americana, selling the American Dream around the world.*

Sailing for pleasure and sport is a feature of wealthy lifestyles the world over, yet it has become particularly associated with the athletic elegance of the New England shoreline: an all-American look found on Ivy League campuses and the yacht clubs of Newport and Nantucket. The look itself sells the accompanying lifestyle, a life of privilege, leisure and pared-back luxury that has become a marker of aspirational East Coast American style. The States came to prominence in yachting during the sport's golden age. The America's Cup is one of the world's oldest sporting trophies and this race between two sailing yachts remains one of the most prestigious events in elite social calendars. Named after the schooner that won the original race in 1851, the Cup itself is held by the victorious yacht club until the time that a rival club is successful in their challenge. Due to the expense of designing and maintaining yachts to compete, it has become synonymous with wealth and luxury.

Louis Vuitton have sponsored the challenger selection series (the qualifying races) since 1983 and regularly create LV Cup Collections to coincide with it, featuring outerwear, watches and luggage with a sporty feel, all of which are water and salt resistant. Omega watches often partner with the New Zealand team, and the Prada sponsorship of the Italian club has seen product tie-ins including accessories and perfume. From the unofficial yachting 'uniform' of blazer and flannels on deck, to the lifestyle brands such as Ralph Lauren and Tommy Hilfiger that capture this privileged essence, sport at sea is a vital facet of marketing the American Dream around the world.

*Page 140: Yachting and its associated garments epitomize American style, even when using European labels, encapsulated here with Sandro jeans and Tod's shoes. Photographed by John Balsom for British* GQ Style *magazine, March 2012.* Opposite: *The Italian team on board their ship during the America's Cup race, 2000.*

## THE GILDED AGE AND THE GOLDEN AGE OF YACHTING

It was the English Restoration Court of Charles II in the 1660s that began the royal obsession with yachting. A century earlier, when the Netherlands was Europe's premier maritime nation, fast, lightweight ships called 'jaghts' were developed for communications and commerce. Competing companies would race their respective boats and when Charles II was reinstated on the throne in London, the Dutch East India Company gifted him a jaght of his own.[1] The King enjoyed racing so much that he ordered further models from local shipwrights, sparking a trend that would trickle down from royalty through the centuries to all of those with a passion for aquatic sports. By 1775, races on the Thames were a reasonably regular occurrence and, that same year, the society was founded that would evolve into the Royal Thames Yacht Club. The first official regatta at Cowes on the Isle of Wight took place in 1812, a week in August that became as much a part of the social calendar as the races at Ascot and grouse shooting in the country. It was in 1851 – the year of the Great Exhibition, when Britain flexed its industrial and cultural muscle to the world – that America first stole the yachting crown from European heads. Members of the recently-formed New York Yacht Club visited Cowes and took part in a race against British ships around the Isle of Wight, a contest which laid the foundations for what would become the America's Cup. America was triumphant, and the New York Yacht Club held the Cup undefeated for the next 132 years.

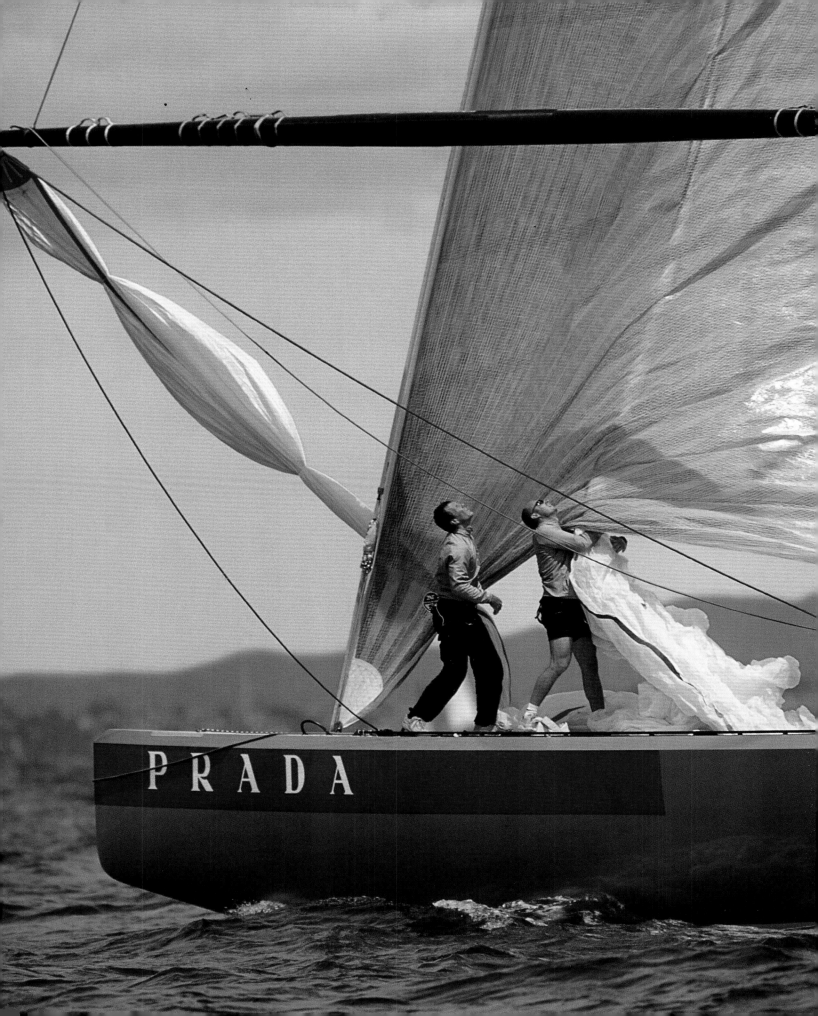

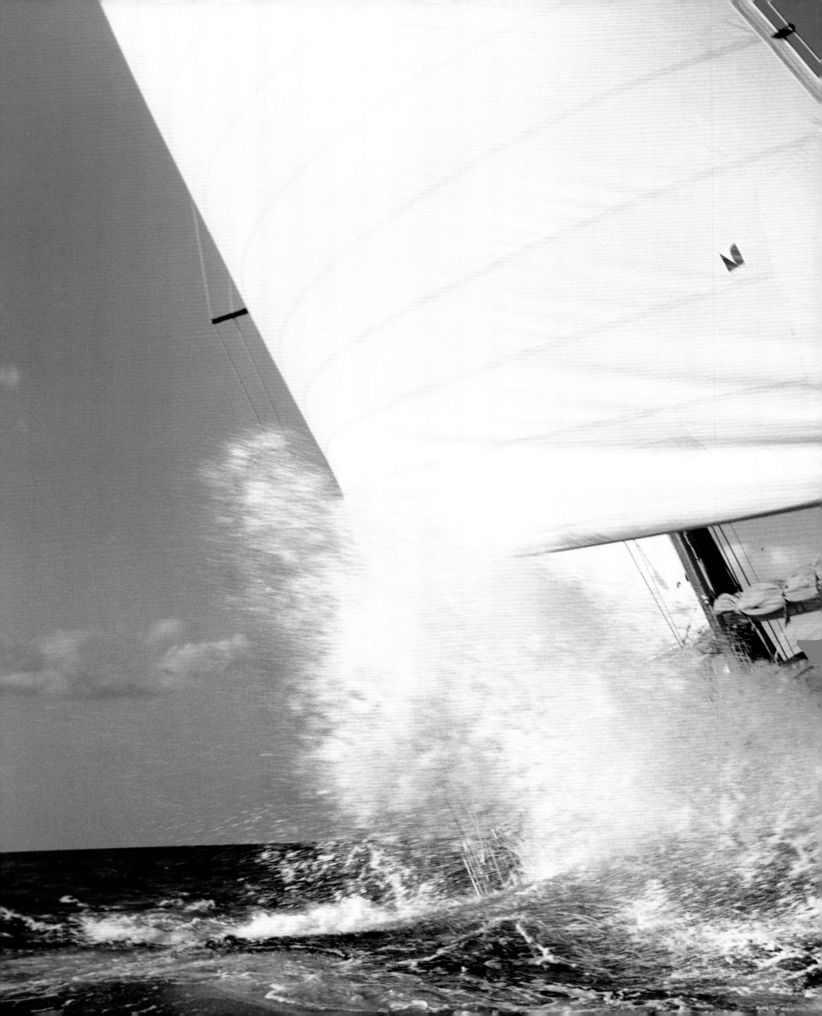

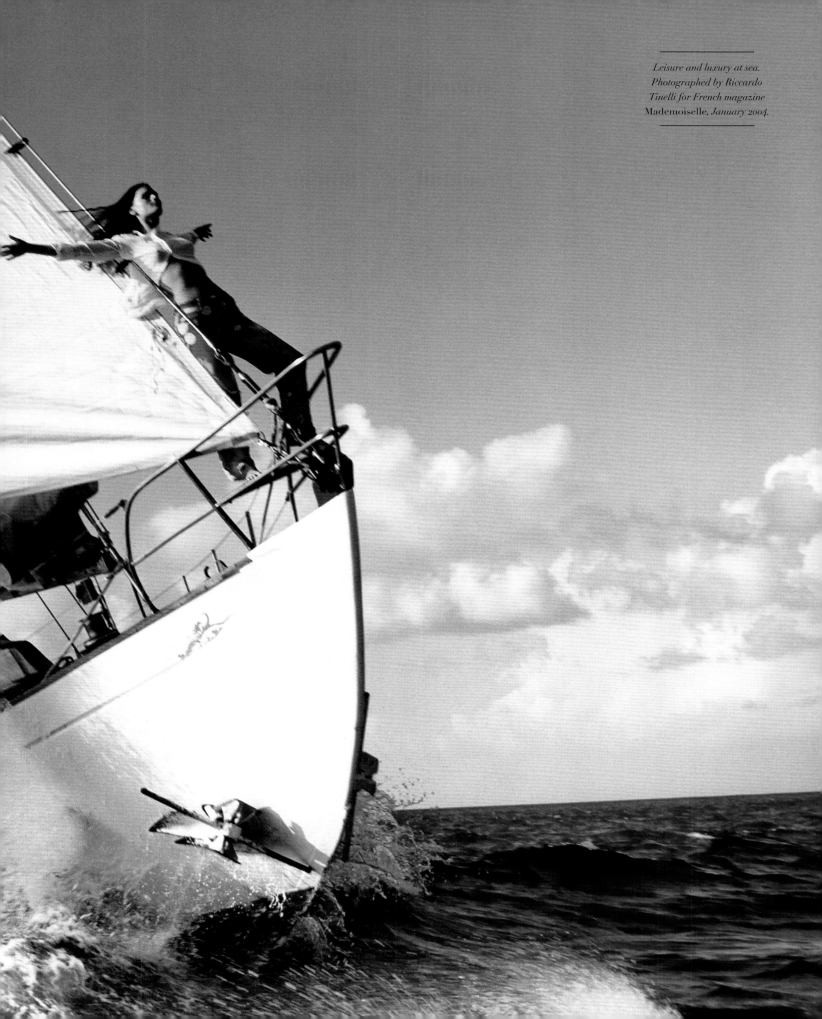

*Leisure and luxury at sea.*
*Photographed by Riccardo*
*Tinelli for French magazine*
Mademoiselle, *January 2004.*

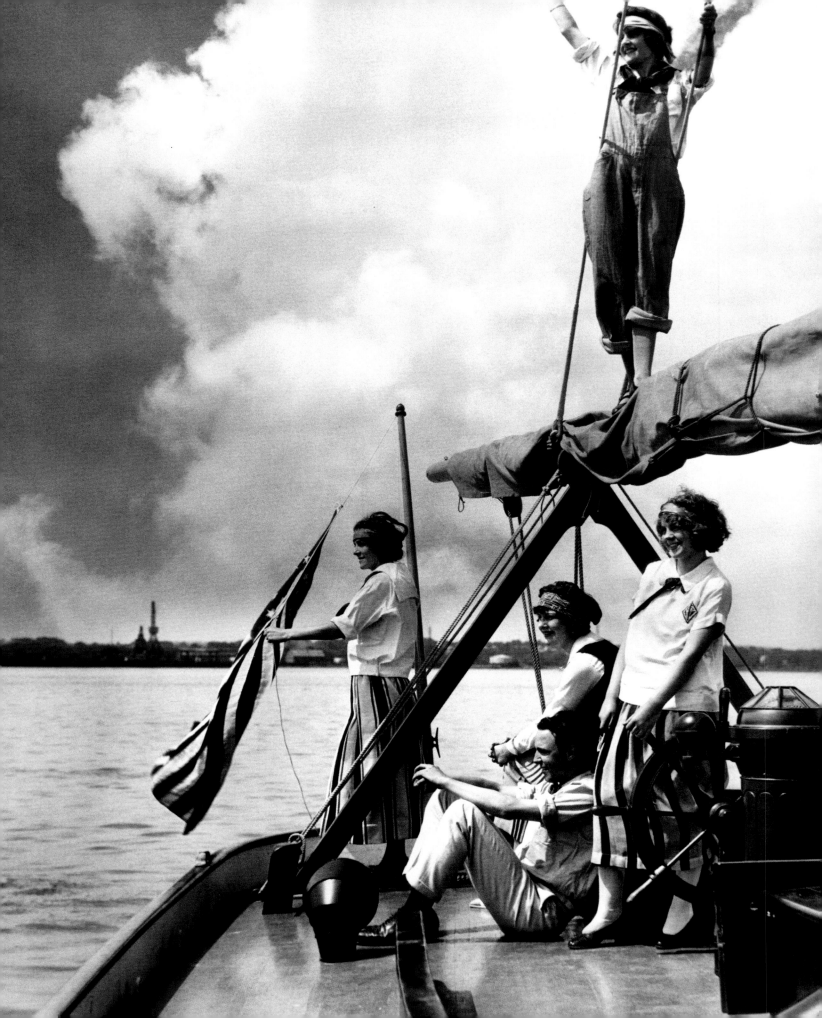

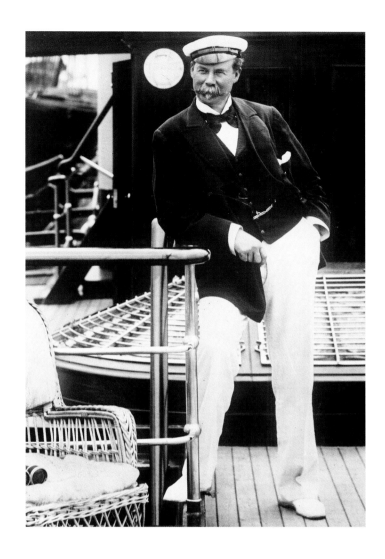

The golden age of yachting coincided with the Belle Époque in Europe and the Gilded Age in America, a period characterized by economic growth; a time when the rapidly expanding middle class came to be defined by its consumer culture. Conspicuous leisure became as much of a marker of success as opulent fashions, leading to the rise of seaside holidays and their accompanying resort wardrobes, when holidaying at the coast became emblematic of a fashionable lifestyle. Owning and racing a yacht became imperative for the American industrialists, bankers and entrepreneurs who made millions throughout the latter half of the 19th century. Lauded millionaires, the likes of John D. Rockefeller and Cornelius Vanderbilt, were owners of lavish yachts, and James Gordon Bennett, son of the founder of the *New York Herald*, even had a Turkish bath and stables complete with cows to provide daily fresh milk on board his boat *Lysistrata*. To own a yacht was a marker of prestige, and they were used not only for racing, but also for entertaining and business meetings. From these early days, places such as Newport and Martha's Vineyard became pivotal stops during group cruises or yachting races. Nantucket, previously a bedrock of the whaling industry, became another quintessential New England retreat, and Long Island and the coast of Cape Cod also benefited from this burgeoning leisure industry, based on sailing for pleasure.

*Above: Scottish businessman and yachtsman Sir Thomas Lipton poses on deck in the quintessential yachting outfit of white flannels and cap, 1910.*
*Opposite: The spirit of the open waves on board a sailboat, 1927.*

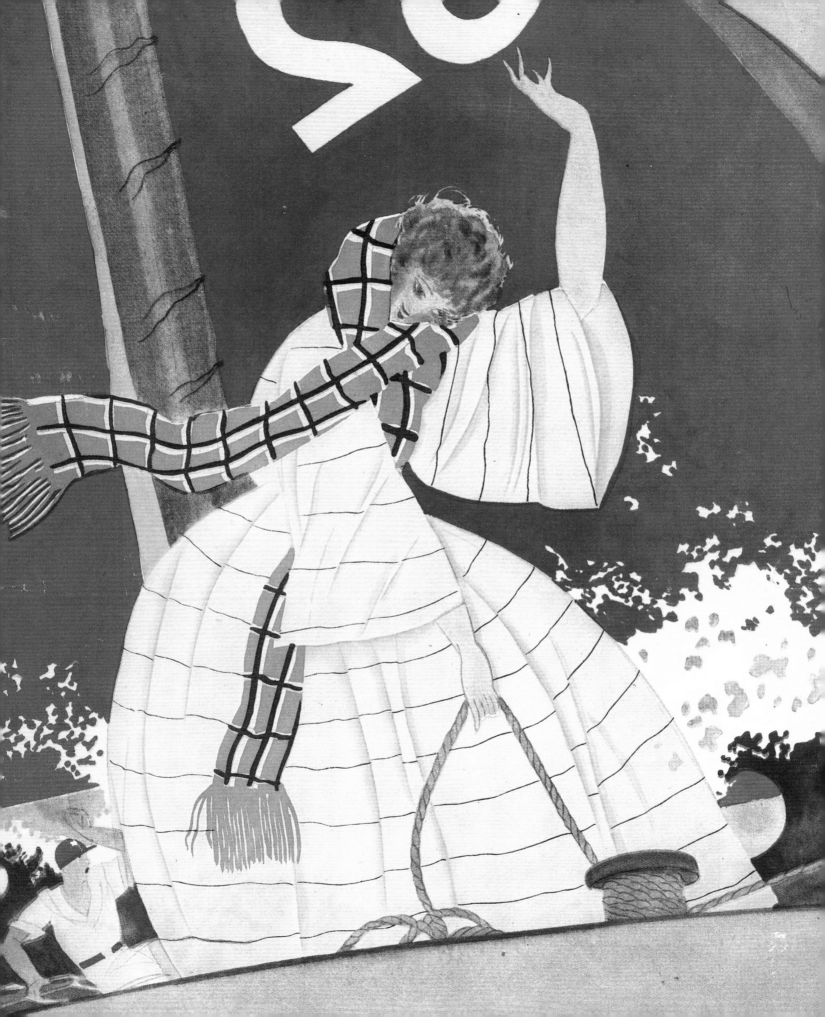

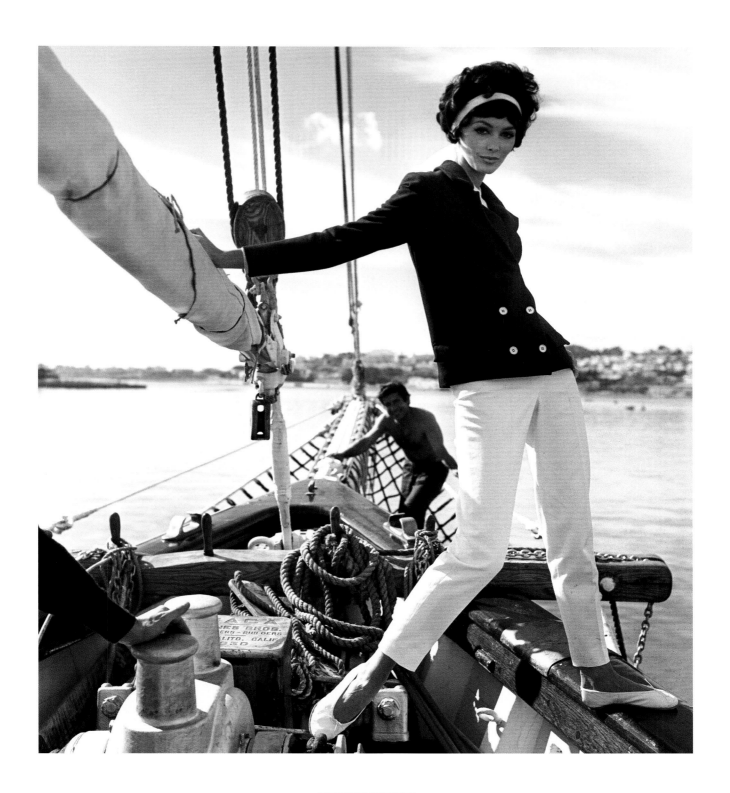

Above: *Model Lucinda Hollingsworth on
board Errol Flynn's yacht* Zaca *in Palma de
Mallorca. Photographed by Georges Dambier
for the Tricosa ready-to-wear catalogue, 1958.*
Opposite: *Au Printemps department store
catalogue capitalizes on the craze for yachting.
Illustration by Eduardo Garcia Benito, 1920.*

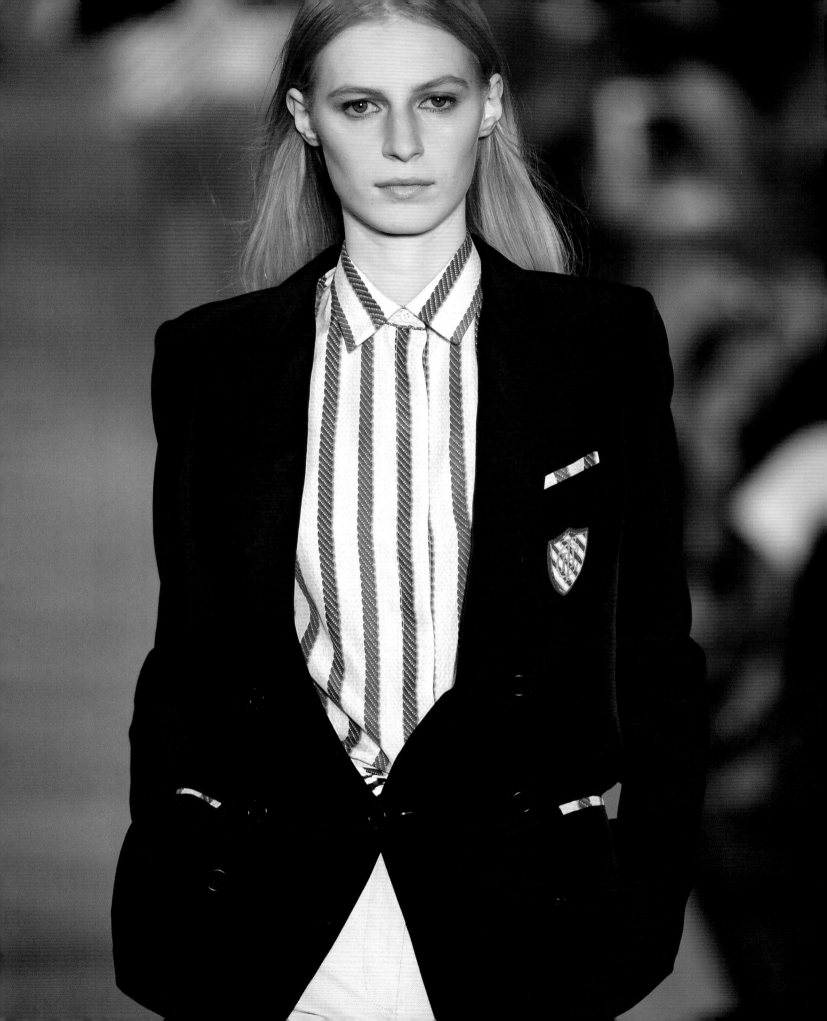

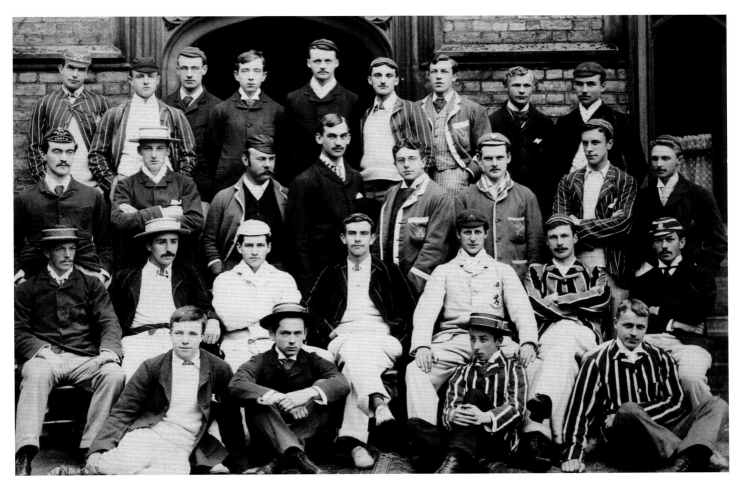

## FROM DECK TO CLUB HOUSE:
## BLAZER AND FLANNELS

The look we associate with the golden age of yachting was worn both ashore and at sea. The *Sartorial Art Journal* in the States, a tailoring trade magazine, had yachting looks firmly entrenched as the double-breasted blazer, cuffed white flannel trousers, white shoes and yachting cap by 1901.[2] This look, coupled with a straw boater, was born from yacht clubs and the rowing teams of elite universities, and was adopted as the uniform of leisure for men in the early 20th century. Wool flannel, woven from the 17th century onwards, became the norm for sportswear throughout the second half of the 19th century, frequently seen behind the wheel of a yacht as well as on tennis courts and cricket fields. The blazer itself originated in university rowing clubs. The Lady Margaret Boat Club of St

**Above:** *Ready for the race: rowing team adorned in striped blazers and boaters, 19th century.* **Right:** *Reinventing the blazer: backstage at the Tommy Hilfiger menswear show at the Maritime Hotel, New York, also for spring/summer 2013.* **Opposite:** *Due to its wealthy yachting credentials, the blazer is a key item for aspirational American brands. Contemporary stripes, blazer and flannels at Tommy Hilfiger, spring/summer 2013.*

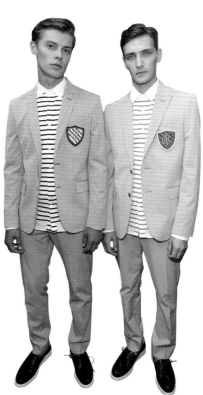

John's College, Cambridge, UK, was founded in 1825, and was pivotal in the establishment of the Oxford and Cambridge University boat race a few years later. Their distinctive, blazing scarlet flannel boating jackets remain part of the uniform today and were referred to as 'blazers' from the 1850s. By the 1880s, the term had spread.[3] American yacht clubs tended to favour a more conservative navy blue, often with double breasted gilt buttons, also known as a reefer jacket in reference to their nautical origins.[4] Each yacht club, initially an extension of the urban gentlemen's club, had their own rules for attire, and blazers often included the club badge embroidered on the breast pocket.

The influence of British men's dress on American style in the first decades of the 20th century should not be underestimated. Yachting and rowing regattas, such as those at Cowes on the Isle of Wight and Henley in Oxfordshire, set the styles for future society events, and reporters were sent to cover the fashions for the American press and trade. A report from Henley in 1924 noted that the blazer was 'enjoying an extraordinary popularity in England this season',[5] and while the double-breasted model could be swapped for a single-breasted version for the club, the look was so persistent during the following decades that, by 1971, the writers of *GQ* talked of rocking the boat of 'the old flannels-and-blazer brigade' when trying to initiate new styles.[6] Moving with ease from

the universities of Oxford and Cambridge to the elite schools of the States, the blazer was also adopted by rowers at Princeton at the turn of the 20th century. Students took to wearing a blazer and flannels for graduation, ensuring the quintessential yachting and rowing 'uniform' became indelibly associated with Ivy League campuses.[7] By the 1920s, white flannels were also established as a fashionable choice for seaside holidays at chic European resorts, as *Vanity Fair* reported in 1928, 'The smart man at Deauville can be seen any morning, after his swim, dressed in spotless white flannel trousers.'[8]

It was also during the 1920s that the blazer became the choice item for women when yachting. Double-breasted blazer and skirt suits feature in a 1929 British *Vogue* piece on yachting, in the requisite colour scheme of white and navy, with a dash of red. The piece features a Jane Regny design and Hermès yachting gloves, and the accompanying text assures the reader, 'Both costumes are ideal for their purpose – they are seaworthy, simple and smart.'[9] It is Chanel, however, who would come to be forever associated with blazers in a high-fashion arena, an interest dating back to her days on board the *Flying Cloud* with the Duke of Westminster. From the mid-1950s, blazer suits were staples of her collections, as well as her own adopted sartorial uniform, and she introduced the house signature, a chain sewn into the hem to weight the jacket, to aid its line. In 1954 American *Vogue* noted that a navy suit in wool jersey with patch pockets was the epitome of her work, 'The suit which represents everything Chanel has believed in all her life.'[10]

*Opposite: Socializing in the sun hits the front page.* Promenade des Planches, *at the French coastal resort of Deauville, is awash with boater hats, blazers and stripes.* Le Petit Journal, *26 August 1923.*

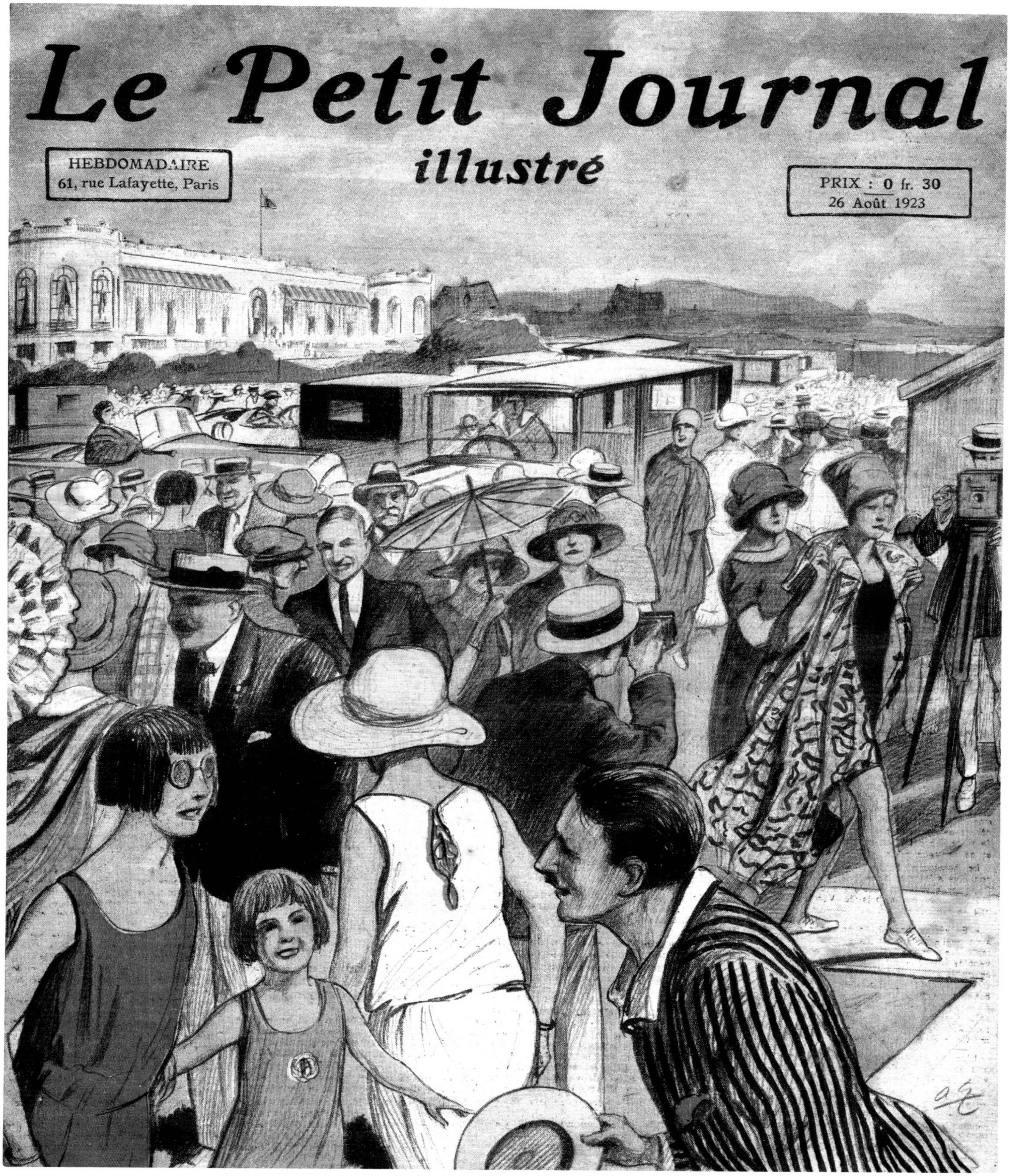

Le Petit Journal illustré

HEBDOMADAIRE
61, rue Lafayette, Paris

illustré

PRIX : 0 fr. 30
26 Août 1923

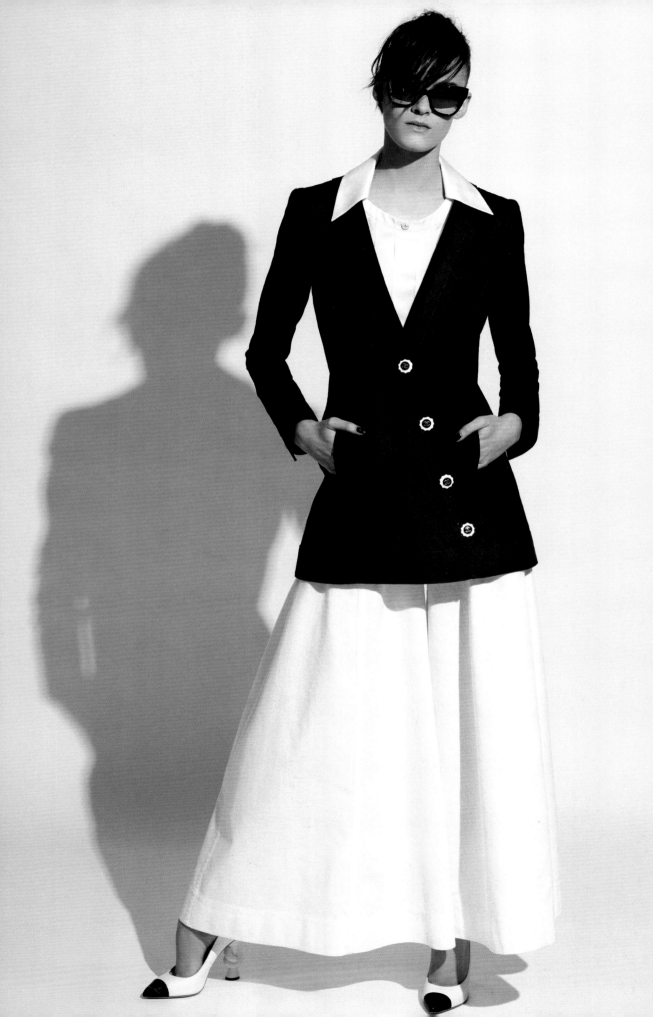

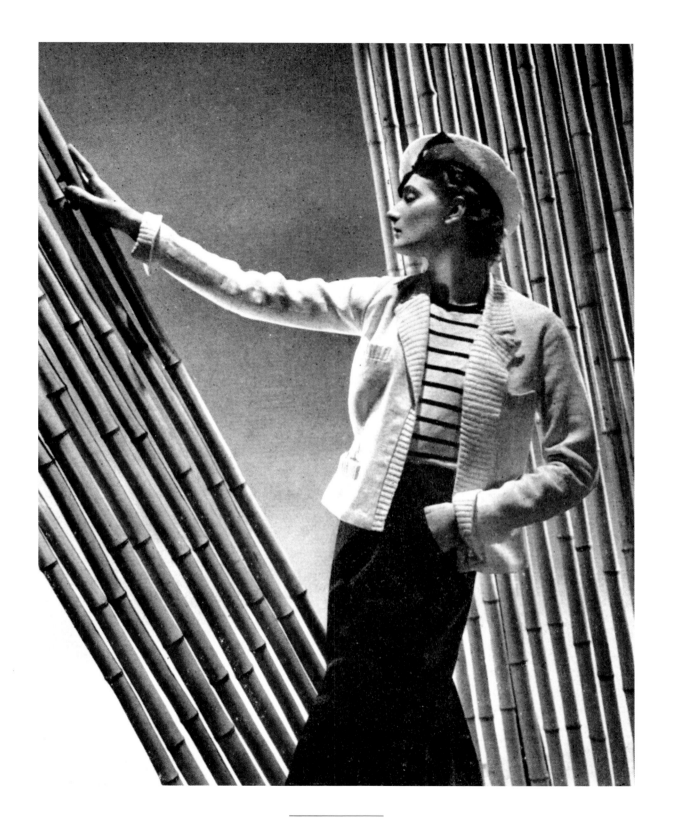

*Above: The blazer-style jacket became a Chanel staple. This ensemble features a white jacket teamed with a navy blue skirt, striped cotton jersey top and white straw beret. It was directly inspired by the outfits that Chanel created for herself. Photographed by André Durst for* Vogue Paris, 1937. *Opposite: Updated sailor look from Chanel's Cruise 2014 collection, photographed by Karl Lagerfeld.*

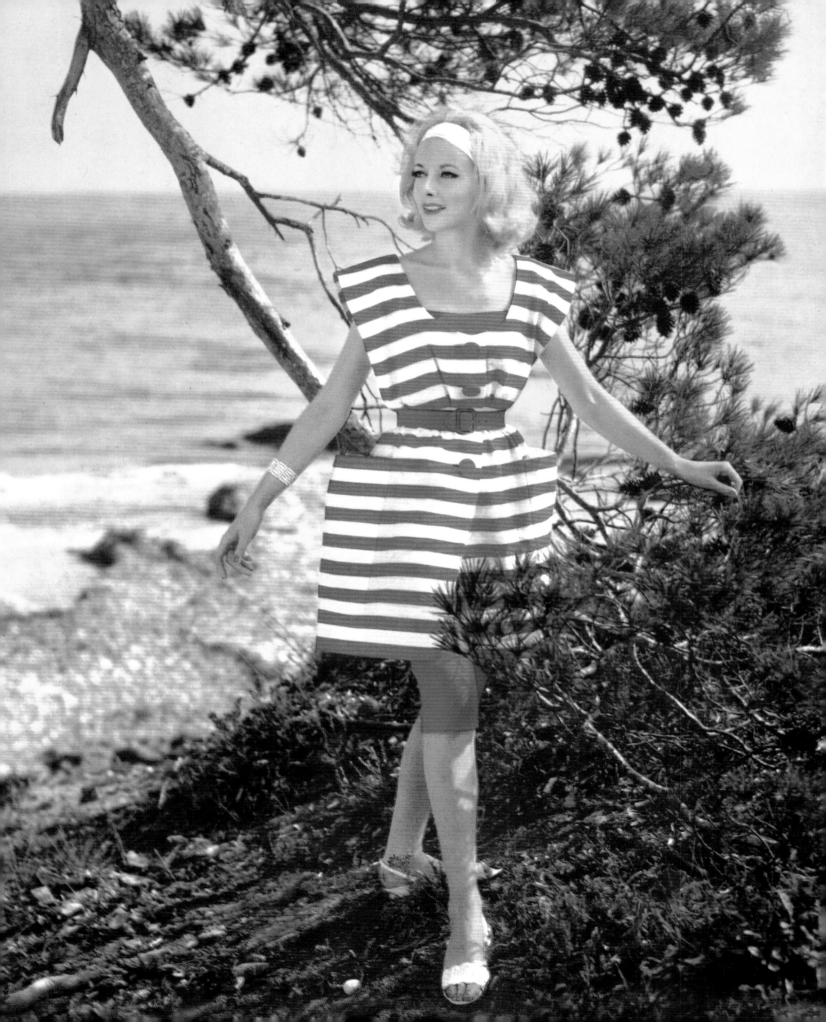

## BEAUTY AND THE BEACH

Tied closely to the sporting life are ideas of leisure and luxury, travel and tourism, which also find their origins on the shorelines of Europe where blazers and flannels were worn from boat to beach. From the earliest days of coastal tourism, when the shoreline crossed over from a place of work to a place of leisure, it has been dominated by the idea of fashionable display; the desire to see and be seen. In European retreats such as San Sebastián and Biarritz, the presence of royalty set the trends for the leisured classes. In Britain, doctors advocated the health-giving qualities of 'taking the water' and 18th-century aristocrats duly responded. The evolution of the railways throughout the following century increased excursions to the sea and discussions of health and wellbeing were gradually superseded by the lure of pleasure. The annual trip to the coast soon became *de rigueur* for the maintenance of a fashionable lifestyle as increasing numbers of resorts evolved from spa towns or picturesque fishing villages. In Britain, the pier and promenade became the forerunner to the catwalk as the season's finest was regularly paraded across the water, the perfect platform for the display of the latest fashions.

During the interwar years, beach chic was also hitting the coastlines of America. Moving away from the pared-down and somewhat functional styles of yachting bays, Palm Beach in Florida soon emerged as a spectacular sartorial destination *par excellence*. Set up by an oil magnate with the aim of creating America's greatest winter playground, the resort had garnered a reputation as *the* hottest place on the east coast to escape the cold by the time the Jazz Age was in full swing. Encouraging a younger crowd than the families who holidayed at Newport or Nantucket, it cultivated an atmosphere that was distinctly modern and *à la mode*.

*Opposite: Coastal resorts are a place to see and be seen. Jacques Griffe sculptural couture stripes, photographed by Philippe Pottier, 1960.*

This is not to say it was without the elite trappings of high society; one anecdote, featured in *Life* magazine in 1952, recounted a fancy dress ball at the prestigious Everglades Club in which one party-goer arrived with a ladder strapped to his back: he had come as a social climber.[11] Palm Beach was notable for its extravagant menswear, often featuring robes or pyjama suits emblazoned with bright patterns ripe for peacocking on the sands. Journalists reported on the Palm Beach social scene for the press and also for the menswear industry, and debated whether it was more advanced in the style stakes than Deauville or Biarritz in France.[12] A 1928 piece in *Men's Wear* extolled the resort for outshining the 'Old World,' proudly asserting 'Palm Beach stands alone and in its own right as one of the world's greatest playgrounds for wealth, luxury, and the blue blood of this land.'[13] 'Palm Beach' lines, shown in early spring, were in effect by the early 1930s[14] and by the middle of the decade even Brooks Brothers were marketing their own seersucker 'Palm Beach' suits. Colourful resort wear later made the names of various designers from Lilly Pulitzer in Florida to Emilio Pucci in Capri.

It was during the 1920s that the 'resort season' first made its mark on the fashion calendar. Parisian couturiers travelled to the resorts of Biarritz and San Sebastian to present their collections to society women.[15] Designer Elizabeth Hawes was sent from New York to the resorts of France as well as to Paris to report on the fashions for an American audience. With a somewhat pithy style, Hawes noted that mid-season collections – what we would now term resort or cruise collections – were being shown in the 1920s, because, 'If Macy's didn't know at once what was worn in chic European spring resorts, how could they hope to do a good summer business?'[16] In 1928, the *New York Times* officially announced that 'Palm Beach Season' was a legitimate season in its own right.[17] The seaside was cemented as a place where trends could be set. The relaxed nature of leisurewear, drawing on sportswear and occupational dress, would impact clothing design throughout the remainder of the century.

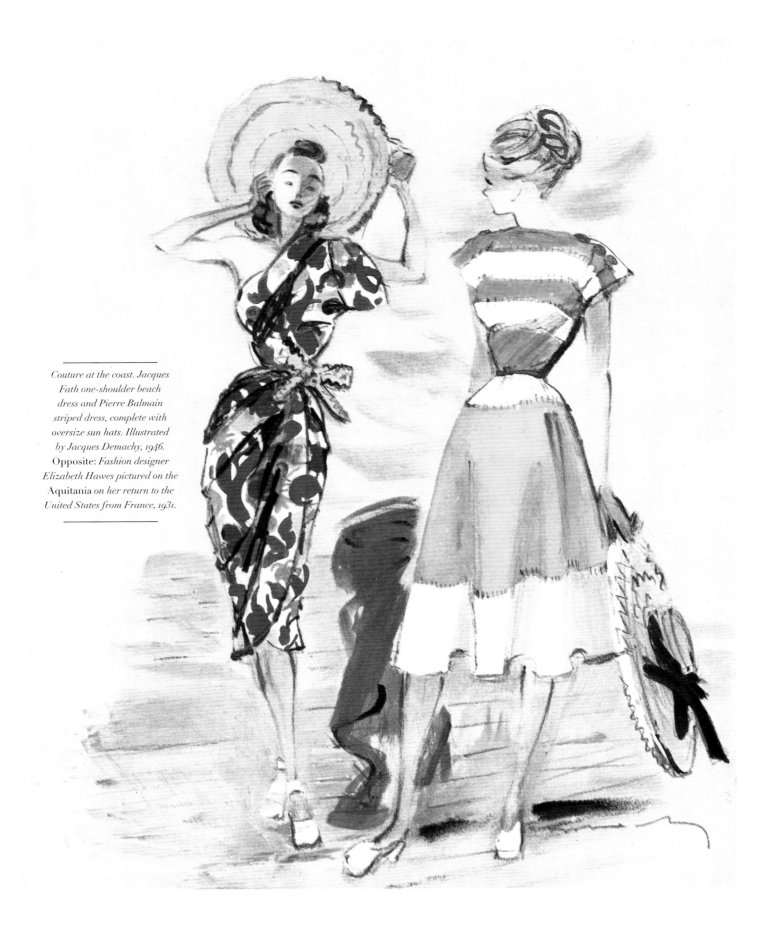

*Couture at the coast. Jacques Fath one-shoulder beach dress and Pierre Balmain striped dress, complete with oversize sun hats. Illustrated by Jacques Demachy, 1946.*
Opposite: *Fashion designer Elizabeth Hawes pictured on the* Aquitania *on her return to the United States from France, 1931.*

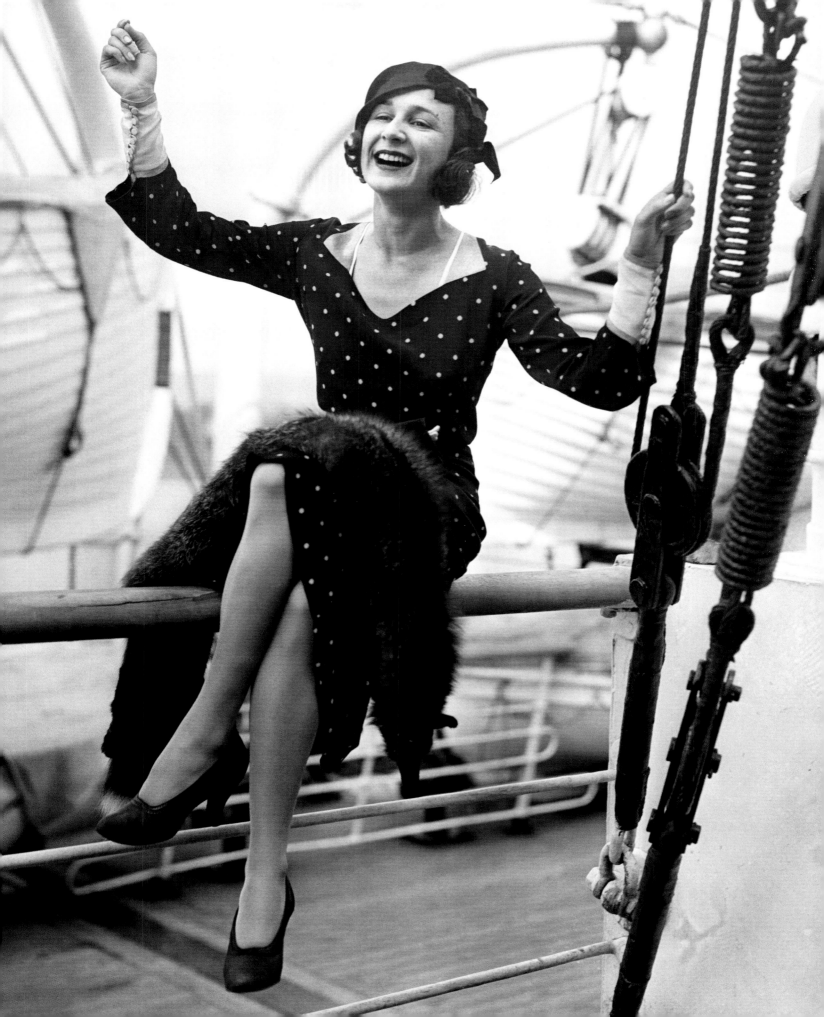

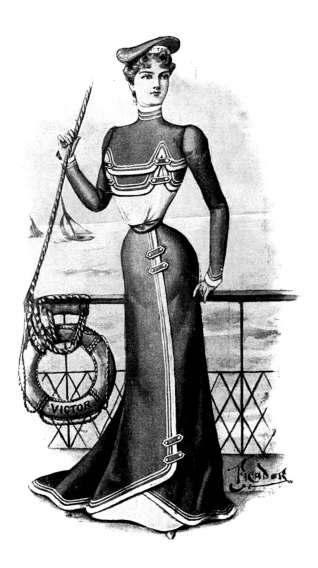

## LUXURY LIFESTYLES: THE LINER

While the beach was blossoming as a fashionable space, transportation was becoming more luxurious for those who could afford to travel in style. For over a century from the mid-1800s, ocean liners were the predominant means of global travel. While routes went all over the world, it was the transatlantic voyages between Europe and the east coast of America that were celebrated for their opulent surroundings, replicating high society on the high seas. The innovators behind the ocean liner were the stalwart of 19th-century engineering, Isambard Kingdom Brunel, and the shipping magnate Samuel Cunard (whose great-granddaughter, Nancy Cunard, would write for *Vogue* in the 1920s). The liner became a reality through the development of steam power, which enabled journeys to be scheduled precisely rather than relying on the vagaries of the wind. By the 1880s, the age of the grand hotel was in full swing, made possible due to the expanding rail networks; a number of the first grand hotels were set up by rail companies themselves.[18] By the end of the century, these hotels had become self-contained destinations, often including facilities for fashionable sports such as golf and tennis.

This ethos was quick to spread to ocean travel. Among the earliest ships to be marketed as 'floating hotels' were Cunard's *Umbria* and *Etruria* built between 1884 and 1885. The architecture and interiors borrowed from the formula of the grand hotels of the Belle Époque, to the extent that César Ritz's architects also designed for ocean voyages. A new kind of ocean-going lifestyle was emerging, one that hinged on the display of the latest fashions and the upkeep of urban social mores. By day, promenade decks ensured passengers engaged in the 'see and be seen' etiquette that dominated public spaces in towns or beaches and by night, protocol was observed regarding rituals such as dressing for dinner among first class passengers. These moneyed travellers were often accompanied by steamer trunks created by the likes of Goyard and Louis Vuitton. Vuitton, formed in 1854, designed luggage specifically for use on luxury liners. Cabin trunks could fit under beds, and the wardrobe trunk, allowing clothing and accessories to be compartmentalized for ease, was created on the advice of

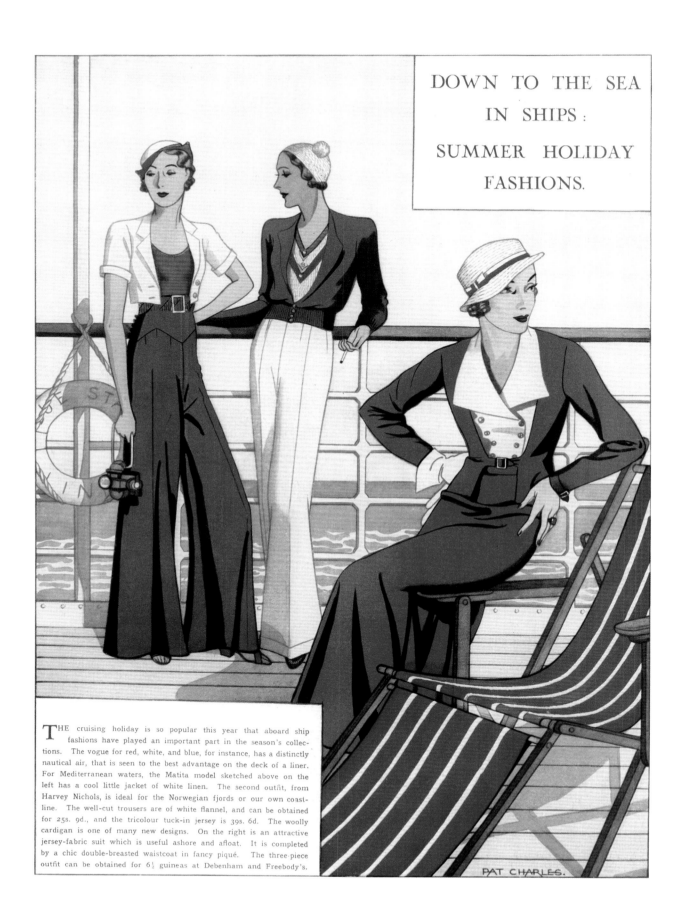

THE cruising holiday is so popular this year that aboard ship fashions have played an important part in the season's collections. The vogue for red, white, and blue, for instance, has a distinctly nautical air, that is seen to the best advantage on the deck of a liner. For Mediterranean waters, the Matita model sketched above on the left has a cool little jacket of white linen. The second outfit, from Harvey Nichols, is ideal for the Norwegian fjords or our own coastline. The well-cut trousers are of white flannel, and can be obtained for 25s. 9d., and the tricolour tuck-in jersey is 39s. 6d. The woolly cardigan is one of many new designs. On the right is an attractive jersey-fabric suit which is useful ashore and afloat. It is completed by a chic double-breasted waistcoat in fancy piqué. The three-piece outfit can be obtained for 6½ guineas at Debenham and Freebody's.

PAT CHARLES.

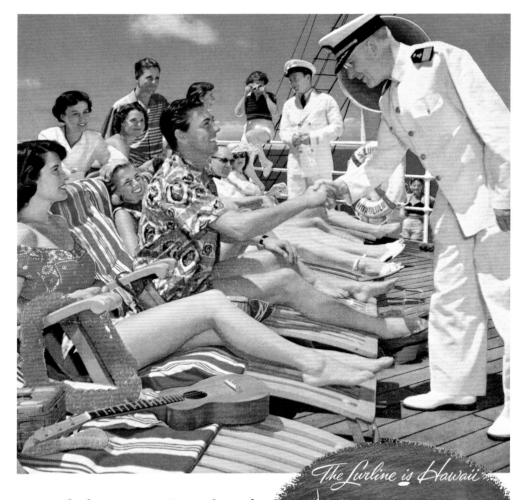

## Glad to Have You Aboard

There are no strangers on the LURLINE. Captain Johnson makes you feel right at home with his cordial "*Aloha*" ...his "Welcome Aboard!" And all around you is the spirit of Hawaii. It invites you to all kinds of fun and relaxation ... seagoing sports, parties, movies, dancing. It adds zest to your enjoyment of matchless food and of well-serviced, luxurious living. Only Matson know-how, product of nearly three-quarters of a century on the Pacific, could weave the gaiety and color of Hawaii so intimately into your voyage on the LURLINE. What a vacation ... all included in your round-trip fare!

*See your Travel Agent or any Matson Lines office: New York, Chicago, San Francisco, Seattle, Portland, Los Angeles, San Diego, Honolulu. And book round trip on the* **LURLINE!**

**THE LURLINE SAILS FROM SAN FRANCISCO AND LOS ANGELES ALTERNATELY**

*The Lurline is Hawaii*

*Matson Lines*

For the finest travel, the **LURLINE**... for the finest freight service, the Matson cargo fleet...to and from Hawaii.

*Dating back to 1882, as the Matson Navigation Company, Matson were instrumental in the growth of Hawaii as a tourist destination. Their steamer, the SS* Lurline, *became one of their finest cruise liners. Matson Lines advertisements to Hawaii, 1953 (above) and 1941 (opposite).*

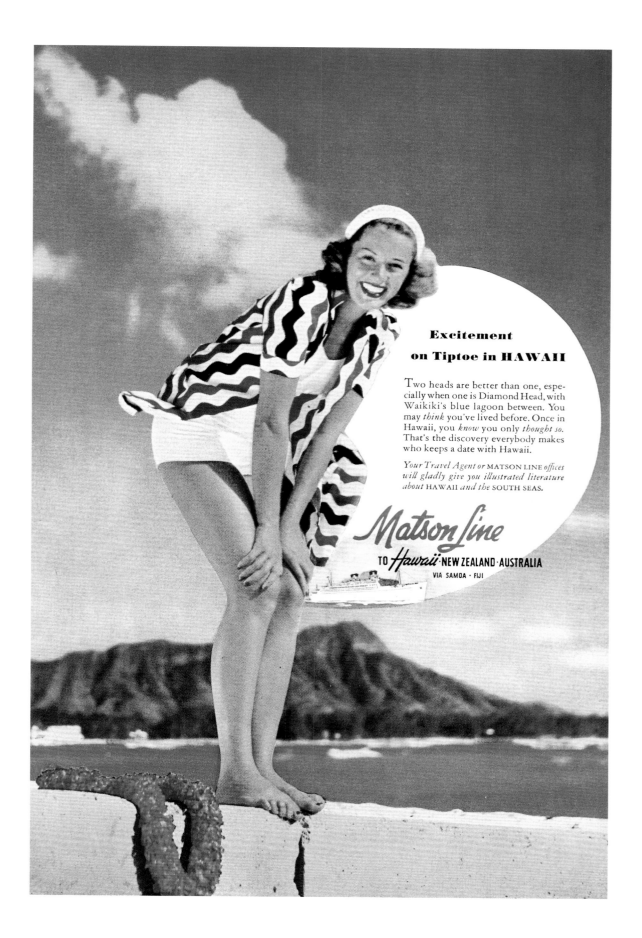

### Excitement
### on Tiptoe in HAWAII

Two heads are better than one, especially when one is Diamond Head, with Waikiki's blue lagoon between. You may *think* you've lived before. Once in Hawaii, you *know* you only *thought so*. That's the discovery everybody makes who keeps a date with Hawaii.

*Your Travel Agent or* MATSON LINE *offices will gladly give you illustrated literature about* HAWAII *and the* SOUTH SEAS.

**Matson Line**
TO *Hawaii* · NEW ZEALAND · AUSTRALIA
VIA SAMOA · FIJI

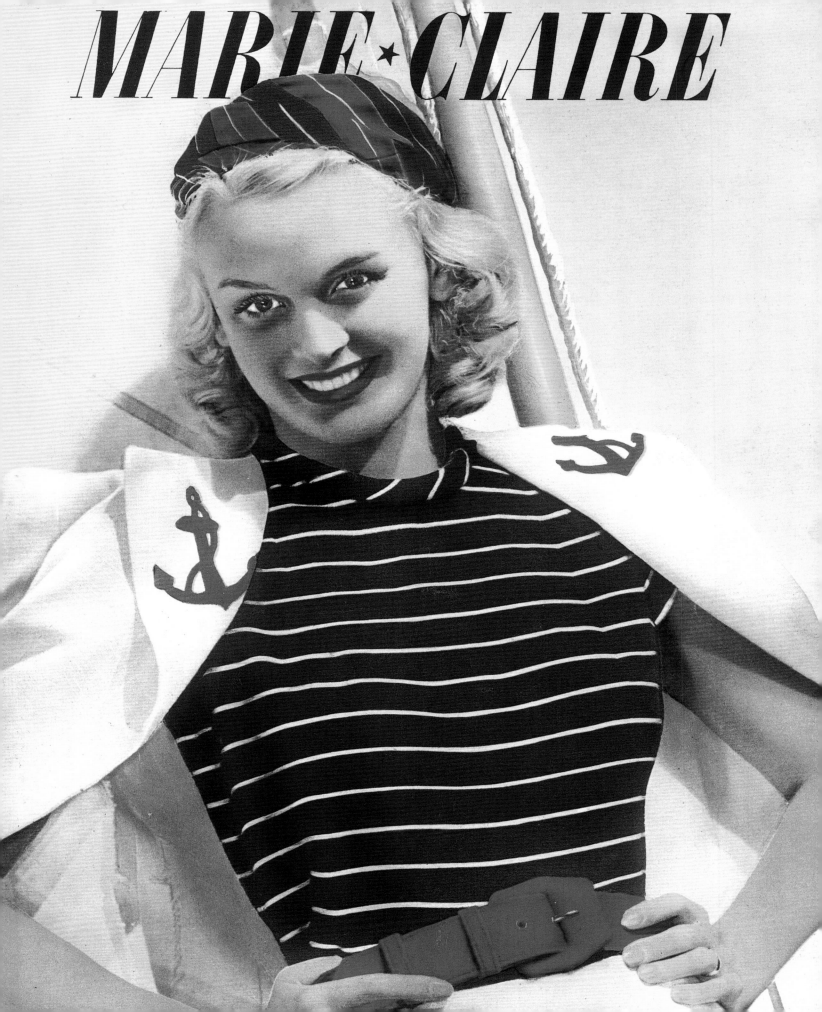

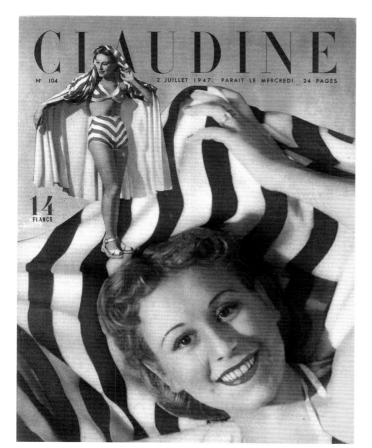
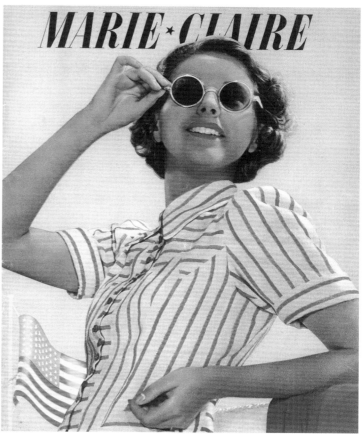

Above, left: *Marcel Rochas couture on the cover of* Claudine *magazine, 1947.* Above, right: *All-American style on the cover of French* Marie Claire, *1939.* Opposite: *Beach chic and the glamour of yachting are often used to sell magazines. Nautical but nice on the cover of French* Marie Claire, *1939.*

couturier Charles Frederick Worth. In 1896, the monogram was developed in an attempt to stave off copycat designs and, by the end of the 19th century, they were selling from outlets in Britain, France and the United States, countries for which sea travel was becoming an essential part of a luxury lifestyle.

As with the navy, class segregation on deck mirrored class stratification on shore, and accommodation on liners varied widely depending on how much you could pay. But, for the first time, sea travel became an option for a wider section of society, and life at sea could be enjoyed rather than endured. Liner travel, complete with sleek modernist design, prevailed

throughout the interwar period, when magazines such as *Vogue* gave advice on what to wear on board and tips on how to pack, fuelling the desire to engage with sea travel. Daywear often had a nautical flavour and during the 1930s wide sailor-style trousers were a favourite of the fashion pages. The luxury liner was finally killed off by the rise of the aeroplane, which would dominate long-distance travel after tourist-class flights began operating in the 1950s. The jet age had begun, but boats were not forgotten. Many liners made the transition to cruise ships where an entire tourist industry developed, yet again based on not just life, but a fully-fledged lifestyle at sea.

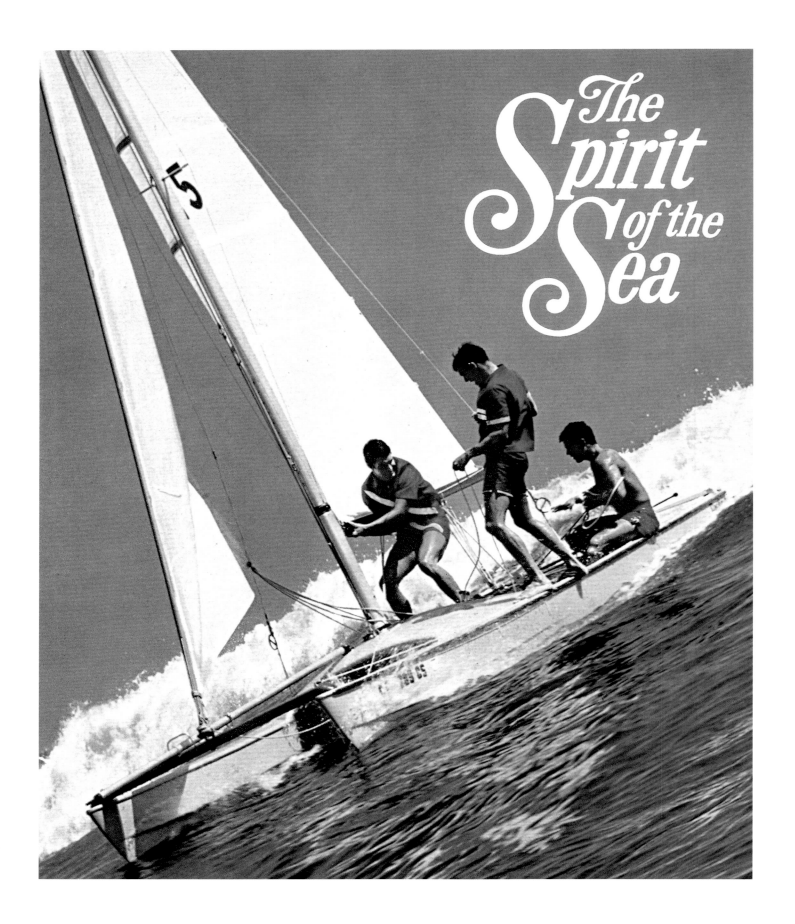

The
Spirit
Of the
Sea

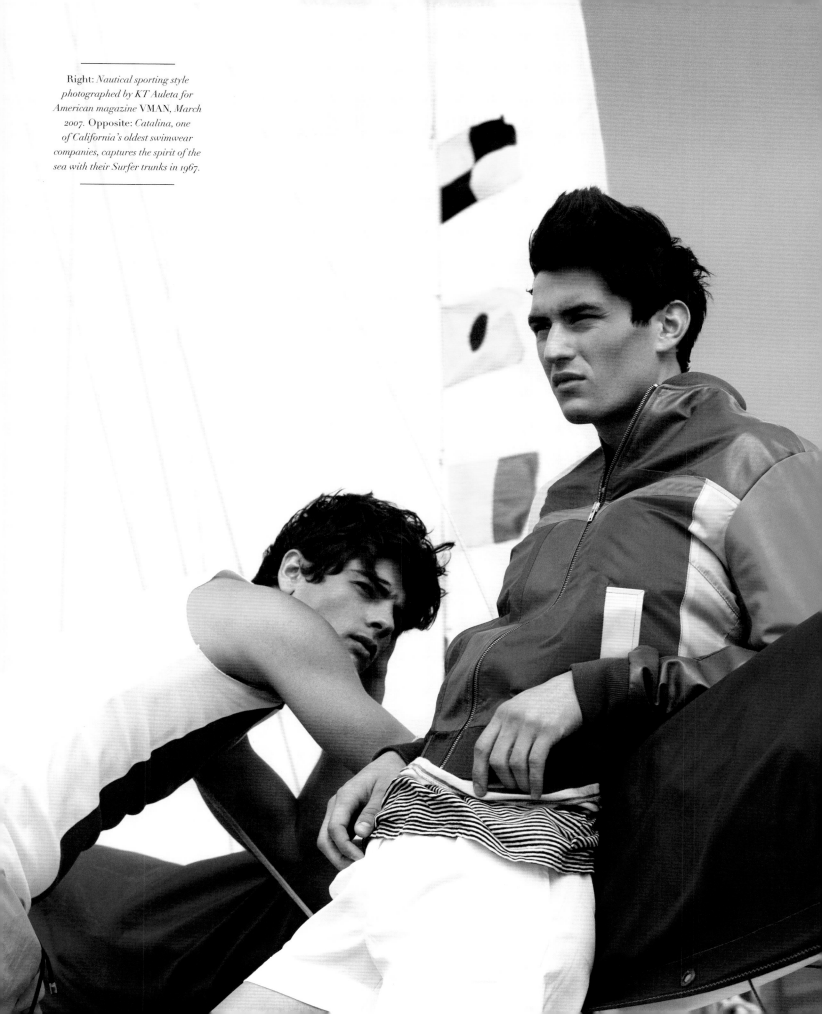

Right: *Nautical sporting style photographed by KT Auleta for American magazine* VMAN, *March 2007.* Opposite: *Catalina, one of California's oldest swimwear companies, captures the spirit of the sea with their Surfer trunks in 1967.*

## FASHION FOR ALL? DEFINING AMERICAN SPORTING STYLE

The story of American style – and of the growth of the US fashion industry – is rooted in the idea of sportswear as typified in yacht clubs and on beaches along much of the eastern seaboard. At the outbreak of the First World War, Paris – home to couture and style arbiter of the western world since the 17th century – was thrown into dire straits leading to a shortage of European fashions across the Atlantic. With Paris temporarily out of the picture, the Editor-in-Chief of US *Vogue*, Edna Woolman Chase, staged a 'Fashion Fête', an early form of catwalk parade showcasing American designs while raising money for the Allied cause. At this time, the Seventh Avenue wholesale trade dominated American fashion, rather than the star-name couturiers of France. Many sportswear lifestyle brands have subsequently grown from this wholesale industry, such as Ralph Lauren and Gant, but initially the industry was anonymous, based on the practice of copying Parisian styles. The 1914 Fashion Fête focused on American design for the first time. Many of the participants were the in-house designers at leading department stores such as Henri Bendel and Bergdorf Goodman, but nonetheless American design was making its own small inroads onto the fashion map.[19] The Second World War was to have similar consequences, including the initiation

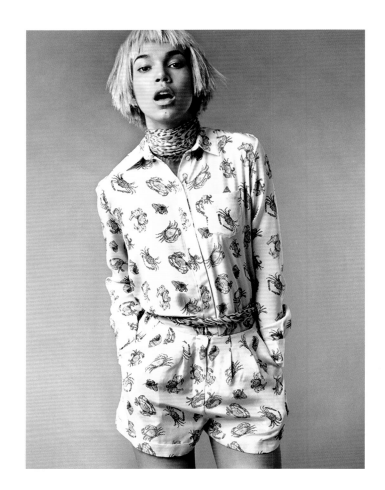

*Above: Seaside prints and sandy shades in contemporary leisurewear. Blouse and shorts by Silken Favours, photographed by Damien Fry, resort collection for spring/summer 2014.*
*Opposite: Claire McCardell became emblematic of mid-century American designers who created active yet stylish sports and leisurewear. Claire McCardell designs, photographed by Genevieve Naylor, 1946.*

of 'Press Week' (which would evolve into New York Fashion Week) by publicist Eleanor Lambert in 1943.

It was the Great Depression, sparked by New York's own Wall Street, that was initially to have the biggest impact on marketing American sportswear as a viable alternative to styles from Paris. Following the Crash, 1930 and 1931 saw a dramatic drop in French couture purchases in the United States due to crippling import duties.[20] A market for domestic fashion was needed to combat the inflated prices from overseas, and the result was the 1932 'American Fashions for American Women' campaign, headed by Dorothy Shaver. Shaver, Vice-President (and later first female President) of Lord & Taylor – one of America's oldest departments stores – had been planning the campaign since 1929, with the aim of creating a cult of personality around previously faceless American designers, whose clothing had been labelled with the manufacturer rather than the designer. The idea that customers would willingly buy clothing promoted as American-designed was revolutionary

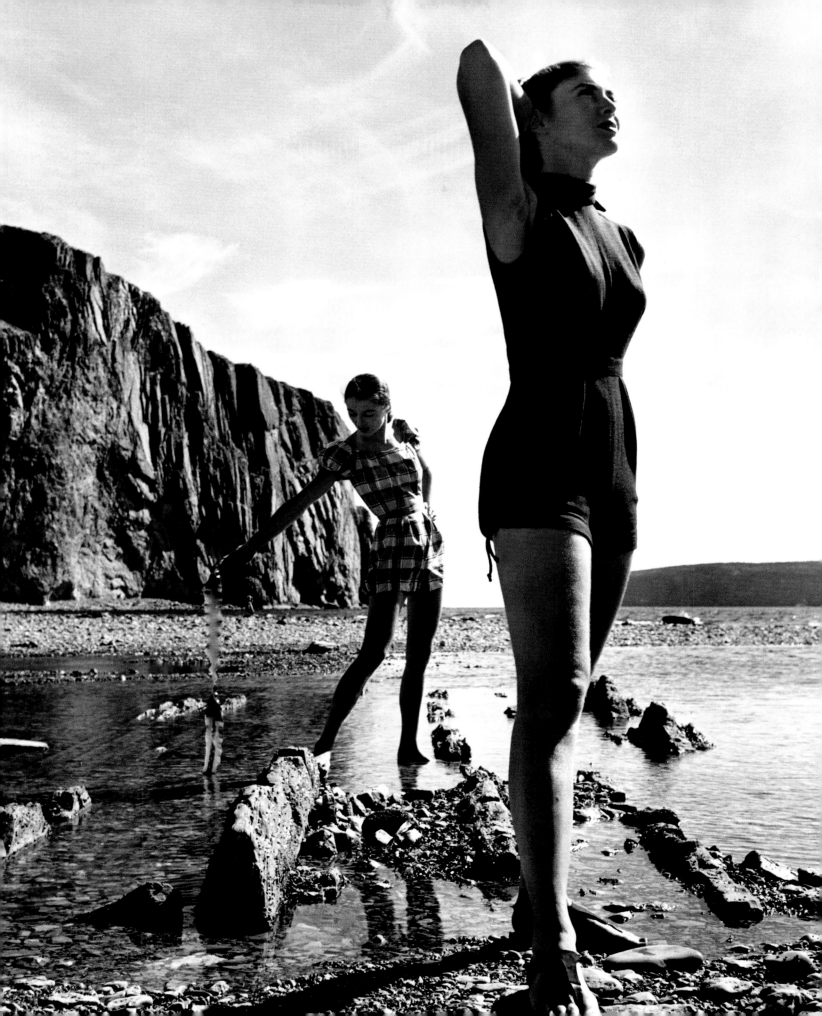

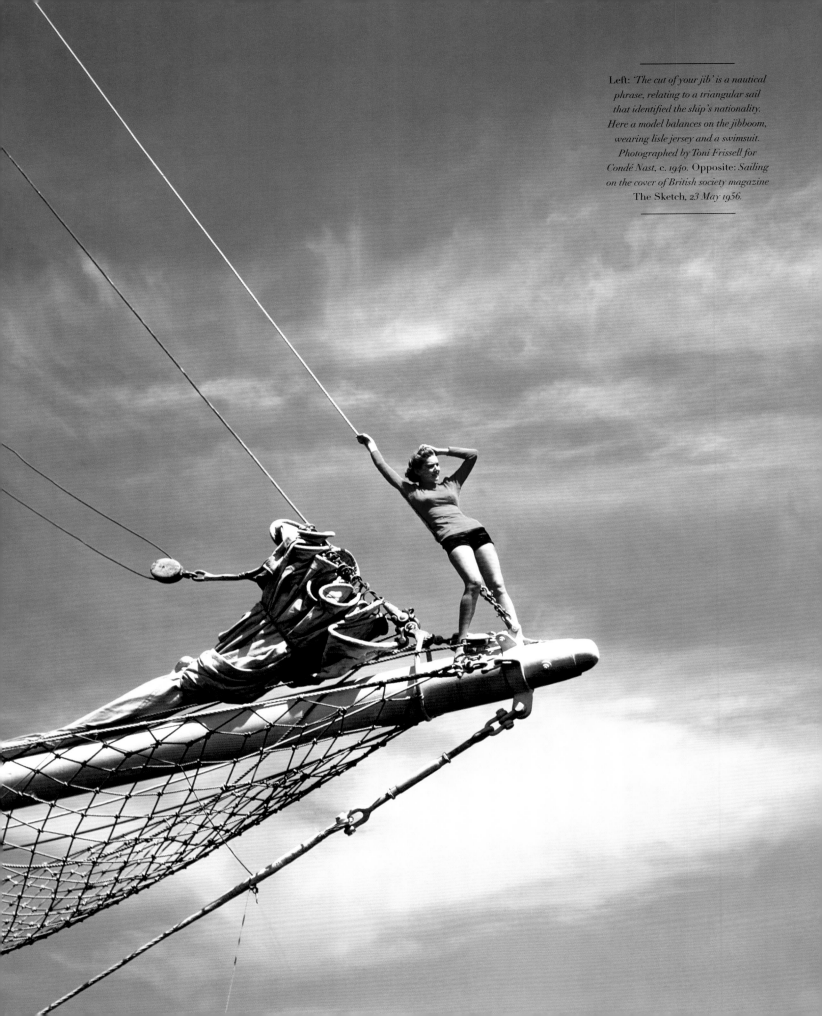

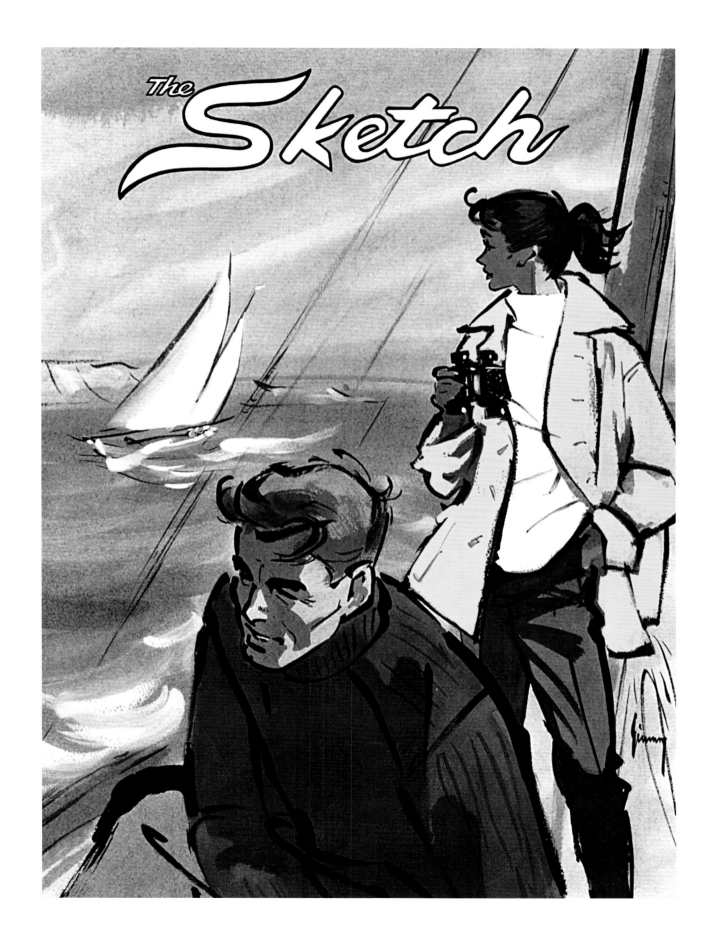

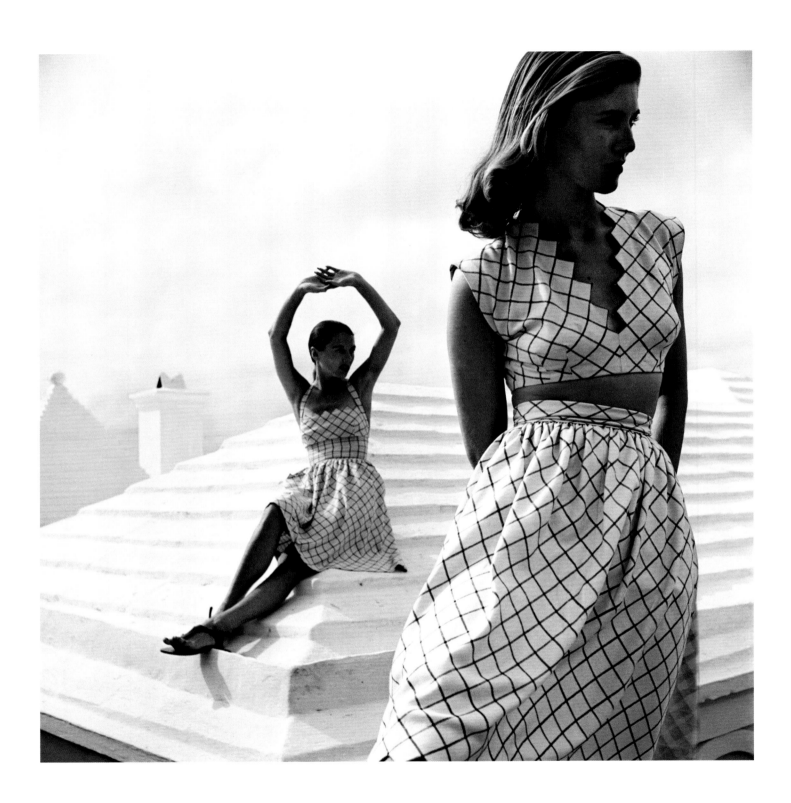

at the time. Three designers were chosen to front the initial campaign, among them Elizabeth Hawes, who had worked in Paris and returned to New York to set up her own business a few years later, determined to work the mass-production industry of Seventh Avenue to her advantage. Optimistic about this method of production she wrote a book, *Fashion is Spinach* (1938), chronicling her conversion from Parisian couture and the continual change of the fashion cycle, to mass production and the notion of timeless style, a mainstay of American sporting chic.

The rhetoric around production line manufacture and the democracy of fashion-for-all would become a key theme in the marketing of 'American style,' along with a focus on the casual, sports-based nature of American clothing. The figurehead of this easy and active American lifestyle design was Claire McCardell. It was yet again Dorothy Shaver at Lord & Taylor who oversaw 'The American Look' campaign in 1945 and featured McCardell as one of the key designers; McCardell quickly became associated with the rise of an autonomous American aesthetic based on athleticism and activewear. The term 'American Look' had been used as a marketing tool to bolster sales of domestic products since the 1920s, when the firm Best & Co. used it as part of their advertising copy.[21] Yet with a national promotional campaign behind it, 'The American Look', as endorsed by Lord & Taylor, would prove to be the most enduring, with McCardell at the forefront of a coterie of predominantly female sportswear designers that also included Clare Potter, Bonnie Cashin and later Anne Klein, who would develop a pared-down, sporty aesthetic that formed the backbone of American design.

*The epitome of democratic American style: summer designs by Claire McCardell, 1946.*

Sportswear, however, was not a uniquely American phenomenon, as outlined in the previous chapter. But it was the rigorous promotion of clothing as accessible, active and functional that came to be uniquely American, carefully situated as more affordable and practical than Parisian couture. McCardell was passionate about the democratization of style, and was a true innovator in sportswear design for mass-production. Many of her garments were ahead of their time and, in their elegant simplicity and contemporary aesthetic, their mid-century origins often come as a surprise. Many of McCardell's leisure items – such as her signature bloomer playsuits – were frequently photographed at the beach, drawing on the active nature of the clothing coupled with the lure of leisure at the coast. Her pieces were regularly shot by Louise Dahl-Wolfe, one of the photographers who would come to be instrumental in defining the American look,[22] along with Toni Frissell, who capitalized on the lure of the great outdoors, and Slim Aarons, whose work for publications such as *Town & Country* captured the quintessential New England socialite WASP lifestyle both in the States and at resorts around Europe.

Sitting slightly outside of the marketing of American style as sporty, casual and democratic was the work of Norman Norell, whose sailor dresses and high-end yacht club chic became his trademark. While distinctly a ready-to-wear label, Norell applied many couture techniques to his work, forming full collections rather than individual pieces, incorporating handwork and featuring a 'fanatical attention to quality', as remarked a prominent *Vogue* editor.[23] He developed a yachting look early when designing for Hattie Carnegie, featuring a navy blazer and white wool skirt, and later developed his design staple of the sailor dress. Inspired by a sailor suit he was dressed in as a child, sailor dresses were a perennial for Norell during the 1950s and '60s, featuring the distinctive square collar and fresh, crisp colour palette of white and blue. Lauded as a master of American design, he put nautical style on the map of American high fashion.

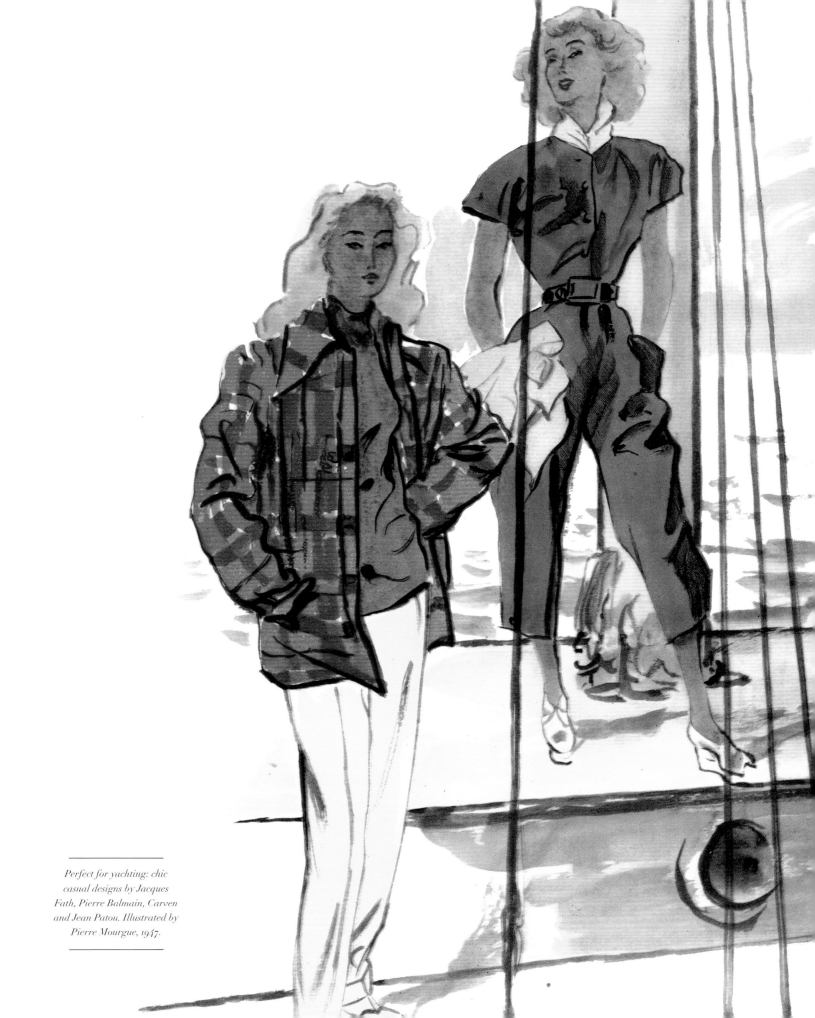

*Perfect for yachting: chic
casual designs by Jacques
Fath, Pierre Balmain, Carven
and Jean Patou. Illustrated by
Pierre Mourgue, 1947.*

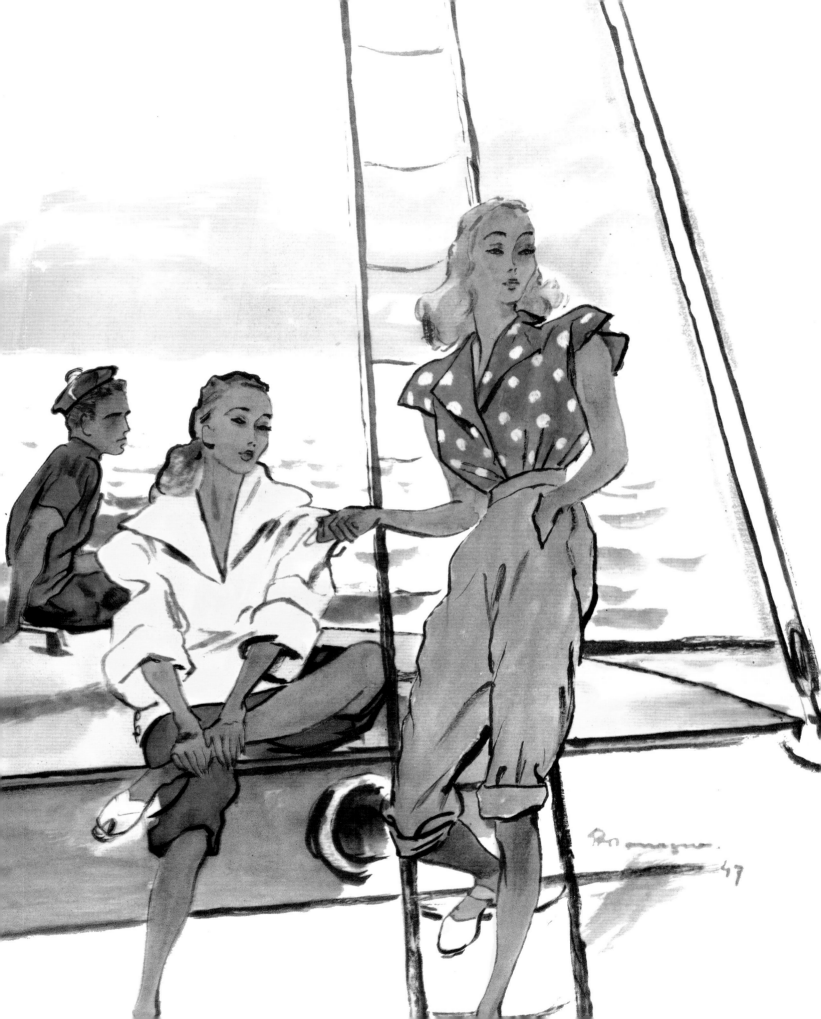

*'I go to Nantucket every summer with my family.... I love the pastimes of New England: we ride bicycles, play tennis, go boating and have clambakes and parties. It's all white picket fences, green grass, blue sky, beige sand. The combinations of these colours and the laid-back, sporty feeling of the lifestyle have been very inspiring to me.'*

TOMMY HILFIGER[24]

*President John F. Kennedy and First Lady Jacqueline Kennedy watch the America's Cup on board USS Joseph P. Kennedy, Jr., off the coast of Newport, Rhode Island, 1962.*

## THE LIFESTYLE LOOK

If the whole notion of American fashion was built on active lifestyles, then it wouldn't take long for a sporting lifestyle to become intrinsic to many American brands. The legacy of yachting and other coastal sports has long been celebrated through the associated clothing. Yet despite the rhetoric of democracy that runs alongside many discussions of Stateside fashion, lots of styles emanating from the shores of New England are anything but. Since 1886, the Social Register directory has provided information on the country's most 'prominent' families, according to their website the 'only reliable, and the most trusted, arbiter of Society in America'. Originally featuring mainly descendants of early Dutch and English settlers, it is telling that the summer edition of the Register also includes a list of yachts and their owners. Nautical sporting pursuits, and corresponding nautical style, have become markers of this lifestyle that is often synonymous with an Ivy League education and other social privileges. The leisure-as-lifestyle aesthetic of many of the brands affiliated with this look may appear casual in comparison to aristocratic court codes of Europe, but it is nonetheless an elite and aspirational style of dress. The Kennedys were the apogee of this lifestyle in the postwar leisure boom. Magazines were keen to capitalize on this aspect of JFK's charm; he was often photographed on his sailboat, *Honey Fitz*, as well as waterskiing or at the beach in swimwear or slacks. It was arguably his lifestyle – as well as his connections to various screen stars – that made him one of the first celebrity politicians and subsequently the president of the USA.

JFK's style drew on modes that were popular on many college campuses. He married Jacqueline Lee Bouvier in 1953 wearing a suit by Brooks Brothers, a company also known for outfitting naval officers with their uniforms. The self-claimed oldest clothing retailer in the States, Brooks Brothers first opened in 1818 and began specializing in ready-to-wear later that century. In 1909, they opened their first store outside of Manhattan, choosing Newport, Rhode Island, where they could dress the likes of the Astors, Vanderbilts and Morgans in their summer retreats. An early presidential fan was Abraham Lincoln; they also provided the naval uniform for Teddy

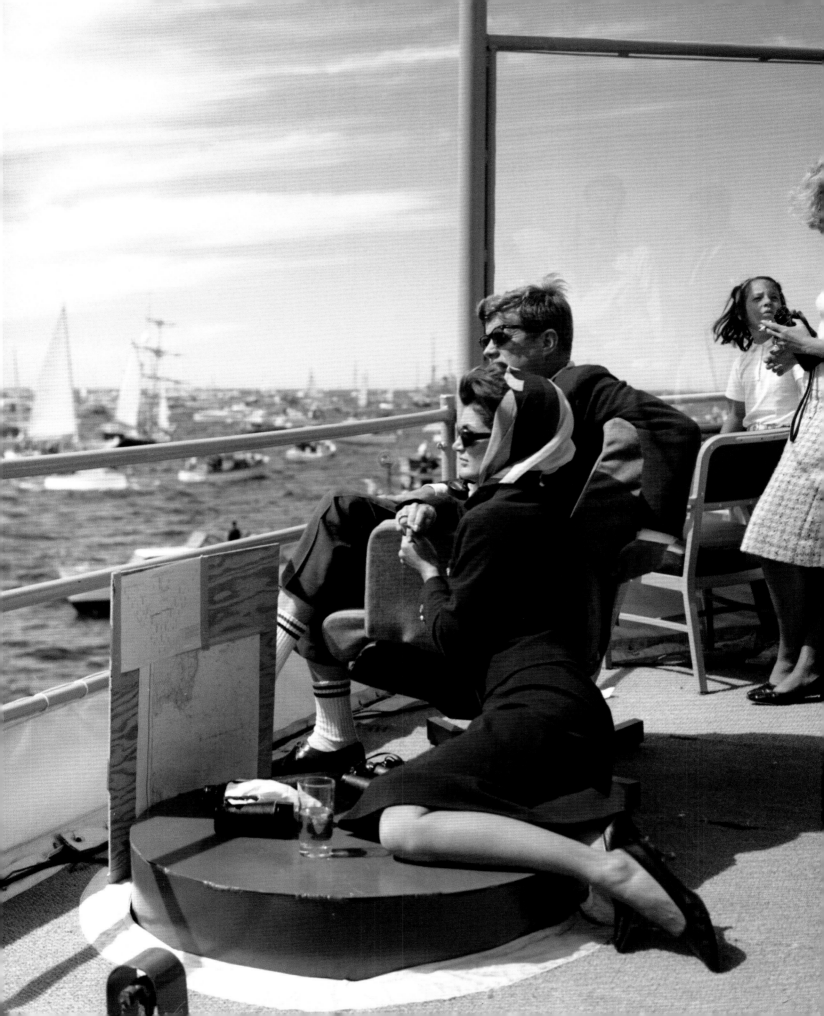

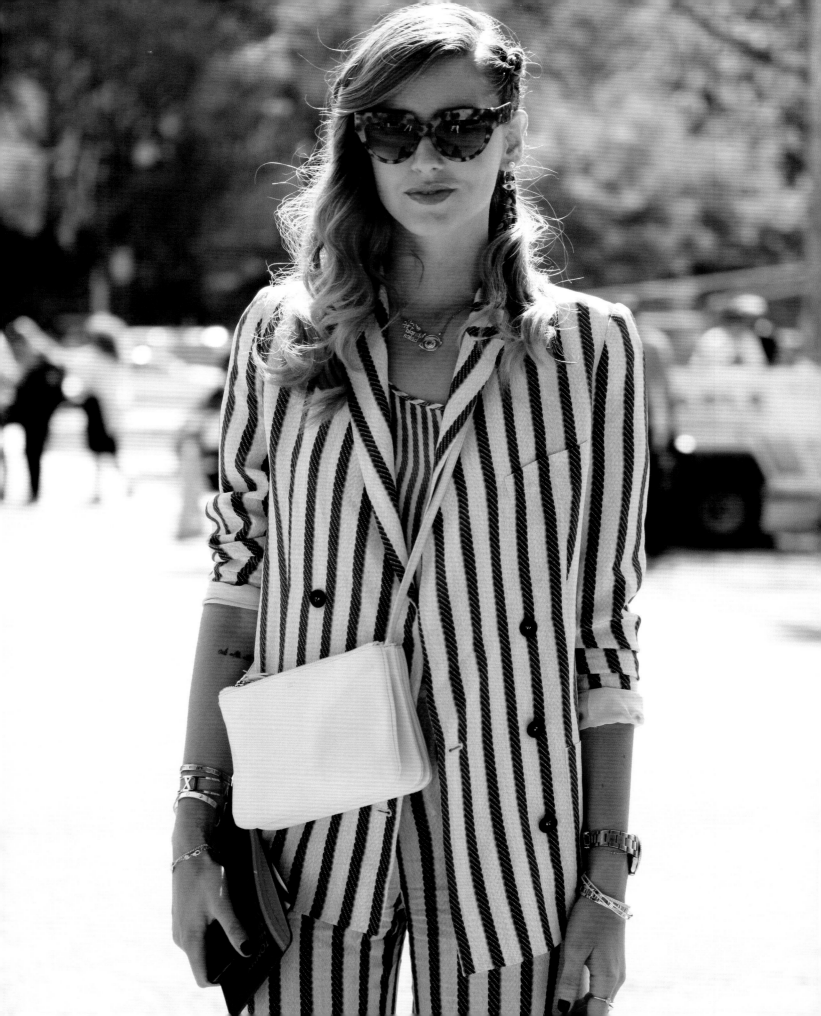

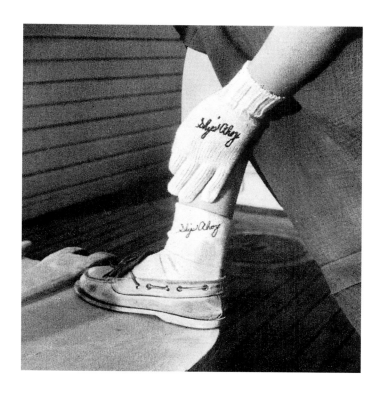

Roosevelt in his pre-White House days. Their button-down collars have become a bastion of American smart casual style, and they were immortalized in Lisa Birnbach's *Official Preppy Handbook* in 1980. JFK was also a regular at Abercrombie & Fitch. Initially a sporting goods store, the company dates back to 1892 and, in its heyday, was patronized by the likes of Amelia Earhart, Katharine Hepburn, Ernest Hemingway and Cole Porter.

Ivy League campuses were often the breeding ground for defining aspects of New England sporting style. Gant is a company with collegiate ties that wouldn't be out of place in any yacht club. Beginning as a shirtmaker in the wholesale business around New York's Seventh Avenue, Ukrainian immigrant Bernard Gantmacher moved to New Haven, Connecticut, in the 1920s. He worked as a sub-contractor supplying shirts, until his sons returned from service in the War and decided to launch their own label. Gant of New Haven was founded in 1949, specializing in the preppy staple of the Oxford button-down collar. These shirts were so popular on campus that, during the 1960s, they produced a range that was sold exclusively through the Yale Co-op college store. The sailing lifestyle associated with the eastern seaboard continues to inspire the brand, as in the spring/summer 2011 'Docking in Newport' collection that featured navy blazers, striped tops and a campaign video shot on board a yacht. Sperry Top-Siders also found favour on college campuses. Paul Sperry created the original deck shoe, himself a New England native from a seafaring family. According to the brand story, in 1935 he was inspired by his dog's paws to create the design for the unique non-slip sole, having watched him gambol effortlessly across the ice. He carved the initial grooves in his soles with a penknife, and they became so popular that the US War

Above: '"Anchors aweigh", "Ship ahoy" or symbols such as compasses, anchors, stars, steering wheels are suggested as embroidered decorations for anklets and gloves.' Deck shoes feature in an article titled, 'Modern Living: Fashion Designers Find New Style Ideas in Navy', Life *magazine, 28 October 1940.* Opposite: *Blogger Chiara Ferragni in Tommy Hilfiger stripes at New York Fashion Week, 2013.*

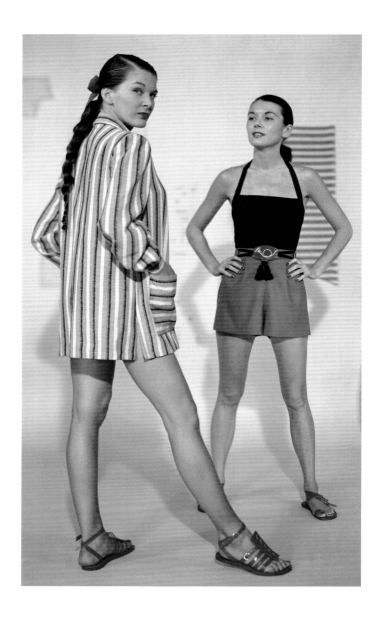

Above: *Mid-century summer leisurewear. A Guatemalan cotton beach jacket on the left, and a beach ensemble with halter-top on the right, 1947.* Opposite: *Model Barbara Mullen wears Lanvin in Saint Tropez for the cover of French* Elle *magazine. Photographed by Georges Dambier, 1957.*

Department issued them as official footwear during the Second World War. Crossing into civilian wear, they became a favourite on campus and at the resorts of New England.

This lifestyle has been captured and sold by aspirational companies such as Ralph Lauren and Tommy Hilfiger, who 'incorporate the nautical aesthetic into their brand handwriting', as noted by Jaana Jätyri, founder of trend forecasting agency Trendstop.[25] Ralph Lauren – originally Ralph Lifshitz – grew up in the Bronx and started out packing gloves, later working as a tie salesman when he started to create his own designs. He launched his first complete women's collection in 1972,[26] with many of his sartorial cues taken from British country life, and he quickly became synonymous with a certain New England lifestyle. Lauren encapsulates the East Coast American Dream, complete with the requisite summerhouse in Montauk. Tommy Hilfiger is adept at mythologizing the all-American lifestyle, venerating hot dogs, baseball, apple pie and the Mickey Mouse Club.[27] He cites his love of sports while growing up as a source of inspiration, along with classic Ivy League campus styles and naval uniform, including pieces he wore as a teenager from bell-bottoms to middy shirts and striped sweaters.[28] The navy blazer is a perennial in the collections of both Hilfiger and Lauren, who constantly reinvent yacht club chic and reaffirm its place in aspirational American living. In recent years, Vineyard Vines and J.Crew have successfully captured nautical-preppy-Americana for a 21st-century customer. Helped again by links to the White House (Michelle Obama has been a regular wearer), since 2012 J.Crew has shown at New York Fashion Week, aligning it with brands such as Lauren and Hilfiger. Beginning in 1983 as a catalogue service, the name 'Crew' was chosen for its power to evoke Ivy League rowing[29] and, by the end of the decade, they had their first retail location in South Street Seaport, a historic area of Manhattan with ties to New York's seafaring past. Creating an accessible yet aspirational brand infused with a smattering of nauticalia, in 2013 they were labelled by *Business Week* as the closest thing America has to 'exportable national style'.[30]

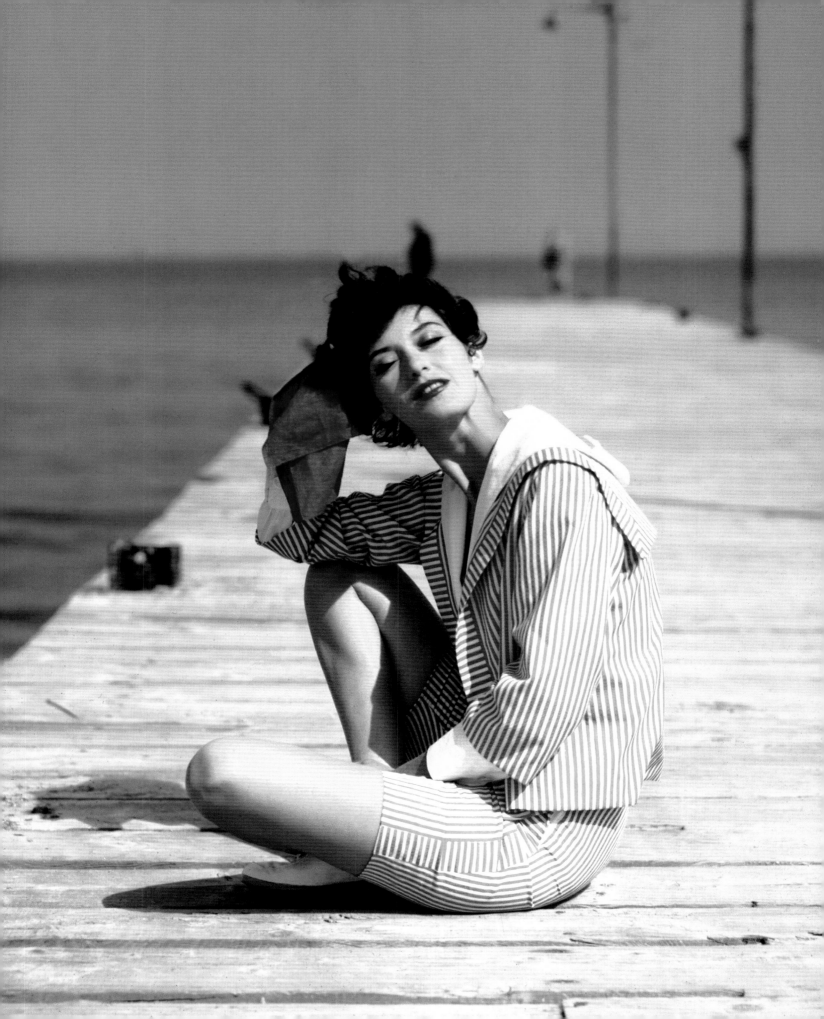

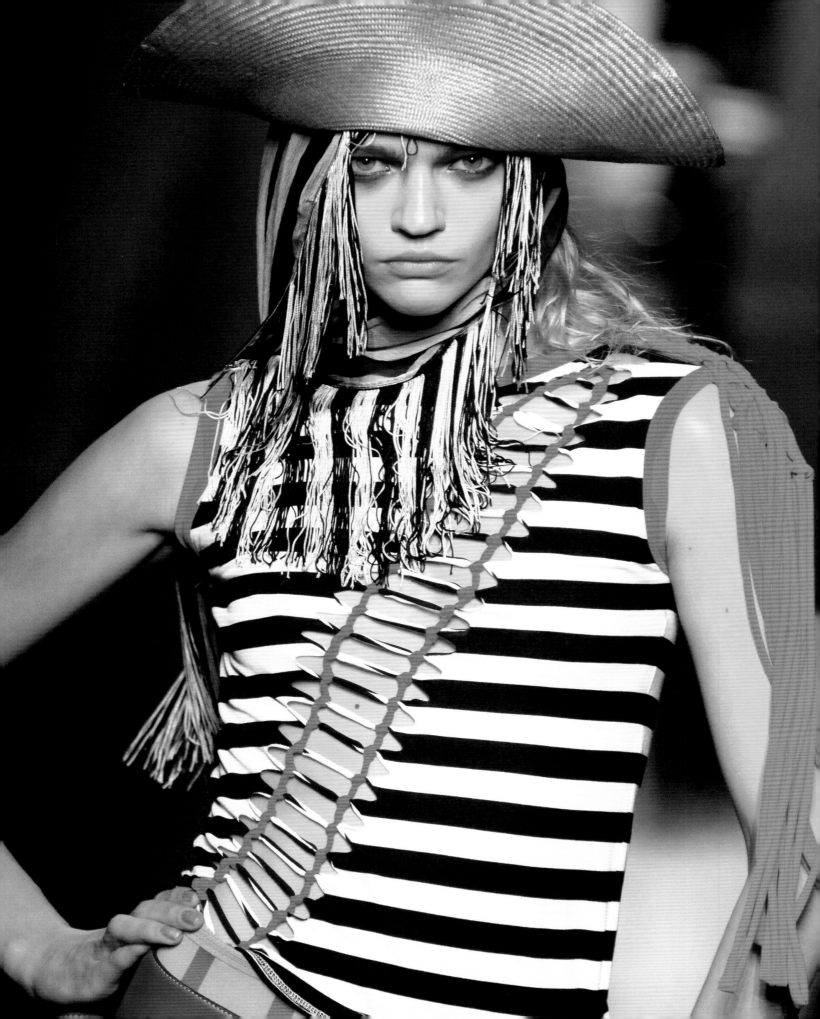

# CHAPTER 5

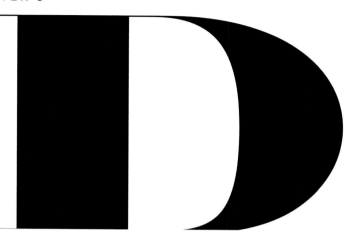

THE PIRATE

*Romance*

*and adventure on the high seas are embodied by the Pirate.
Designers with a penchant for historical detail and the spirit
of rebellion, from McLaren and Westwood to Galliano and de
Castelbajac, are drawn to his excess. Embodying aristocratic
17th-century opulence, as well as shipwrecked stripes and
rags, the Pirate's style is drawn as much from fiction as from
fact: a theatrical villain recast as a swashbuckling hero.*

On its publication in 1814, the poem *The Corsair* became a bestseller, infecting early 18th-century London with pirate fever. The poet, Lord Byron, added his own romantic image to the growing mythology surrounding the pirate – he was well qualified, as the original 'mad, bad and dangerous to know' – and cast the pirate as a heroic outlaw. During the heyday of piracy, a century earlier, there was no such sympathetic portrayal, but time had granted Byron the privilege of poetic licence. Once the terror of the seas, over the centuries these often violent, occasionally cruel, felons have been reconstructed as adventurous heroes on a par with Robin Hood in the popular imagination. The pirate has come to symbolize passion and adventure on the high seas. This glamorous intrigue brings with it a host of associations that have enchanted the fashion world, from the anarchic rebellion of McLaren and Westwood to the historical references incorporated by Galliano, Gaultier and McQueen. Our knowledge of the appearance of pirates is often taken from fantasy rather than history. Works of fiction, from *Treasure Island* (1883) to *Pirates of the Caribbean*, have defined how we think of the pirate today, adding to the mystery of these quasi-mythical figures. With this lineage of dashing derring-do, the pirate has a seductive quality, and elements of rebellion, romance and a hint of danger lay the foundations for pirate style.

*O'er the glad waters of the dark blue sea,*
*Our thoughts as boundless, and our souls as free*
*Far as the breeze can bear, the billows foam,*
*Survey our empire and behold our home!*
*These are our realms, no limits to their sway –*
*Our flag the sceptre all who meet obey.*
BYRON, *THE CORSAIR*, 1814

## THE GOLDEN AGE OF PIRACY

Piracy's 'Golden Age' lasted roughly from 1650 to 1720, after which the increasing professionalization of national navies were better able to police the waters. During this period, there were various different types of piracy. The privateer was essentially a pirate operating by licence on behalf of a specific country. A 'letter of marque', issued by the sovereign, would allow a captain and his crew to attack and plunder enemy ships, legalizing a crime otherwise punishable by death. Sir Francis Drake is the most well-known privateer: depending on your geographical location, history paints him as either a national hero or a common pirate. A full-blown pirate, in contrast, operated for no one but himself and his crew, defying international laws and attacking ships from all nations, even his own. Corsairs were pirates operating in the Mediterranean, predominantly along the Barbary coast of north Africa, while buccaneers were found in the Caribbean and around the coast of South America, an area of rich pickings as the New World was colonized and raided and the slave trade was a growing economic force.[1] Against the backdrop of these atrocities, it is

*Page 182: Jean Paul Gaultier's spring/summer 2008 collection captured the essence of the pirate: swashbuckling style on the high seas.* Opposite: *The Scottish sailor John Paul Jones became an American naval commander in the 1770s, during the Revolutionary Wars. In revenge, the British depicted him as a pirate. Published by A. Park, London, first half of 19th century.*

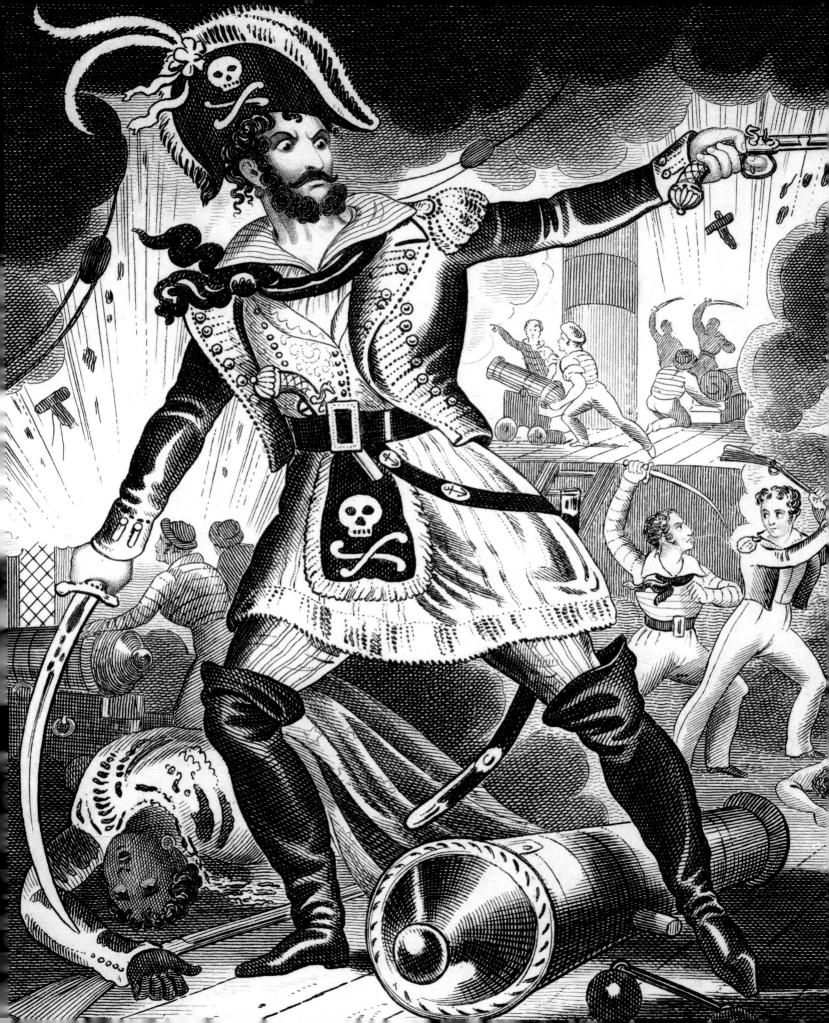

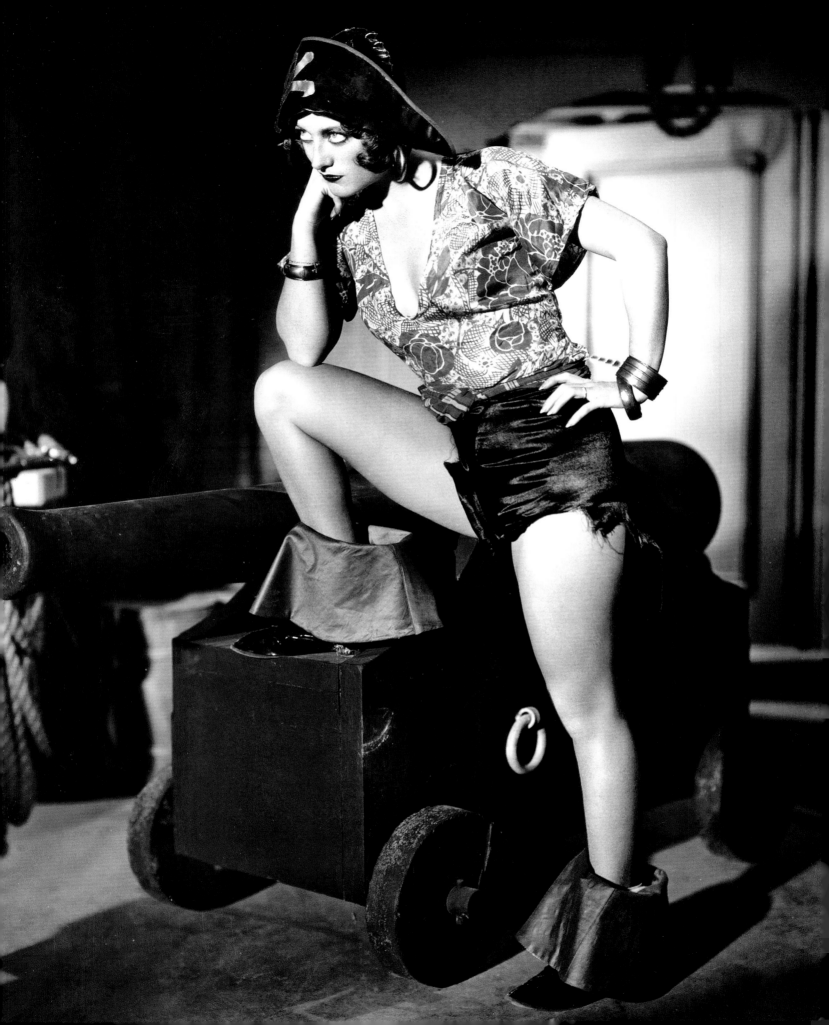

Below: *Hand-knitted cardigan from the Mary Maxim 'Pirate' pattern. The Mary Maxim company was founded in Canada in the 1950s, with knitwear patterns initially inspired by the crafts and motifs of the Cowichan First Nations people who in turn had been influenced by British and Scottish fishermen's knit traditions. From the Beyond Retro archive, 1950s.*

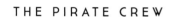

perhaps not surprising that today the pirate is viewed through distinctly rose-coloured glasses, as a heroic figure in opposition to this state-sanctioned barbarity. But in reality the pirate profited from exploitation, colonial plundering and slavery as much as the European nations who ratified these actions.

While very few first-hand descriptions of pirates remain we can be sure that they were a far cry from Errol Flynn or Johnny Depp. An account from 1699 describes 'a man of middle Stature, Square-Shouldered, Large jointed, Lean, much disfigured with the small pox, broad Speech, thick Lipped, a blemish or Cast in his left eye'.[2] Whether they were merchant seamen from captured ships or naval sailors out of work in peacetime, the vast majority of pirates were men from maritime backgrounds and their clothing would have reflected this.[3] However, in an era preceding official uniforms, this could be somewhat diverse. What has become widespread in pirate fiction is the idea of class stratification, as existed on naval ships: that the pirate captain came from the upper echelons of society and the crew from further down the social scale. J.M. Barrie's Captain Hook is the best-known version of the affectedly aristocratic pirate captain. This largely mythical distinction has led to a perceived disparity in dress between the pirate crew – the lower orders – and the pirate captain.

## THE PIRATE CREW

Based on the clothing of working seamen, the imagined dress of the pirate crew tends to be fairly accurate. Stripes are a prominent feature of the pirate wardrobe, from the anachronistic matelot tops to the striped cotton ticking trousers common to pre-regulation mariners. Trousers were worn by seafarers and other working men long before they were fashionable in high society: breeches were mandatory at court in Britain until the early 19th century. The cutlass was the pirate's weapon of choice, being easier to handle than the more elegant rapier often depicted in films. It came into use around 1590, and featured in Royal Navy regulations until 1936.[4] As for headwear, the handkerchief or scarf worn around the sailor's neck could easily be transferred to the head.[5] The red cap that often adorns the First Mate – reminiscent of Disney's 1953 Mr Smee, and a favourite of Jacques Cousteau and later

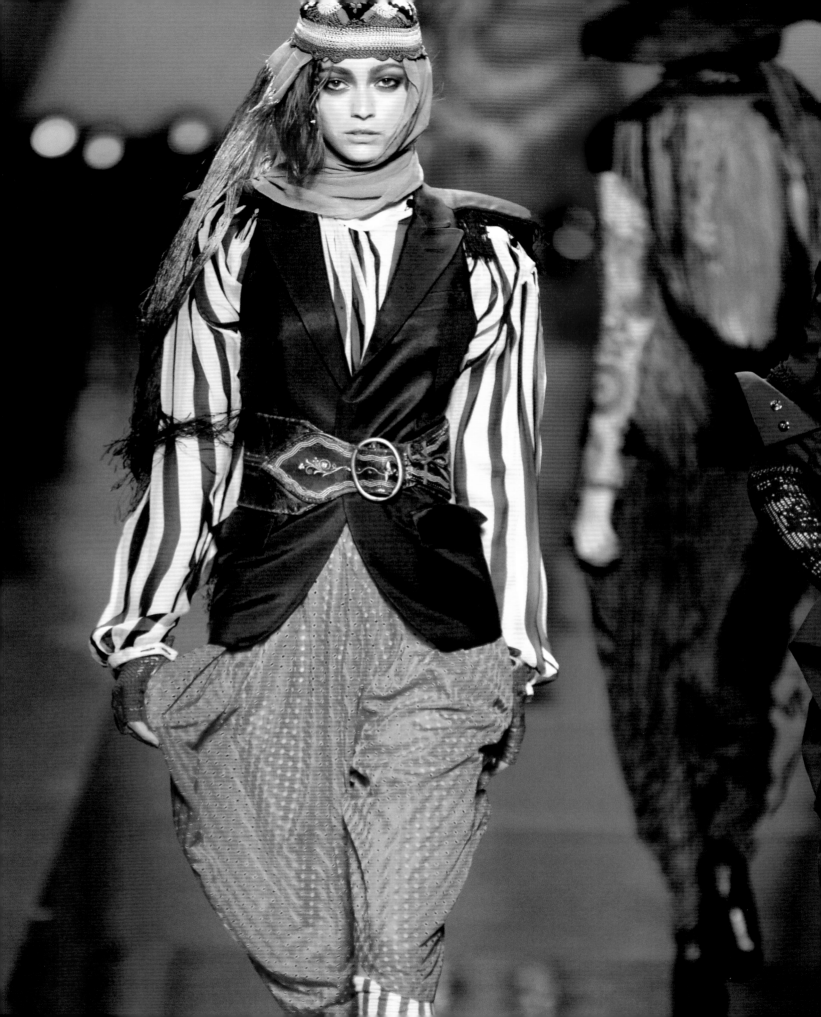

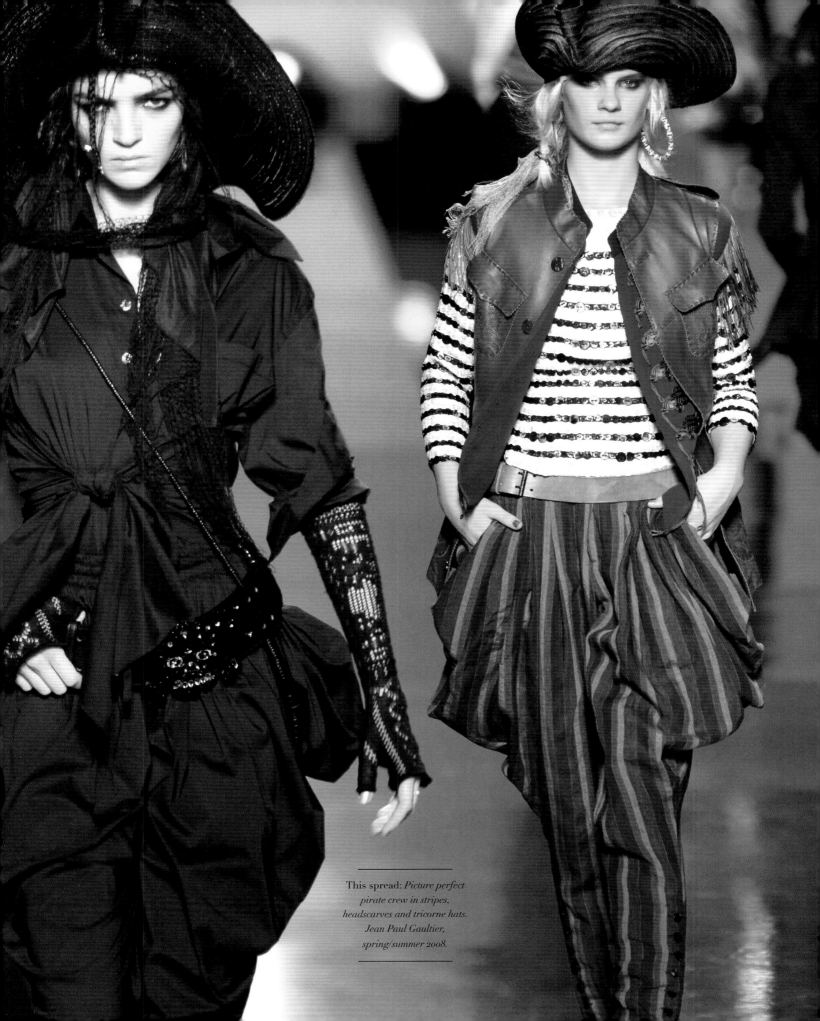

This spread: *Picture perfect
pirate crew in stripes,
headscarves and tricorne hats.
Jean Paul Gaultier,
spring/summer 2008.*

Wes Anderson's Steve Zissou – is derived from the red woollen 'Monmouth' caps incorporated into the slop chest in the 17th century.[6] The sash around the waist was a stylistic fad in the second half of that century,[7] but had been associated with the military since the Middle Ages, befitting a man whose life and income was dependent on fighting.[8]

Many of these elements have been used, combined with a certain ragged, shipwrecked aesthetic, to indicate a hint of danger and the spirit of adventure. This was a recurrent theme throughout the first years of the 21st century, sparked by the *Pirates of the Caribbean* movies, which resurrected the pirate genre on the silver screen. The Disney series saw four films released between 2003 and 2011. Based on a theme park ride at Disneyland in California, it is considered one of the most successful film franchises of all time, having earned $3.7 billion at the global box office.[9] The film was name checked in reviews of Jean Paul Gaultier's spring/summer 2008 ready-to-wear collection, which featured theatrical pirates in breeches-style cropped trousers, playing on the military theme with details such as frogging and fringed epaulettes. Stripes and headscarves resembling skullcaps also featured in this motley crew. Marni sent a subtler version of the pirate gang down the runway for spring/summer 2010. Oversize shell earrings were combined with sash-style belts and knotted headscarves. A multitude of stripes and silk layers hinted at pyjama dressing, adding a déshabillé feel that was reminiscent of bodice-ripper historical romances.

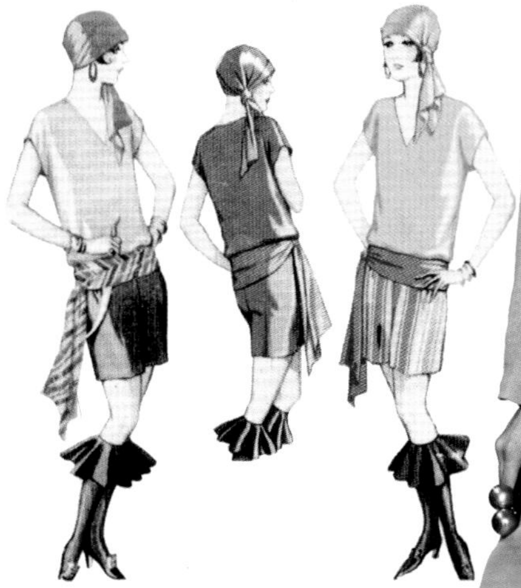

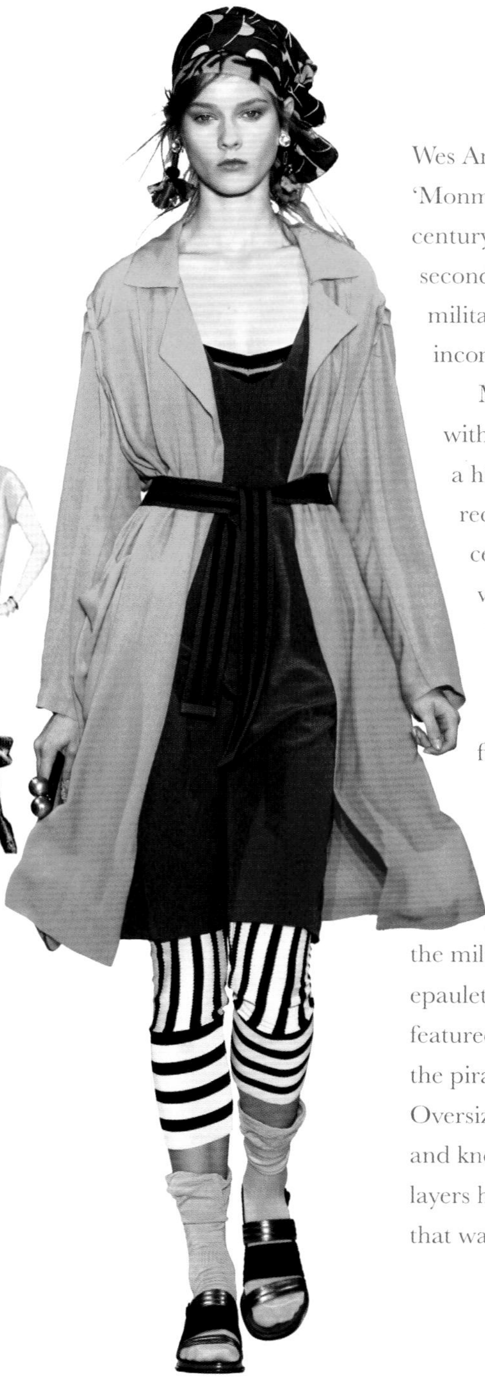

Above: *The pirate has always been a popular option for fancy dress, shown here in* McCall's Printed Patterns Counter Book, *1930.* Right: *The pirate crew with a déshabillé feel at Marni spring/summer 2010.*

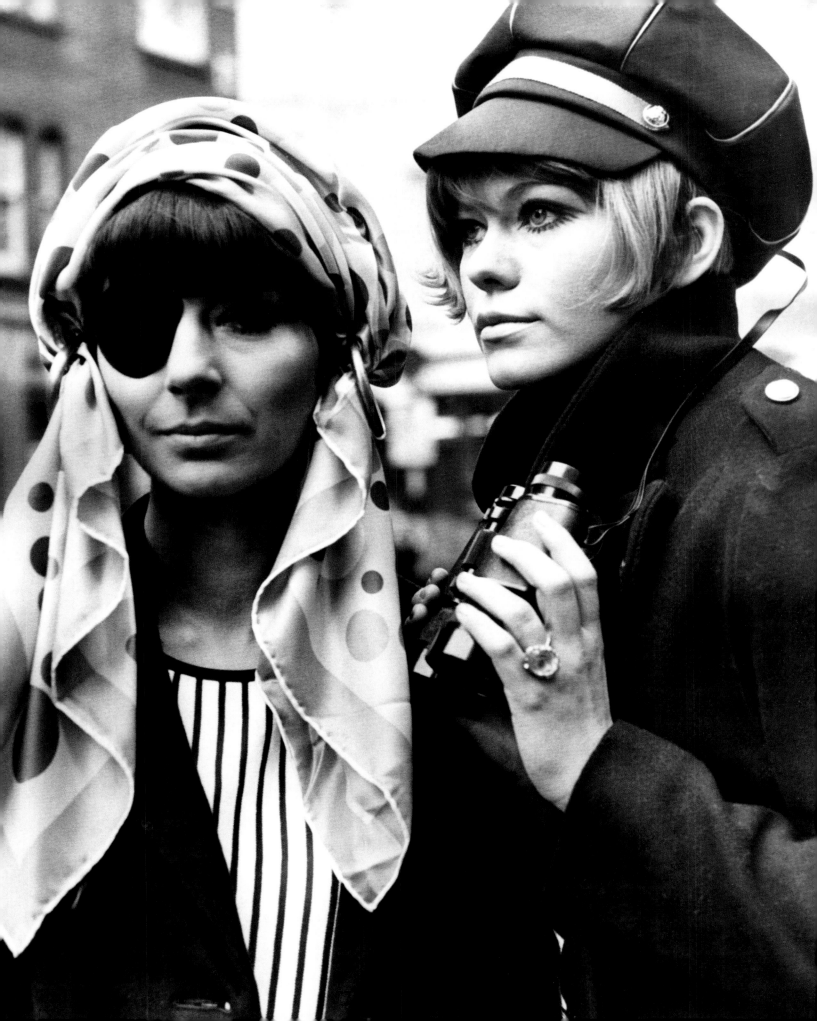

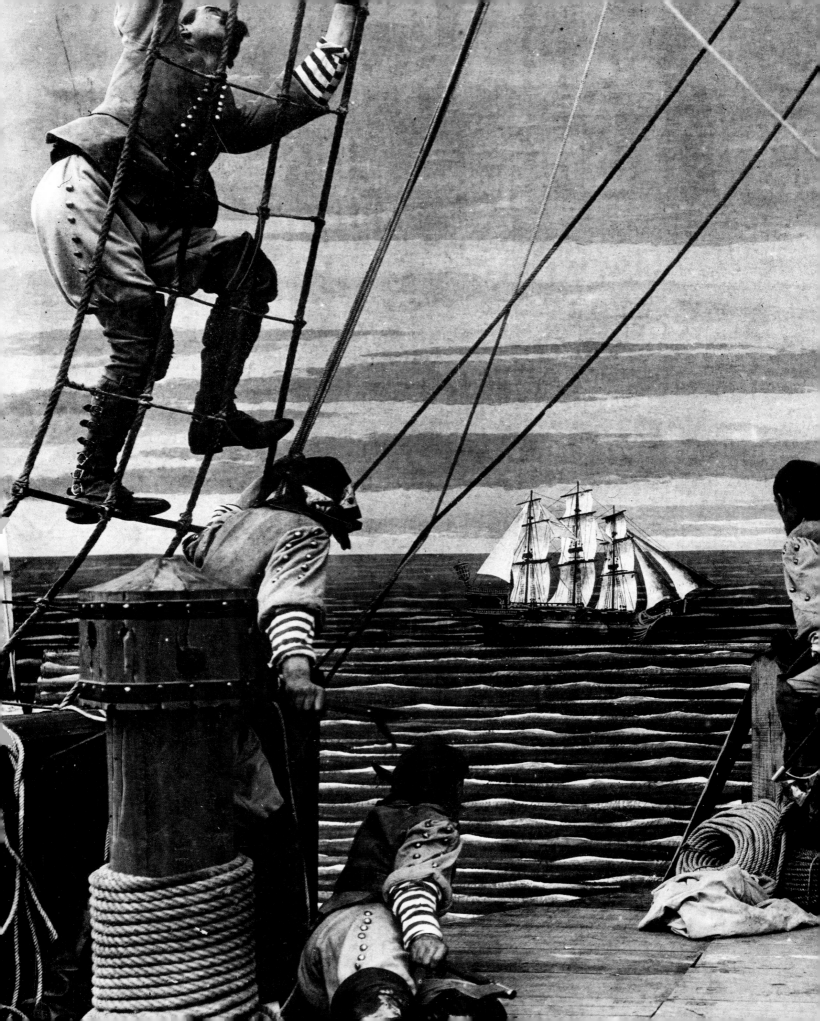

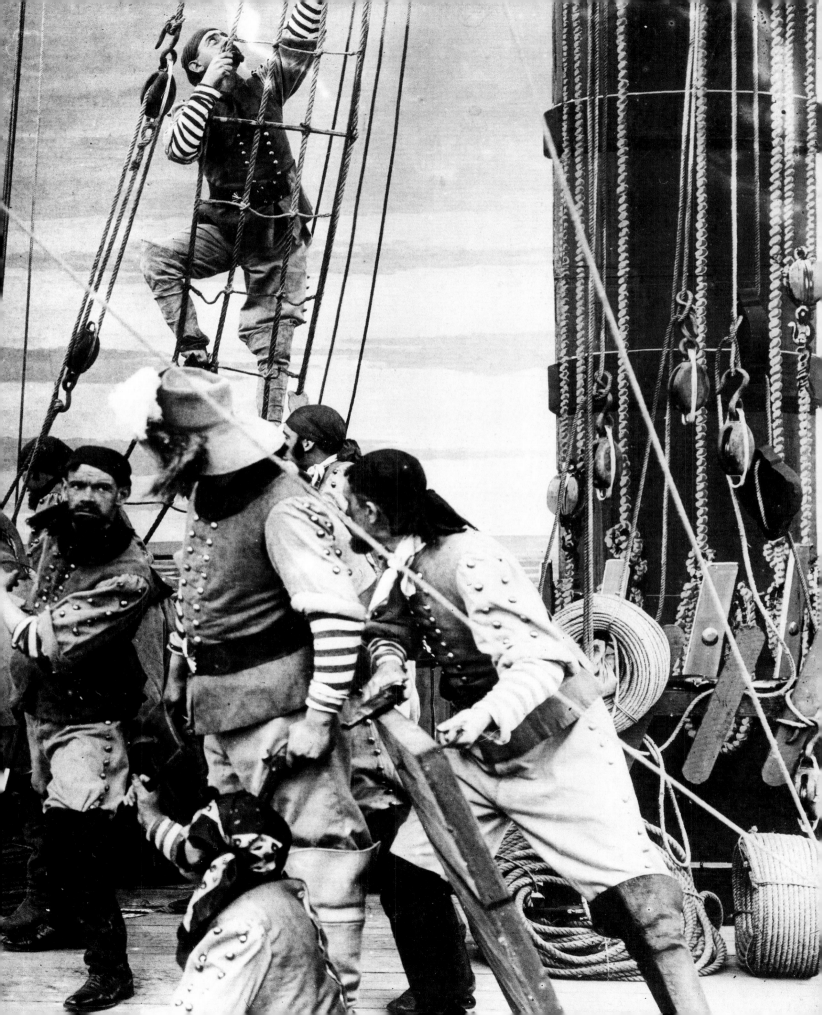

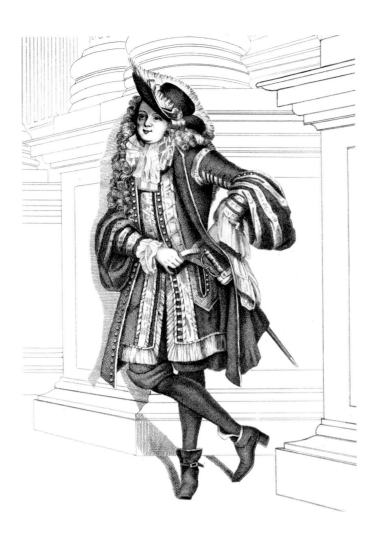

## THE PIRATE CAPTAIN: RESTORATION STYLE

The pirate captain is generally dressed more sumptuously than the crew. In reality, it wasn't unknown for pirates to don fancy apparel depending on what spoils came their way. Execution reports tell us that velvets and silks were frequently part of plundered pirate treasure, and a love of finery is evident in an account of Bartholomew Roberts at his last battle 'dressed in a rich crimson damask waistcoat and breeches, a red feather in his hat, a gold chain round his neck, with a diamond cross hanging to it'.[11] Captains' style is generally a rough historical mix of fashions from the 1660s – concurrent with the Golden Age of Piracy – and later styles from the 18th century. The 1660s was a transitional time for menswear, as the doublet was renounced in favour of a more streamlined silhouette that would form the basis of today's three-piece suit. In October 1666, six years after the reinstatement of Charles II on the English throne, Samuel Pepys noted in his diary that the King had declared a new fashion for clothes. This fashion was the vest, now known as the waistcoat. According to the diary of John Evelyn, this stylistic innovation was introduced to break from the elaborately ribboned and decorative styles of the King's cousin Louis XIV's court in France, where Charles had spent time during exile.

*'In dress he somewhat aped the attire associated with the name of Charles II, having heard it said in some earlier period of his career that he bore a strange resemblance to the ill-fated Stuarts'*

CAPTAIN HOOK, AS DESCRIBED IN J.M. BARRIE'S *PETER AND WENDY* (1911)[10]

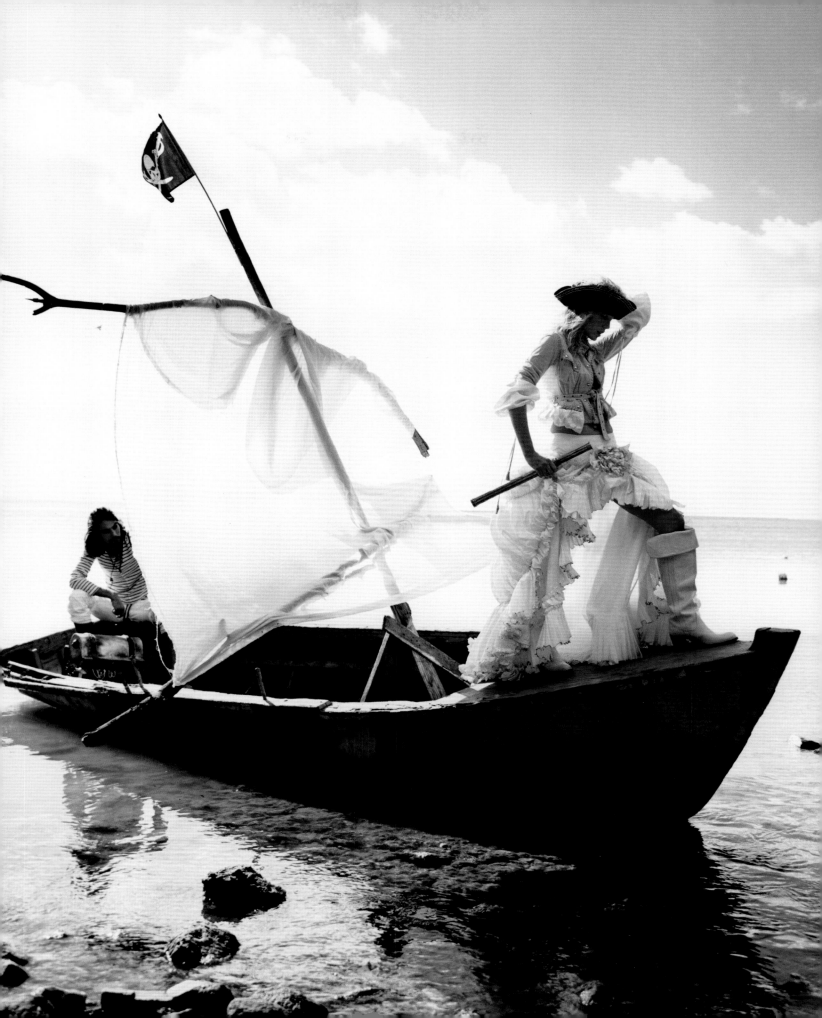

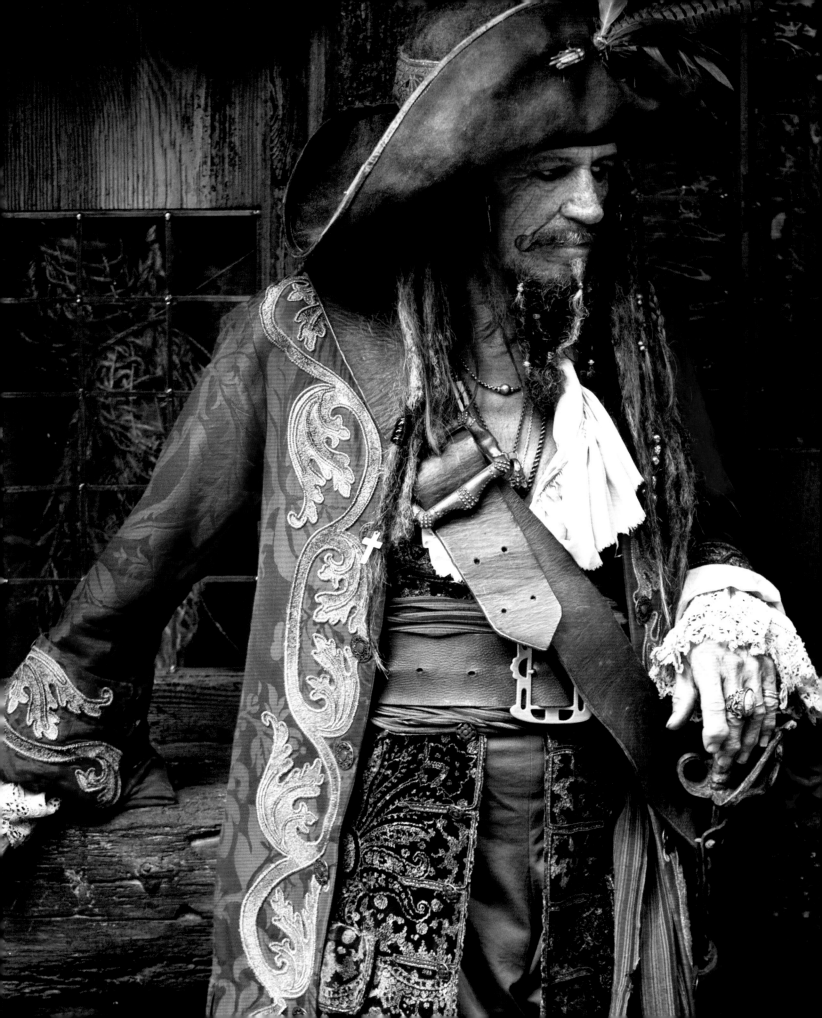

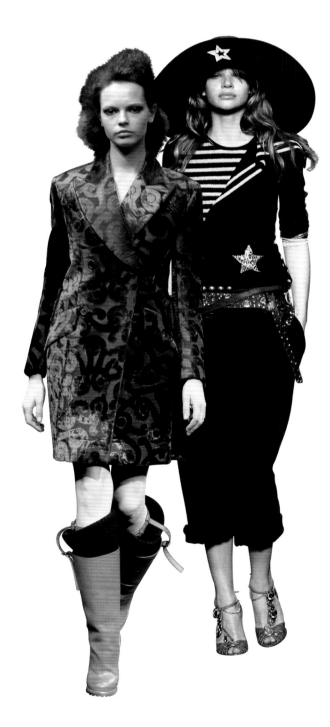

That's not to say that the new style was without adornment. The coat worn over the vest was known as the *justaucorp*, as it was cut close to the body, and could be decorated with braids and embroidery, especially around the buttonholes and deep cuffs.[12] For men of fashion, this was coupled with a wide-brimmed beaver hat trimmed with ribbons and feathers, and a tightly curled periwig which, at their height of popularity, could reach down to the waist and be sprinkled with gold dust to sparkle in the light.[13] The military also plays a role in our perception of pirate captains. Red – the colour of pirate coats from Howard Pyle's *Book of Pirates* (published 1921) to Keith Richards' Captain Teague – has long associations with the army. The first European military uniforms appeared towards the end of the 17th century and, in England, the ravages of the Civil War had played a big part. Cromwell's New Model Army was associated with red jackets, as madder, the dye used to create red, was abundant and relatively cheap. From the middle of the century, the army garnered the long-running nickname 'red coats' that would send Jane Austen characters into a frenzy in later centuries.[14] The lavish red coat in velvet or damask is an enduring symbol of the elegant and foppish pirate captain.

The three-cornered tricorne hat was also worn from the end of the 17th century, and it is the world of millinery that has most often embraced the pirate aesthetic. The fashion for cloche hats in the 1920s led to a number of close-fitting 'pirate' or tricorne models towards the end of the decade. 'Cornered hats are among the most flattering type of any period,' read an article in *Vogue* in 1929 and, just two months earlier, Cecile of South Molton Street advertised 'The New Pirate Hat in Felt'.[15] Many of the hats featured during this period were stocked at the Army & Navy Stores, a department store originally founded as a co-operative in 1871 by army and navy officers to supply domestic goods at reasonable prices. It was taken over by House of Fraser in the 20th century. Oversized hats are often used as shorthand for pirate style. In 2005, Sonia Rykiel used wide cocked sunhats to top off a collection that also featured breeches, decorative skulls, a cutlass motif and 'pieces of eight' gold coin trimming. Wide sunhats were folded into tricornes for Gaultier's spring/ summer 2008 pirate-inspired show, and Chanel's 2010 cruise collection opened with black tricorne hats coupled with sweeping black cloaks that also referenced the show's Venetian Lido boardwalk setting.

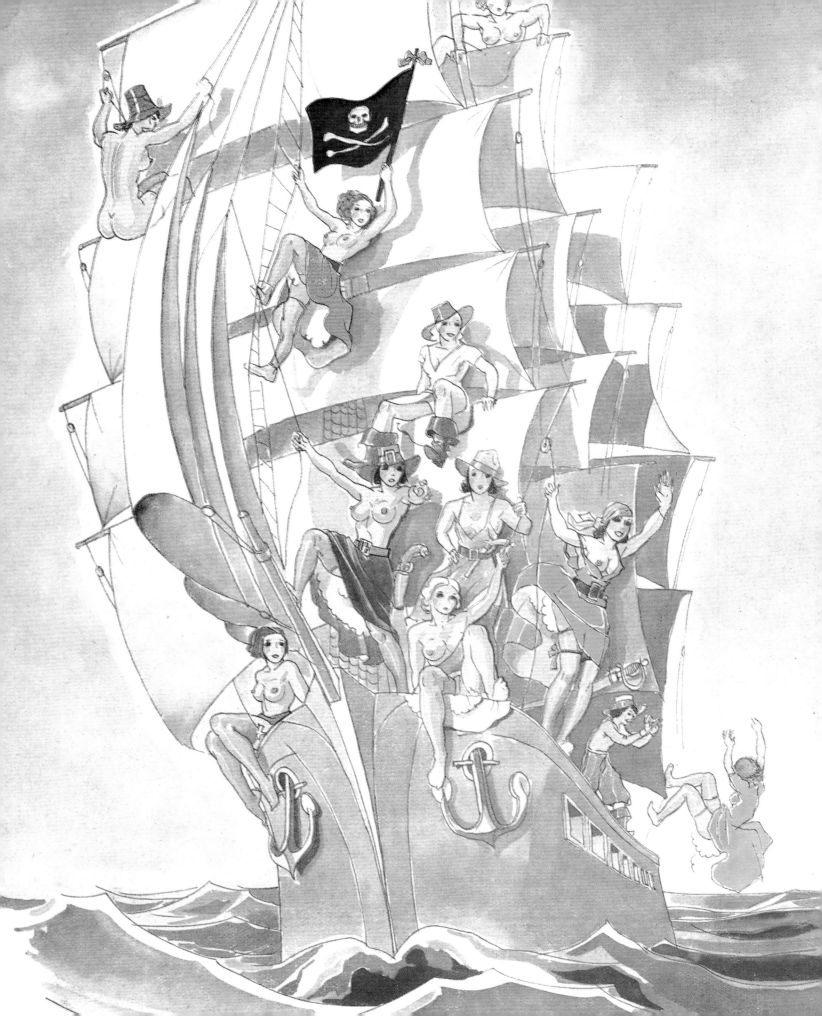

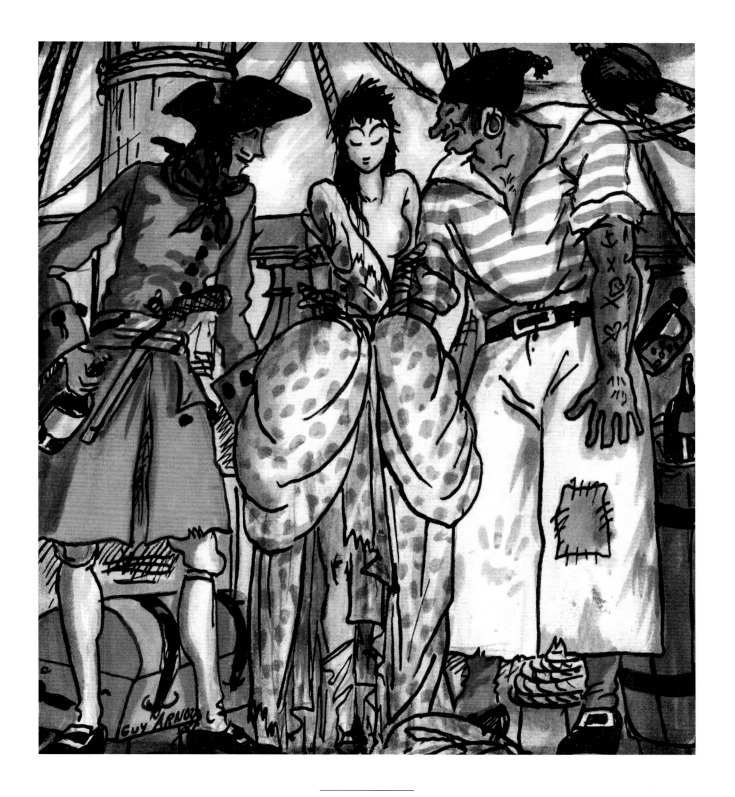

Above: *The popular perception of the aristocratic
pirate captain contrasted with the crew hailing from
the lower orders is captured in the illustration 'In
the Time of the Corsair' by Guy Arnoux for* La Vie
Parisienne *magazine, 1934.* Opposite: *The risqué side
of pirate style is the subject of this illustration in* Le
Sourire *erotic magazine. By Noël Cerutti, 1933.*

> '*You should be able to get*
> anybody *wearing pirate*
> clothes, if you can get across
> those clothes' politics.'
>
> MALCOLM McLAREN[16]

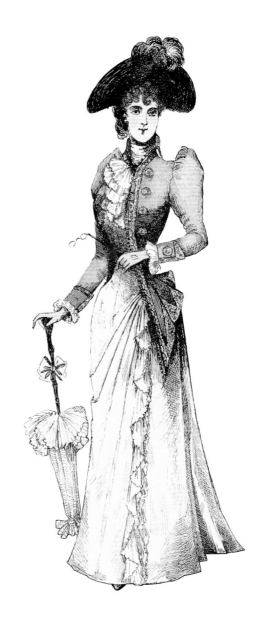

---

## POSTMODERN PIRATES:
## McLAREN AND WESTWOOD

Of all the incarnations of pirate style, none has made such
an enduring mark on pop culture as Malcolm McLaren and
Vivienne Westwood's 'World's End' collection. The unisex
collection for autumn/winter 1981 included damask trousers,
tasselled sashes, gold brooches, asymmetrical billowing shirts,
bicorne cocked hats, muslin stockings and rolled-down boots.
It was available in-store before it debuted on the catwalk and
the maritime theme was evident in more than just the clothes:
the World's End store at 430 Kings Road had been reimagined
as a pirate galleon, complete with uneven decking floor, and
the clothing label featured Blackbeard's cutlass. Westwood
had turned to history for her inspiration, drawing heavily on
Norah Waugh's *The Cut of Men's Clothes 1600–1900* that she
had found in the National Art Library at London's Victoria
and Albert Museum, kick-starting the interest in historical
costume that has continued to play a huge role throughout
her career. McLaren added the piracy element. Pirates, such
as Blackbeard, held a fascination for him since childhood,[17]
but his interest in piracy incorporated much more than a
romanticized figure on the high seas.

*Above: A Louis XVI style jacket,*
*referencing the second half of*
*the 18th century, features in this*
*hand-coloured fashion plate in*
*luxury journal* L'Art et la Mode,
*by G. de Billy, 1890. Opposite:*
*Blitz Kid, model and singer Lizzie*
*Tear in the 'World's End' collection,*
*outside the World's End shop on the*
*King's Road in London's Chelsea.*
*Cocked hats were regulation for the*
*British Navy from 1795 until 1827.*
*Photograph by Ted Polhemus, 1981.*

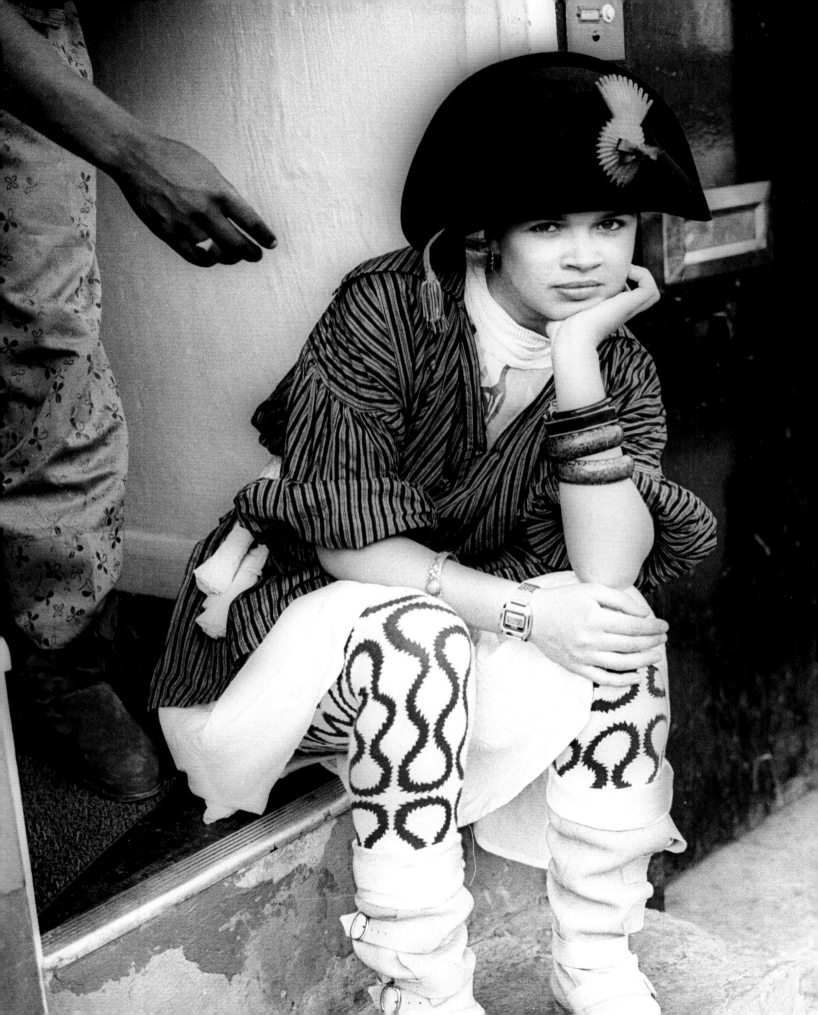

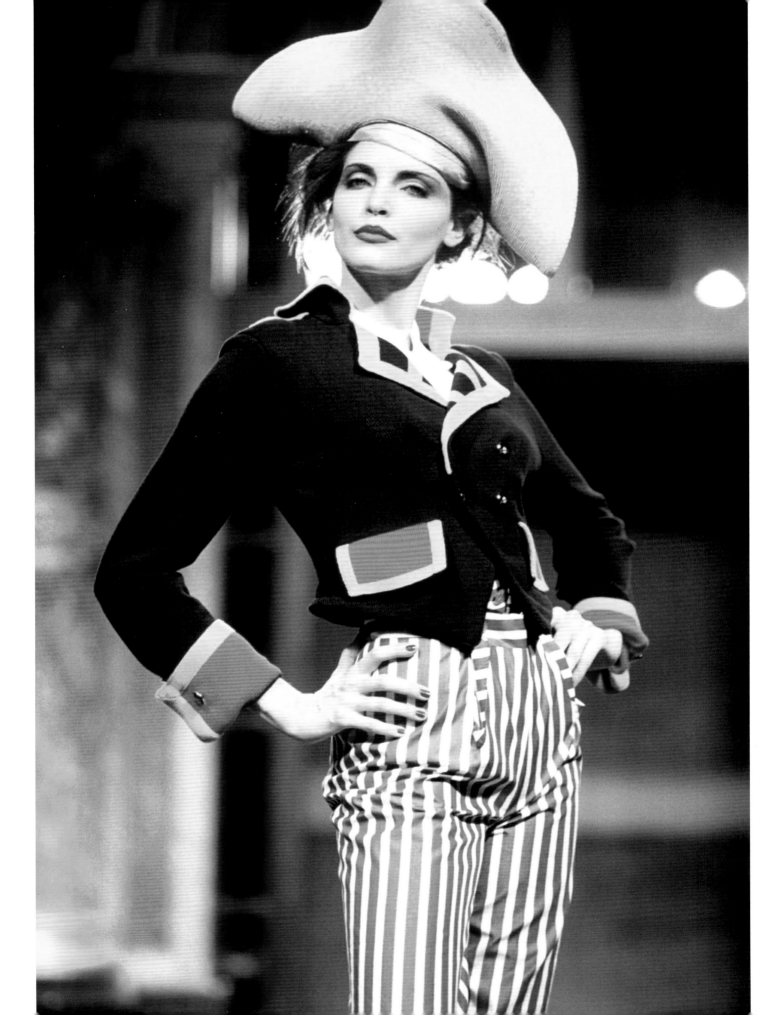

Music and fashion were inseparable for McLaren. He dressed his group Bow Wow Wow in the 'World's End' collection and their music, a mixture of global influences including the 'Burundi beat', was played at the catwalk show, punctuated by the sound of cannon fire. McLaren was also interested in undermining the dominance of the corporate music industry. The introduction of the Sony Walkman a couple of years earlier, as well as the growth of pirate radio, meant that music piracy was high on the agenda. A Sony Walkman featured on the 'World's End' collection invite, and they also adorned the models on the catwalk after McLaren persuaded Sony to lend them for the show.[18] The single 'C30, C60, C90, Go!' by Bow Wow Wow was an explicit reference to tape recording that somehow slipped past the record label. As with so much of McLaren's work, the 'World's End' collection chimed with the cultural zeitgeist and the extravagant New Romantic club kids out in force at London nightspots like Billies and Blitz. A pop culture phenomenon, the New Romantic movement birthed stars like Boy George and bands such as Spandau Ballet, who celebrated the theatrical side of historical costume in flowing ruffled shirts and ostentatious military jackets. In the same year the collection debuted, both *The Face* and UK *Vogue* noted the influence of the New Romantics on various London designers, with *Vogue* labelling Westwood the 'originator of the buccaneer spirit'.[19] The collection was a commercial and critical success. High-end retailer Joseph placed an order, and the Victoria and Albert Museum requested a custom-made version to add to their permanent fashion collection. The collection was also the focus of a Bruce Weber-shot British *Vogue* editorial, marking its approval by the mainstream fashion press.[20]

Opposite: *The pirate influence was later revisited by Vivienne Westwood for spring/summer 1996.*

Some of the key pieces from the collection specifically reference what we think of today as 'pirate clothing'. While high-heeled buckled shoes were all the rage for the aristocracy towards the end of the 17th century, thigh-high boots were favoured by the military. These could be folded down to resemble bucket-topped boots, and the jackboots of the 18th century are another influence on the styles associated with pirates. The McLaren and Westwood version featured straps and buckles and are now variously slouchy suede or stiff leather. After Kate Moss was photographed wearing an original pair of the boots in the early 21st century, the style proved to be so popular that Westwood reissued them.

One of the first garments McLaren and Westwood created for the collection – and one that was to become the most commercially viable – was the shirt. For men of fashion during the Golden Age of Piracy (and until relatively recently), the shirt was considered underwear, a protective layer between the body and the expensive silks of the vest. However, that's not to say it was lacking in luxury. Created from the finest linens or silk cambric, they had voluminous sleeves culminating in detachable ruffled lace at the wrist, which could be seen beneath the deep cuff of the coat. Equally, the lace cravat was visible over the layers of coat and vest, and reached various lengths depending on the vagaries of fashion. It was disparagingly labelled a 'slabbering bib' by a 17th-century commentator upon reaching a particularly robust width.[21] The popularity of the shirt in the early 1980s wasn't the reserve of McLaren and Westwood fans alone. Even *Harpers & Queen* sang the praises of the soft voluminous shirt. In a spread entitled 'Beauty and the Blouse', they extolled the virtues of this 'feminine fairy-tale come true' and featured billowing designs from the likes of Bellville Sassoon and Valentino, designers who represented the antithesis of McLaren and Westwood's punk-fuelled legacy.[22]

## POLITICAL PIRATES: A FASHION REVOLUTION

Despite becoming known as the pirate collection, piracy wasn't the only influence on McLaren and Westwood in 1981. Les Incroyables, extravagantly dressed men in post-Revolutionary France, were also an inspiration.[23] After France became a republic in 1792, all symbols of monarchy were abolished and tricolour patches were used to cover the Royalist fleur-de-lis.[24] The same year, there was a failed attempt to make the liberty cap or *bonnet rouge* – reminiscent of the red woollen hat of sailors – compulsory wear for Jacobins, the most radical revolutionary group.[25] However, Les Incroyables, and their female counterparts Les Merveilleuses, embraced fashion at a time when clothing had taken on a heightened political air. Luxury was equated with the overthrown aristocracy, and the Incroyables' reversion in part to pre-Revolutionary styles led to accusations of Royalist sympathies. Their dress consisted of a greatcoat coupled with tight, often striped calf-length breeches and the bicorne hat.[26] When adopted by various navies in the late 18th century, the bicorne was often worn with a cockade to signify political allegiance. The tricolour cockade became the defining marker of Republicanism in Revolutionary France, a stylistic feature replicated in the 'World's End' collection.

While occurring in a different time frame to piracy's Golden Age, the spirit of democracy of the Revolution remains. Life on board the pirate ship was more egalitarian than strictly stratified naval ships. Captains were voted in by the free men of the crew and could be voted out just as easily.[27] While the degree to which this was for ideological or practical reasons can never be fully acknowledged, this apparent appeal to democracy in an age of searing social inequality has resonance with the anti-establishment ethos of McLaren and Westwood. With her background in the punk movement, it comes as no surprise that Westwood was describing herself as an anarchist around the time that the collection debuted.[28] Despite referencing the post-revolutionary Incroyables, McLaren and Westwood's collection captured the spirit of the sans-culottes, the working class faction of Revolutionary France who took pride in their occupational trousers, as opposed to the breeches (culottes) of their aristocratic forebears.

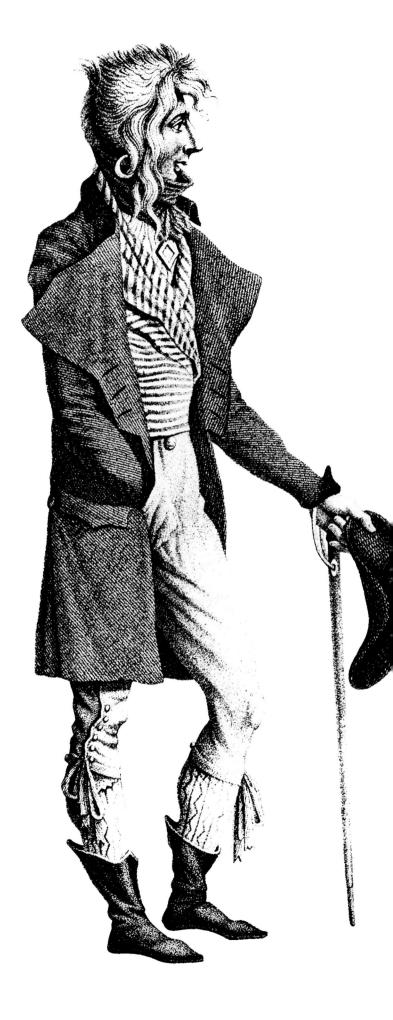

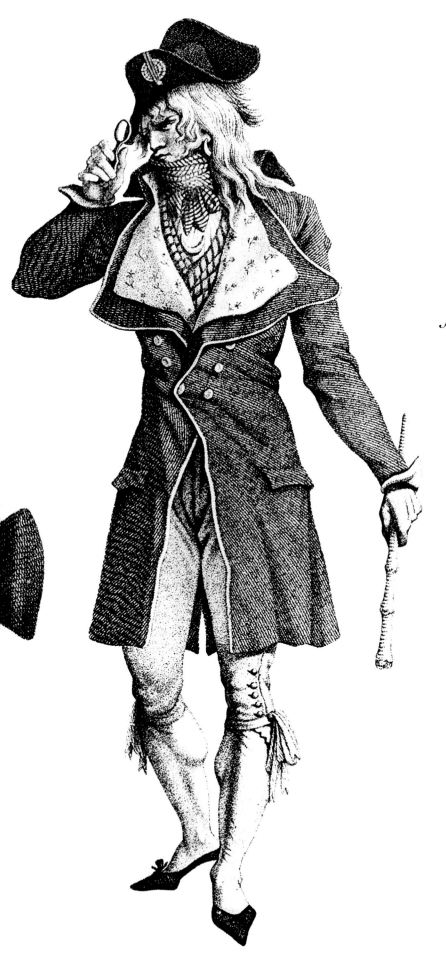

'I don't really want to talk that much about fashion. It's only interesting to me if it's subversive: that's the only reason I'm in fashion, to destroy the world "conformity".'

– VIVIENNE WESTWOOD, 1981[29]

*Les Incroyables – men of fashion in post-Revolutionary France – were an influence on McLaren and Westwood's 'World's End' collection of 1981. This very print appears in Norah Waugh's* The Cut of Men's Clothes, *which provided the historical basis for the collection. Copper engraving, c. 1795.*

## EYE PATCHES AND PARROTS

Wooden legs and eye patches, while appearing to be among the more fantastical elements of pirate garb, actually have some basis in reality. Like any seamen, pirates were susceptible to occupational hazards, which could range from accidental injuries on board the ship to wounds sustained during fighting. Missing limbs and eyes were not as uncommon as might be expected and disabled sailors often became the ship's cook, hence the profession of the one-legged Long John Silver.[30] Parrots were also no fictional gimmick. Bringing back birds and beasts from travels was popular among seamen both for company and to make a profit at home. Wild animal emporiums were a feature of dockside towns and there were many bird markets throughout 18th-century London. Parrots, with their canny knack of mimicking speech and their striking plumage, were a popular choice.[31] Parrots heighten the exotic element of pirate style, offering space for fantasy and escapism, a key factor in its continued popularity. Gaultier's 1997 parrot-shouldered bolero worn over a black crepe jumpsuit with plunging neckline added an exotic element to Hollywood Golden Age-style glamour for his first-ever couture collection. Not one to take a theme lightly, Jean-Charles de Castelbajac featured oversize parrots and eye patches for his spring/summer 2010 collection. The floor of the set resembled the ocean complete with menacing shark fins, and the collection featured other nautical icons such as sailor hats and stripes, as well as treasure maps and Hawaiian florals: the tropical excess of buccaneer style.

## THE JOLLY ROGER

The symbol that truly epitomizes the pirate is the Jolly Roger flag. What has become the homogenized skull and crossbones was originally a plethora of designs, produced by individual pirates. Before black, red was the preferred choice as the colour of blood and danger, and this also leads to one theory behind the name, that it stems from the French *jolie rouge*. Another theory is that it originates from 'Old Roger', a nickname for the devil. The skull, or 'death's head' has been a *memento mori* emblem since the Middle Ages, so its use as a warning of death and danger comes as no surprise. But there was more variety in the individual pirate flags: blazing balls, bleeding hearts, whole skeletons and hourglasses to name a few. Calico Jack used a skull above crossed cutlasses. By the 1730s, it is thought the skull and crossbones as we know it today had become the predominant marker for a pirate vessel.[32] Alexander McQueen became synonymous with the skull, a brand motif that successfully distilled his gothic interests into a commercial package. The skull scarf was introduced in 2004, the same year that Kate Moss wore a whole dress emblazoned with the print at a charity auction. In 'What A Merry-Go-Round' for autumn/winter 2001 gold skeletons were accessories, draped around shoulders and clinging to the hems of black-clad models. The skull and crossbones also appeared on a knitted dress, a piece that appeared to be unravelling and decomposing like a flag tattered and torn by stormy weather. In later work the skull came to represent evolutionary themes and the human destruction of the planet, a *memento mori* for the 21st-century.[33]

*Following spread: The ultimate in stylish skull and crossbones: the Alexander McQueen skull print scarf was introduced in 2004 (left). The parrot's bright plumage is a favourite with fashion designers. Combined with eye patch for Jean-Charles de Castelbajac, spring/summer 2010 (centre). Jolly Roger: skull dress by Jean-Charles de Castelbajac, autumn/winter 2011 (right).*

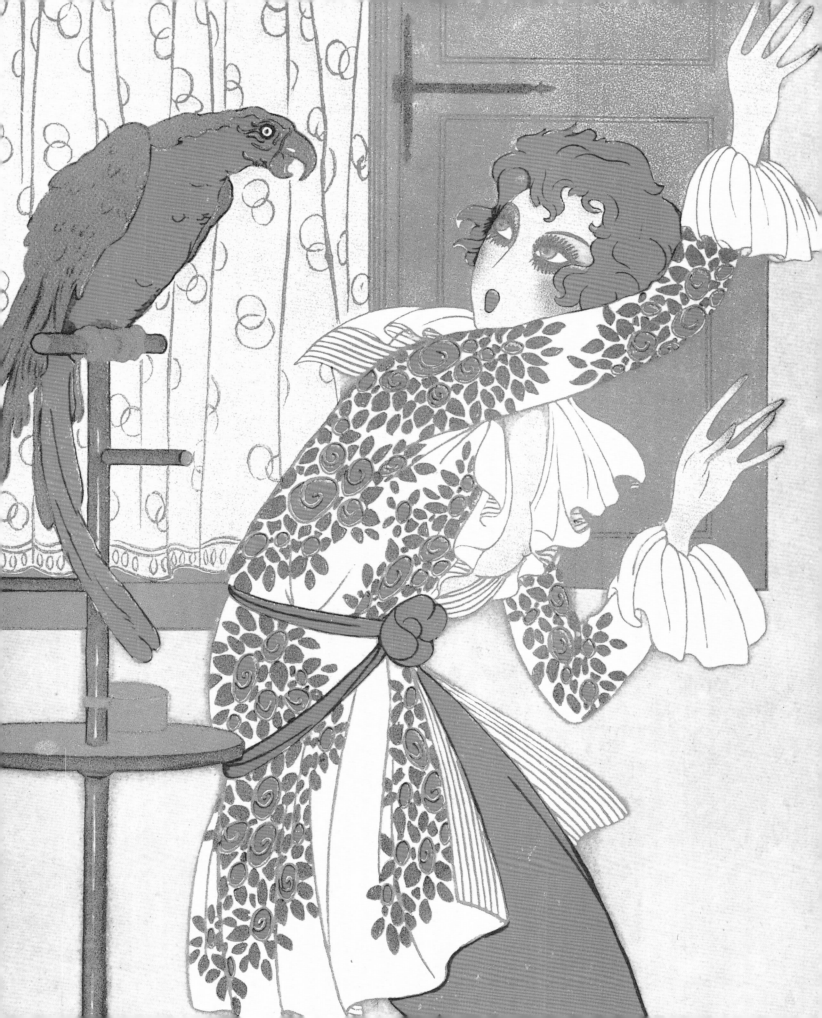

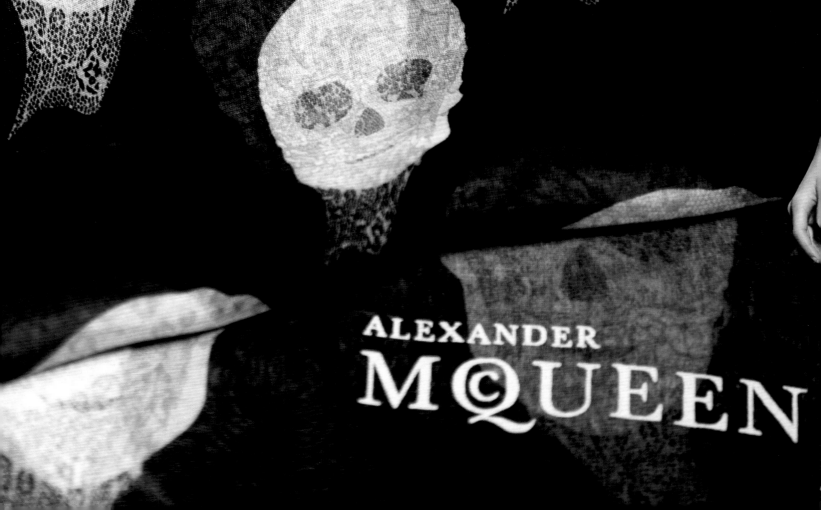

ALEXANDER
M©QUEEN

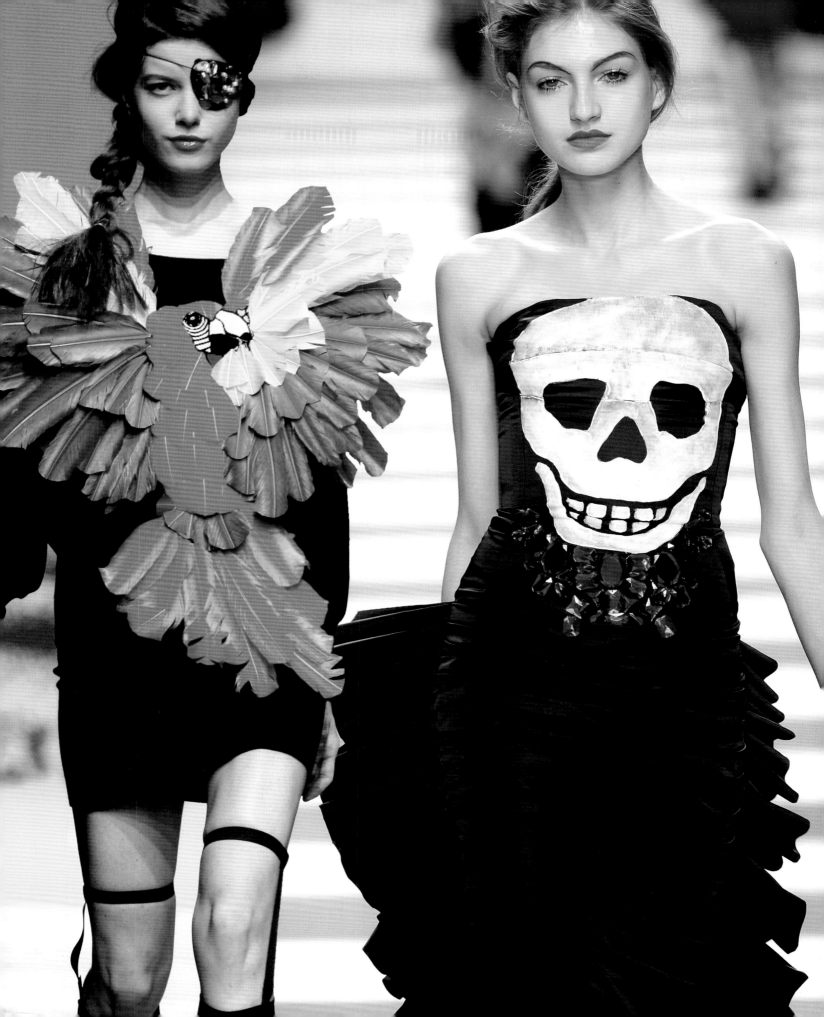

## THE MERMAID MYTH

An equally compelling maritime myth known to seafarers
the world over is the mermaid. Many sightings were reported
during the 17th century, around the time of the Golden Age of
Piracy. Mermaids exist in centuries-old tales around the globe
from *Arabian Nights* to the *Ramayana*, and as folkloric characters
from the ningyo of Japan, the rusalka of Slavic mythology,
the jengu of Cameroon and the Mami Wata of Africa, the
Caribbean and South America. In Europe, it is in Denmark
that the lasting legacy was born in Hans Christian Andersen's
fairytale *The Little Mermaid* (1837). The desire for mermaids
to exist has been around since antiquity and the idea of a lost
Atlantis or marine paradise has persisted throughout history.
'Mermaids' (more likely manatees) were spotted on Columbus's
voyages, and celluloid mermaids are nearly as old as film itself,
from the lost movies of Annette Kellerman to Esther Williams.
The siren-call of mermaids has seduced many design houses.
Their aquatic allure cast spells during the high glamour of
the 1930s and 1950s, when couturiers constructed mermaid
gowns with luxurious fishtail hems. In 1933, Rochas' mermaid
gown featured velvet scales; later in the decade Charles James
created the 'La Sirène' dress, using complex construction to
create drapes and ripples in the fabric. The silhouette of the
mermaid gown remains a red carpet favourite.

Alexander McQueen combined aquatic life with
privateers for his 2003 'Irere' collection. 'Underwater, I feel
most at peace,' he had told *Vogue* the year before,[34] but the
serenity is shattered by the shipwreck narrative running through
the collection. 16th-century conquistadors, complete with
leather doublets and jerkins, morph into cascading chiffon in
his 'Oyster' and 'Shipwreck' dresses. Gaultier took mermaids
as inspiration for his entire couture spring/summer 2008
collection, the same year his ready-to-wear show focused on
the pirate. Nautical motifs such as sailor pants were rendered
in scaly silver sequins, and paillettes added the sheen of
fish scales and mother-of-pearl. An underwater element
ran through many collections for spring/summer 2012.
At Alexander McQueen, Sarah Burton offered a poetic take
on marine inspiration with patterns drawn from oysters and
barnacles and pleating that was likened to pirate's buried
treasure.[35] Karl Lagerfeld staged an underwater kingdom
for his Chanel ready-to-wear collection, taking the house's
long-established pearl obsession back to its aquatic origin.
Pearls were strewn through models' hair and around their
waists, while mother-of-pearl glistened through fabrics and
on seaweed-like ruffles.

*Opposite: Mermaids inspired an
entire haute couture collection by
Jean Paul Gaultier, spring/summer
2008 (left and right). The mermaid on
the runway at Alexander McQueen,
spring/summer 2012 (centre).*

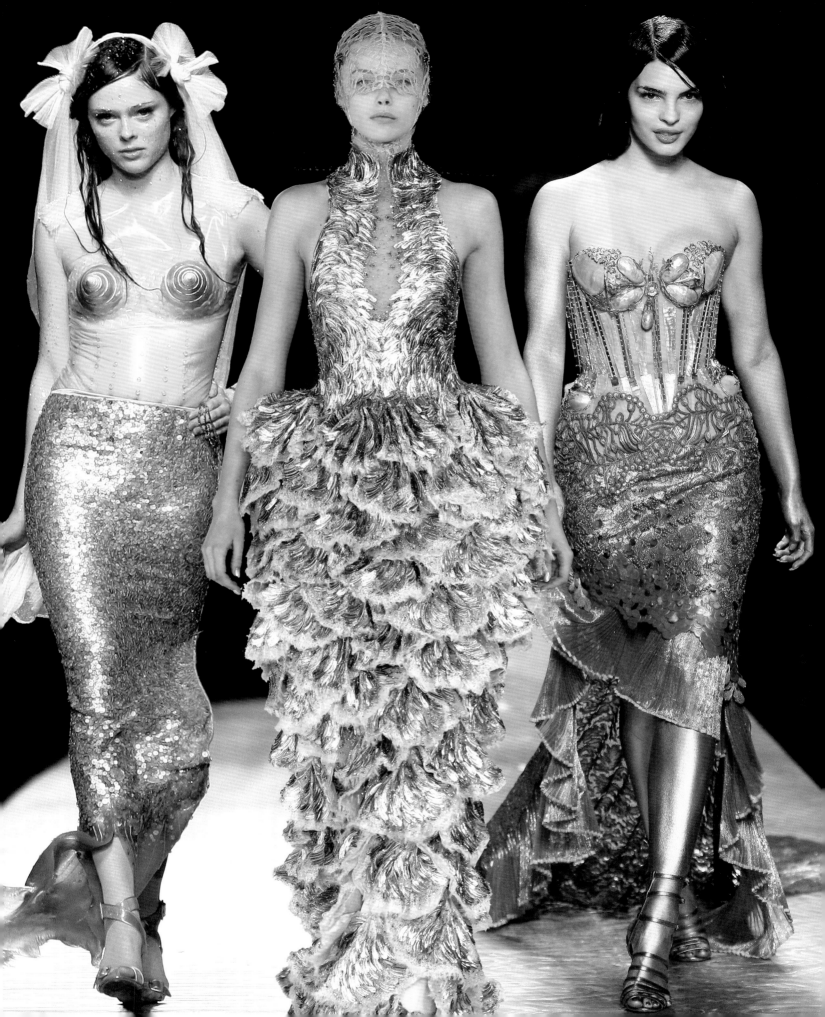

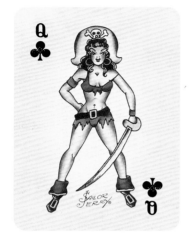 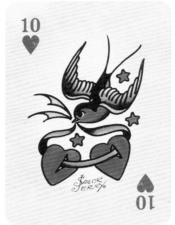 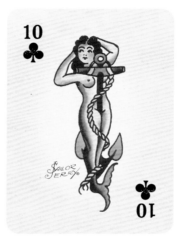 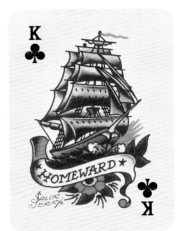

## SEA STYLE: TATTOOS

Mermaids were a popular choice of tattoo for 19th-century seafarers. Much history dates the introduction of tattoos in the west to James Cook's voyage to the South Sea Islands in 1774, giving us the word – from the Polynesian *tatu* – and starting a craze among sailors. But more thorough scholarship reveals that while the etymology may date from then, the practice stretches back much further.[36] A form of folk art, similar inscriptions to these nautical designs could also be found on scrimshaw: engravings on shells, whale bone or ivory that were produced to pass the time when at sea. In the early 19th century, the most popular symbol for sailors were initials, followed by anchors, mermaids – often holding a looking glass and comb – and ships and fish.[37] The popularity of these motifs indicates that they were used in part to mark out group identity as men of the sea. Often executed by other sailors, by the middle of the century the practice was increasingly professionalized with tattoo parlours opening in many British and American port towns, especially from the 1860s.[38]

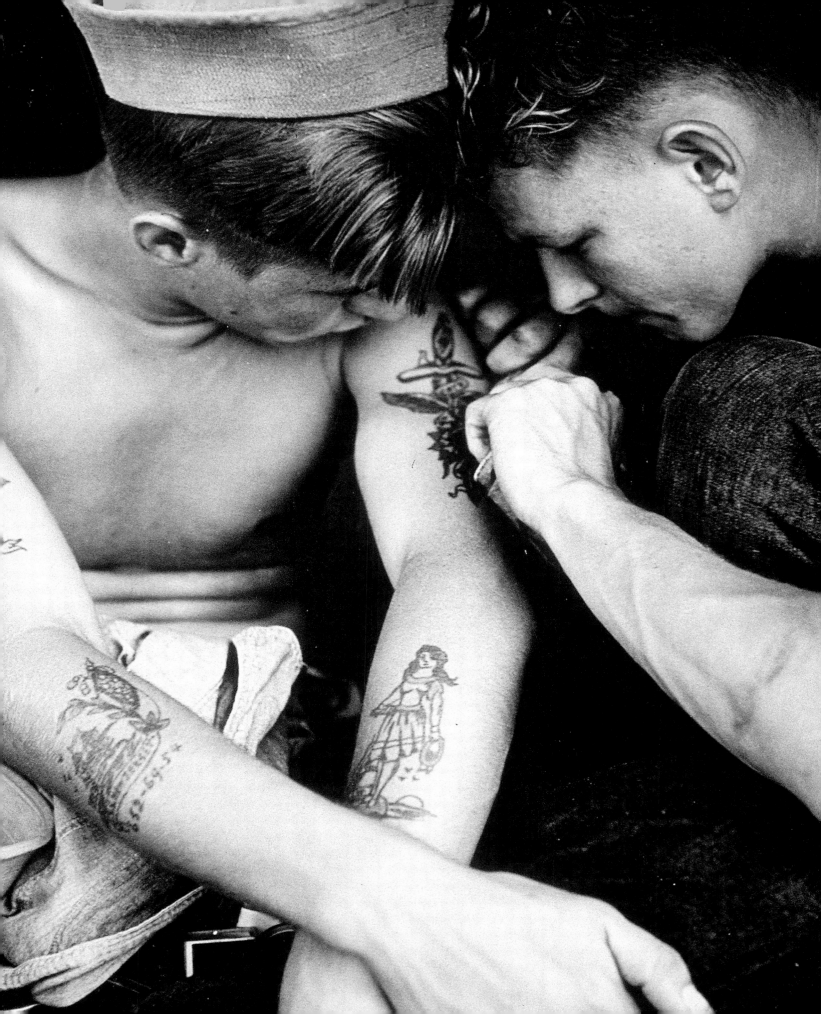

Opposite: *The royal tattoo craze.*
*Princess Waldemar of Denmark*
*reportedly had many interesting*
*experiences in the Far East before*
*she married, including visiting*
*Chinese opium dens and getting*
*her anchor tattoo. Cover of*
The Sketch, *1907.*

Tattooing has a long history of association with the sea. By 1914, a surgeon estimated that sixty per cent of American sailors were tattooed.[39] In contrast, only five to ten per cent of French sailors were inked by the late 19th century, possibly because the practice was regularly outlawed on French ships.[40] Despite this, some of the most popular designs found in French prisons were pirate's heads with cutlasses.[41] Many common beliefs persist about the symbolism of maritime tattoos: a swallow represents 5000 nautical miles covered and an anchor indicates the sailor has crossed the Atlantic. But it is more likely that different ships and crews would attach different significance to the same symbols depending on their experiences, so 'reading' a sailor's voyages through tattoos becomes a futile task; meanings were localized rather than spread across whole navies.[42]

Despite the long-standing association of tattoos with groups at the margins of society in the West, such as prisoners and sailors, the 1880s saw an unexpected trend for tattooing among the aristocracy. This was said to be sparked by a tattoo the Prince of Wales (and future Edward VII) got in the Holy Land in the 1860s that had only come to attention two decades later.[43] By the end of the 1880s, McDonald's tattoo studio – located on fashionable Jermyn Street – was flooded with London high society looking for permanent inky status symbols.[44] In the following decade the phenomenon was covered in the press. In an article called 'Tattooed Royalty,' *Harmsworth Magazine* speculated that such eminent names as the Grand Duke Alexis of Russia, Prince and Princess Waldemar of Denmark and the Duke of York had all been seduced by the power of ink.[45] *The English Illustrated Magazine*

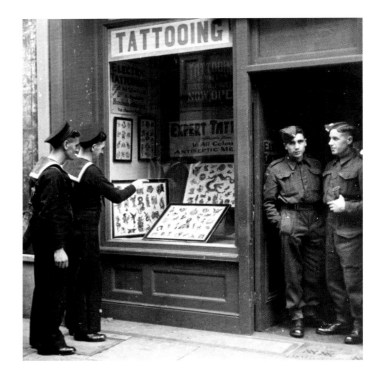

and *Tatler* also ran pieces on this craze in the early years of the 20th century. The interwar period has become known as the 'golden age of tattooing' as the practice became more socially acceptable. The influential designs of 'Sailor' Jerry Collins date from around this time. Beginning his career in Chicago in the 1920s, Collins moved to Hawaii in the following decade and opened a tattoo parlour.[46] The recent resurgence in maritime tattoos both on flesh and on fabric owes much to Sailor Jerry's legacy. His designs were the inspiration behind embroidered tops shown on the Maison Martin Margiela couture catwalk for spring/summer 2014, which featured swallows and mermaid pin-up girls. Rodarte's autumn/winter 2013 collection was also inspired by tattoo imagery, featuring stylized roses on flesh-coloured socks.

Above: *From the 1860s, tattoo*
*parlours sprung up in British*
*and American port towns.*
*Seaman Sydney Collins and*
*his shipmate peruse the options*
*at Professor Cecil Rhodes'*
*Dover tattoo parlour, 1941.*

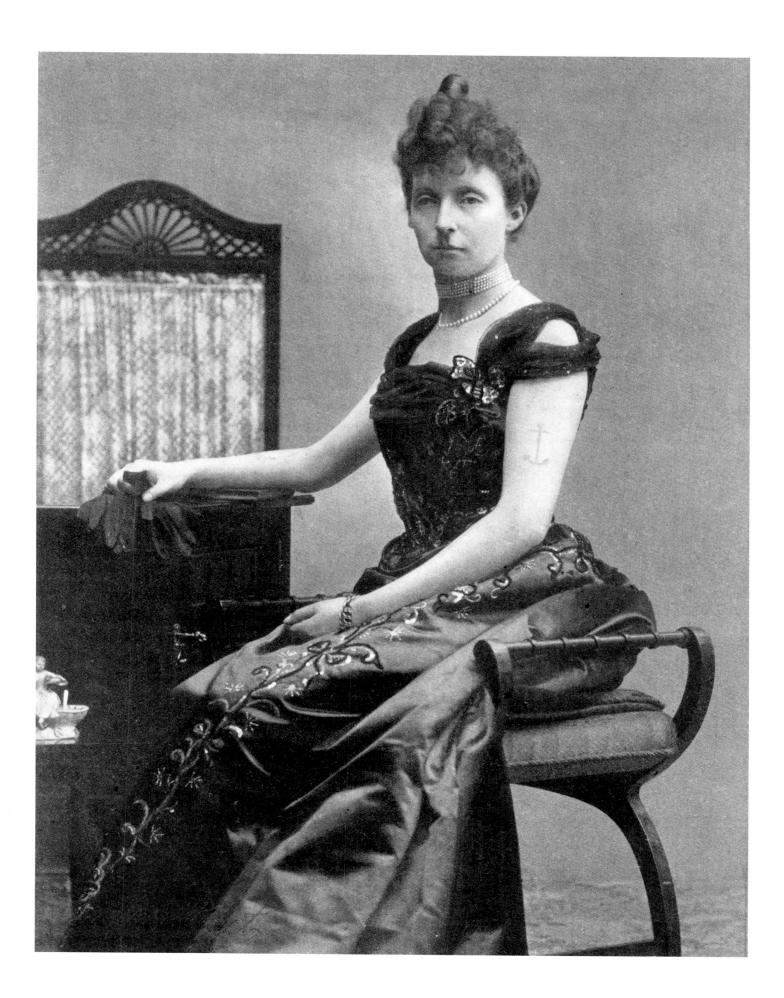

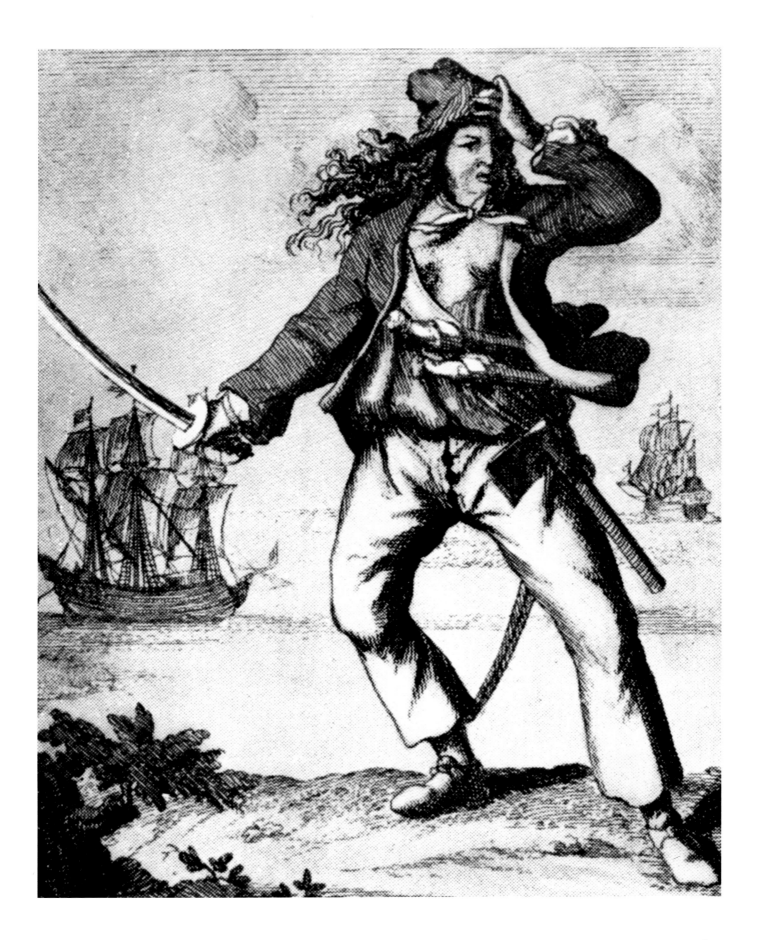

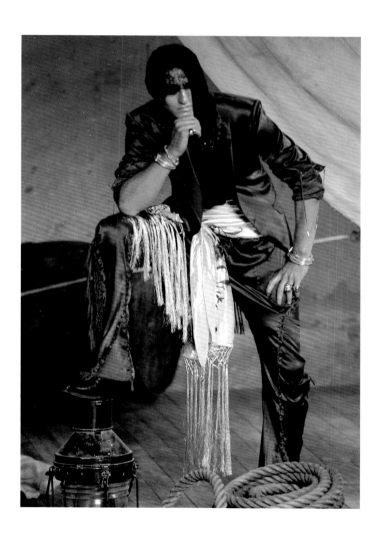

Above: *John Galliano revisited a host of historical characters, including the buccaneer, for his menswear collection of spring/summer 2005.*

## ROMANCE AND REBELLION

The pirate remains a larger-than-life character, an antihero as likely to appear at costume balls as on the catwalk. This tradition stretches back a long way: fancy dress manuals from the late 19th century recommended Gilbert & Sullivan pirate characters, advocating a risqué approach still associated with fancy dress by suggesting a 'red and black short skirt, with much gold trimming; low black gold-bedizened bodice, and gold armlets, with a chain of sequins from the shoulder to wrist'.[47] According to British *Vogue*, it was also a 'pirate ship' owned by the Guinness family that was the party destination of choice for the 'super-bright young persons' of the 1920s when visiting the Cowes yachting regatta.[48] In fashion, the ideological and aesthetic influences initiated by McLaren and Westwood can be traced in later adaptations of pirate style that have been as much informed by their legacy as by historical dress. John Galliano has a long-standing interest in both rebellion and historical inspiration, stretching back to his graduate collection, 'Les Incroyables' in 1984, just three years after McLaren and Westwood's 'World's End'. His 'Pirate' jacket first appeared for autumn/winter 2001. Asymmetrical and deconstructed, it uses corsetry as its foundation while giving the impression of being held together by sail rivets. The pirate is also a staple of Galliano's menswear. Spring/summer 2005 featured a host of historical figures, mixing buccaneer with beachwear, while for autumn/winter 2009 he again revisited the French Revolution, featuring tricorne hats and cuffed boots alongside red bonnets and tops emblazoned with 'cockade' prints implying a flash of revolutionary zeal. These ideals of romantic rebellion have fed into our perception of the pirate in contemporary culture, an enduring maritime myth of swashbuckling proportions.

# PICTURE CREDITS

**a** = above
**c** = centre
**b** = below
**l** = left
**r** = right

**1** Gamma/Camera Press; **2–3** Photo Sofia Sanchez and Mauro Mongiello/Trunk Archive; **6** Courtesy Hearst Archive UK; **8** Bibliothèque nationale de France, Paris; **9** Photo Chris Moore; **10–11** Photo Giampaolo Sgura/Trunk Archive; **12** Paramount/The Kobal Collection; **14** © CHANEL; **17** The Granger Collection/Topfoto; **18** Mary Evans Picture Library; **19** Photo © Anthea Simms; **20** Photo Frédérique Dumoulin-Bonnet. Courtesy Sonia Rykiel; **21ʀ** © Woolmark Archive (Australian Wool Innovation Ltd.) and the London College of Fashion; **23** Photo Boo George/Trunk Archive. Model Alessandra Ambrosio represented by dna model management, New York; **24** Rex Features/Richard Young; **25** Photo © Anthea Simms; **27** Photo Stephen Crawley. Image courtesy the Gieves & Hawkes Archive, Savile Row, London; **28** Courtesy Givenchy; **29** © Woolmark Archive (Australian Wool Innovation Ltd) and the London College of Fashion; **30** © Condé Nast Archive/Corbis; **31** Universal/The Kobal Collection/Ray Jones; **32** Courtesy David Sassoon. © Bellville Sassoon; **35ᴀ** National Maritime Museum, London; **36–7** Photo IWM via Getty Images; **37ʀ** Courtesy Gloverall Archive. Model Chris Doe at Select Models; **39ʙ** *The New York Sun*, June 15, 1919; **40, 41** Courtesy Moschino; **42** Rex Features/Keith Waldegrave/Associated Newspapers; **43** Courtesy Gloverall Archive; **44** © Jacques Haillot/Apis/Sygma/Corbis; **45ʟ** © Fondation Pierre Bergé – Yves Saint Laurent; **45ʀ** University of Newcastle (Australia) Archives A6590 (iv); **47** Photo © Anthea Simms; **48** © Pierre et Gilles; **52** Library of Congress, Prints and Photographs Division, Washington, D.C. (LC–USZC2–2980); **53** Photo Gilles Bensimon/Trunk Archive; **54** Gaiety Girl Collection, London College of Fashion Archive, courtesy of Robert Waters; **55** Courtesy Hearst Archive, UK; **55c** Mary Evans Picture Library; **55ʀ** Courtesy Hearst Archive, UK; **56** Mary Evans/Everett Collection; **57** © Matthew Frost; **59** GraphicaArtis/Corbis; **60** © Woolmark Archive (Australian Wool Innovation Ltd.) and the London College of Fashion; **61** © Matthew Frost; **62** MGM/The Kobal Collection; **63** © Condé Nast Archive/Corbis; **64** © Matthew Frost; **66** © Courtesy Olympia Le-Tan. Photo Shoji Fujii; **67** © Camera Press; **69** Time Life Pictures/Pictures Inc./The LIFE Picture Collection/Getty Images; **72** © Condé Nast Archive/Corbis; **73** © Courtesy Olympia Le-Tan. Photo Shoji Fujii; **74** Courtesy Marc Jacobs; **75ʟ, 75ʀ, 76, 77** Photo © Anthea Simms; **79** © Pierre et Gilles; **81** Planet-Film/Albatross/Gaumont/Kobal; **82ʟ** Philadelphia Museum of Art, Pennsylvania/Bridgeman Art Library; **82ʀ** Photo © Anthea Simms; **83** Yohji Yamamoto Femme S/S 2007 collection. Photo © Monica Feudi; **84** Keystone-France/Gamma-Keystone via Getty Images; **85** Rex Features/Chris Barham/Associated Newspapers; **86** trunkarchive.com; **88–9** © Illustrated London News Ltd/Mary Evans; **91** Photo Corrie Bond. Courtesy Viviens Creative Australia. Models: Roksana at Networkmodels, Kaila Hart at IMG Models; **92ʀ** Photo © Anthea Simms; **93ʟ** Courtesy Jean Paul Gaultier Archives. Model Lindsey Wixson at Storm Models; **93ʀ** Courtesy Jean Paul Gaultier Archives. Model Hannelore Knuts at Models 1; **94** Courtesy Saint James; **95ʟ** © CHANEL; **95ʀ** © All rights reserved; **96** Photo Philippe Pottier; **97** © Genevieve Naylor/Corbis; **99** Alexandra Danilova Collection, Music Division, Library of Congress, Washington, D.C. (022.00.00); **100** © Collection CHANEL/All rights reserved; **101** Mary Evans Picture Library; **102** © Bettmann/Corbis; **103** Photo Guy Aroch/Trunk Archive; **104** Rome-Paris-Films/The Kobal Collection; **106** Imagno/Getty Images; **107** Photo © Anthea Simms; **108** Photo Andrey Yakovlev 2010. Art Director Lili Aleeva. Model Alena Churakova. Make-up Lili Aleeva, Hair Oxana Zavarzina for magazine Leonardo. All Sonia Rykiel; **109ʟ** Courtesy Moschino; **109ʀ** Photo Alex Lambrechts for The Rodnik Band; **110ʟ, 110ʀ, 111** Photo © Anthea Simms; **112, 113** © Woolmark Archive (Australian Wool Innovation Ltd.) and the London College of Fashion; **114** Photo Chris Brooks/Trunk Archive; **115** Courtesy Lowestoft Maritime Museum, UK; **117** © Fairchild Photo Service/Condé Nast/Corbis; **118** © Woolmark Archive (Australian Wool Innovation Ltd.) and the London College of Fashion; **121** New York Public Library/Bridgeman Images; **122** Photo Kublin; **123ᴀ** Courtesy Southwold Museum, UK; **123ʙ** © CHANEL; **124** George Pickow/Three Lions/Getty Images; **125ʟ, 125ʀ** Courtesy Prada; **126** Courtesy Gant; **127, 128, 129** © Woolmark Archive (Australian Wool Innovation Ltd.) and the London College of Fashion; **131** © Succession Roger Descombes; **132** Photo © Anthea Simms; **133** © The Estate of Georges Dambier; **136** © Fairchild Photo Service/Condé Nast/Corbis; **137** The Fine Arts Museums of San Francisco, gift of Mrs Eloise Heidland, 1982.18.1a–c; **138** © Condé Nast Archive/Corbis; **139** © The Estate of Georges Dambier; **140** Photo John Balsom/Trunk Archive; **143** © Onne van der Wal/Corbis; **144–5** Photo Riccardo Tinelli/Trunk Archive; **146** ClassicStock/Corbis; **147** Buyenlarge/Getty Images; **149** © The Estate of Georges Dambier; **150** Photo © Anthea Simms; **151ᴀ** Hulton-Deutsch Collection/Corbis; **151ʙ** Jamie McCarthy/WireImage for Tommy Hilfiger/Getty Images; **153** Leemage/UIG via Getty Images; **154** © CHANEL/Photo Karl Lagerfeld; **155** © André Durst/Vogue Paris; **159** Corbis; **160, 161** © Illustrated London News Ltd Mary Evans; **167** Photo KT Auleta/Trunk Archive; **168** Photo Damien Fry; **169** © Genevieve Naylor/Corbis; **170** © Condé Nast Archive Corbis; **171** © Illustrated London News Ltd/Mary Evans; **172** © Genevieve Naylor/Corbis; **177** Robert Knudsen, White House/John F. Kennedy Presidential Library and Museum, Boston; **178** Rex Features; **180** © Genevieve Naylor/Corbis; **181** © The Estate of Georges Dambier; **182** Photo © Anthea Simms; **185** Mary Evans Picture Library; **186** The Kobal Collection; **187** Beyond Retro Archive; **188, 189c, 189ʀ** Photo © Anthea Simms; **190ʀ** Photo © Anthea Simms; **191** Keystone/Hulton Archive/Getty Images; **192–93** adoc-photos/Corbis; **194** Mary Evans Picture Library; **195** Photo Anne Menke/Trunk Archive; **196** Keith Richards on set for The Pirates of the Caribbean: On Stranger Tides (Dir. Rob Marshall, 2011). Walt Disney Pictures/The Kobal Collection; **197ʟ** Courtesy Prada; **197ʀ** Photo Frédérique Dumoulin-Bonnet. Courtesy Sonia Rykiel; **201** © PYMCA/Alamy; **202** Rex Features; **204–205** Interfoto/Sammlung Rauch/Mary Evans; **209c, 209ʀ** Photo © Anthea Simms; **211ʟ** © Stephane Cardinale/People Avenue/Corbis; **211c** Photo © Anthea Simms; **211ʀ** Photo Francois Guillot/AFP/Getty Images; **212** sailorjerry.com; **213** MPI/Getty Images; **214** Getty Images; **215** © Illustrated London News Ltd/Mary Evans; **216** Mary Evans/Epic/Tallandier; **217** Pierre Verdy/AFP/Getty Images; **221** Courtesy of Anthony Randle, Gill and Sadie Doherty

Other images supplied by the author.

# NOTES

## INTRODUCTION

**1** Foucault, M., 'Of Other Spaces: Utopias and Heterotopias', 1967
**2** The English Navy, made up of a permanent fleet of military warships, was formed under Henry VIII in the early 16th century, who also set up the Office of Admiralty for administration. It officially became 'Royal' with the Restoration of King Charles II in 1660. The French Marine Nationale, meanwhile, dates back to the Middle Ages, but was formalized in the 1620s, and was expanded by Louis XIV later in the century. The American Navy cites its beginning as 1775, the year the Revolution started.
**3** Miller, A., *Dressed to Kill: British Naval Uniform … 1748–1857* (London, 2007), p. 9

## CHAPTER 1, THE OFFICER

**1** Flügel, J.C., *The Psychology of Clothes* (London, 1930), p. 104
**2** Miller (2007), pp. 13, 16, 17
**3** Thanks to Dr Phil Weir and to Samuel McLean at King's College London for discussions on institutional identity.
**4** Haythornthwaite, P. & Younghusband, B., *Nelson's Navy* (Oxford, 1993) and also letters in *The Literary Gazette*, 14, 1830

**5** Dickens, G., *The Dress of the British Sailor* (London, 1957), p. 3

**6** Miller (2007), p. 19

**7** *Les Marins Font la Mode* (Paris, 2009), p. 9

**8** Ibid.

**9** See Harding, R., *The Emergence of Britain's Global Naval Supremacy: The War of 1739–1748* (Woodbridge, 2010)

**10** Miller (2007); Wilkinson-Latham, R., *Royal Navy 1790–1970* (Oxford, 1977), p. 14; Hobbs (1997)

**11** Hobbs (1997)

**12** Ibid., pp. 9, 42

**13** Ibid., pp. 67, 75; Wilkinson-Latham (1977), p. 14; Hobbs (1997)

**14** Miller (2007), p. 9

**15** Deslandes, Paul. R., 'Exposing, Adorning and Dressing the Body in the Modern Era' in Toulalan, S. and Fisher, K. (eds), *The Routledge History of Sex and the Body* (Abingdon and New York, 2013), p. 192; Craik, J., *Uniforms Exposed* (Oxford, 2005), pp. 34, 36

**16** Cole, S., *The Story of Men's Underwear* (London, 2012), p. 50; Matthews David, A., 'Decorated Men: Fashioning the French Soldier, 1852–1914', in *Fashion Theory*, 7:1, 2003, p. 12

**17** Austen, J., *Pride and Prejudice* (London, 2007 [1813]), p. 251

**18** For more on tailoring and sex appeal, see Hollander, A., *Sex and Suits* (Brinkworth, 1994)

**19** Matthews David (2003), p. 11

**20** *The Literary Gazette*, 14, 1830

**21** Wilkinson-Latham (1977), p. 5

**22** Miller (2007), pp. 27–8

**23** Jarrett, D., *British Naval Dress* (London, 1960), p. 95

**24** Lester, R., *Boutique London, A History* (Woodbridge, 2010), p. 129

**25** Lester (2010), p. 70

**26** Sherwood, J., *Savile Row* (London, 2010), pp. 106, 108, 120–126. Also discussions with Peter Tilley, Curator at Gieves & Hawkes, and Amy Miller, Curator of Decorative Arts and Material Culture at the National Maritime Museum, Greenwich, London.

**27** Craik (2005), p. 33

**28** See collections at the National Maritime Museum (NMM), Greenwich

**29** McDowell cited in Craik (2005), p. 35

**30** See collections at the NMM, Greenwich, and Royal Naval Museum, Portsmouth, UK

**31** See the ribbons used as textile tokens in the archive at the Foundling Hospital Collection, London

**32** See examples at Lowestoft Maritime Museum and the Fan Museum, Greenwich, London

**33** Barreto, C. and Lancaster, M., *Napoleon and the Empire of Fashion 1795–1815* (Milan and London, 2010), p. 20

**34** Ibid., p. 35

**35** Ibid., pp. 116–17

**36** Myerly, S., *British Military Spectacle* (Cambridge, MA, and London, 1996), p. 149

**37** *Illustrated London News*, 30 December 1854, p. 700

**38** See, for example, Howell, G., *Wartime Fashion, 1939–1945* (Oxford, 2013)

**39** 'Monty's Beret', *Life*, 5 April 1943, pp. 51–2

**40** 'Fashion Designers Find New Style Ideas in Navy', *Life*, 28 October 1940, pp. 83–6

**41** Jarrett (1960), pp. 136–37

**42** Newark, T., Newark, Q., Borsarello, J.F., *Brassey's Book of Camouflage* (London, 2002), p. 15

**43** Ibid., p. 17

**44** Newark, T., *Camouflage* (London, 2007), p. 78

**45** For more see Behrens, R., *Camoupedia* (Dysart, IA, 2009)

**46** *New-York Tribune*, 15 June 1919, p. 4

**47** Interview with Nigel Calladine, consultant to Original Montgomery, 10 December 2013

**48** Interview with Mark van Beek, 11 December 2013

**49** Leach, R., *Fashion Resource Book: Men* (London, 2014), p. 166

**50** *London Gazette*, 18 May 1757, issue 9688, p. 3

**51** *General Regulations for the Government of the Navy of the United States* (Washington, 1841), pp. 5–14

**52** *Les Marins Font la Mode* (2009), p. 23

**53** Rawsthorn, A., *Yves Saint Laurent* (London, 1996), p. 83

**54** Müller, F., 'Dressing for Modern Times: Yves Saint Laurent's "Essentials"', in *Yves Saint Laurent* (Paris, 2010), pp. 66, 125–6

**55** Watt, J., *Alexander McQueen: Fashion Visionary* (London, 2012), p. 16

**56** Quoted in *Muse* magazine, December 2008, referenced on blog.metmuseum.org/ alexandermcqueen/jacket-joan, accessed 23 May 2014

## CHAPTER 2, THE SAILOR

**1** Herman Melville, *Moby-Dick; or, The Whale* (Boston, 1892 [1851]), p. 12

**2** Interview with Olympia Le-Tan, December 2013

**3** Styles, J., *The Dress of the People: Everyday Fashion in 18th-Century England* (New Haven and London, 2007), pp. 45, 49, 51

**4** Dickens (1957), p. 4

**5** Christie's lot notes, Sale 1229, Orders, Decorations, Campaign Medals and Militaria, 27 April 1999

**6** For uniform information see Miller (2007); Wilkinson-Latham (1977); Joseph, N., *Uniforms and Nonuniforms* (New York, 1986); Dickens (1957) and Jarrett (1960)

**7** Rose, C., 'What Was Uniform about the Fin-de-Siècle Sailor Suit?', *Journal of Design History*, 24:2, May 2011, pp. 105–124

**8** Jarrett (1960) p. 19

**9** Miller (2007), p. 88

**10** See for example, 'Military Uniforms', *Life*, 19 May 1941, p. 70

**11** 'Jack's Uniform, A Brief History of the Sailor Shirt', *The Literary Digest*, 14 April 1917

**12** Firth, C.H. (ed.), *Naval Songs and Ballads* (London, 1908), quoted in Cordingly, D., *Heroines and Harlots: Women at Sea in the Great Age of Sail* (Basingstoke, 2001), appendix

**13** See collections at the NMM, Greenwich

**14** Joll, J., *Europe Since 1870* (Harmondsworth, 1976), p. 83

**15** Cole, S., *The Story of Men's Underwear* (New York, 2010), p. 61; also 'T-shirt History', *Men's Wear*, 10 February 1950, p. 234

**16** Black, S., *Knitting: Fashion, Industry, Craft* (London, 2012), p. 69

**17** See Summerfield, P., 'Patriotism and Empire: Music Hall Entertainment 1870–1914' in MacKenzie, J.M. (ed.), *Imperialism and Popular Culture* (Manchester, 1986). Also chapter 4 of Fuller, S. and Whitesell, L. (eds), *Queer Episodes in Music and Modern Identity*, (Urbana, 2002)

**18** Craik (2005), pp. 97–98

**19** 'Introducing Some of the New Features of the Indispensable Middy', *The Toronto World*, 6 April 1916, p. 3

**20** Tuite, R., *Seven Sisters Style* (New York, 2014), p. 33

**21** Rose (2011)

**22** Patent filed for convertible middy blouses by Morris Sobelman of Baltimore, April 1924. Also advert for the Two-In-One Middy by Morris & Co., Paul Jones Middies, 1922

**23** Dickens (1957); Jarrett (1960) p. 120

**24** *New York Press*, 29 May 1894. Thanks to Nancy Bruseker for sending me these clippings

**25** *Vanity Fair*, June 1915

**26** Hensgen, Marke A., 'To Cap It All Off … A Fond Look at a Navy Trademark: Uses (and Abuses) of the "Dixie Cup"', *All Hands*, 860, November 1988, pp. 33–5. Found at the Navy Department Library, US Navy website, part of the Naval History & Heritage Command http://www.history.navy.mil/library/online/ uniform_hats.htm, accessed 23 May 2014

**27** Letter in *Yank, the Army Weekly*, August 1945

**28** Dickens (1957), p. 5

**29** Ibid., p. 7

**30** Liberty cuffs information from Daniel D. Smith, retired Senior Chief Petty Officer, US Navy Reserve http://navydp.com/NavyCollector/Navy_ Traditions.htm, accessed 23 May 2014

**31** *Les Marins Font la Mode* (2009), pp. 39–40

**32** *Proceedings of the United States Naval Institute*, 58, 1932

**33** For more, see 'No More Bell Bottoms?', *All Hands*, 347, February 1946, pp. 6–9

**34** Rennolds Milbank, C., *Resort Fashion* (New York, 2009), p. 167

**35** Maglio, D., 'Peacocks in the sands: Flamboyant men's beachwear 1920–30', *Critical Studies in Men's Fashion*, 1:1, 2014, p. 31; Blum, D., *Shocking! The Art and Fashion of Elsa Schiaparelli* (Philadelphia, PA, and London, 2003), p. 28

**36** Blume, M., *Côte d'Azur* (London, 1992), p. 91

**37** 'Woollen Suits for the Beach', British *Vogue*, 24 June 1931

**38** Schoeffler, O.E. & Gale, W., *Esquire's Encyclopedia of 20th-Century Men's Fashions* (New York and London, 1973), p. 91

**39** British *Vogue*, July 1966, pp. 46–47

**40** Ibid., pp. 68–69

**41** British *Vogue*, June 1973, pp. 150–157

**42** Miller (2007), p. 94; see also Deslandes in Toulalan and Fisher (2013), p. 187

**43** Crisp, *The Naked Civil Servant* (London, 1985 [1967]), p. 99

**44** See Cole (2000), pp. 21–22, and Baker, P. and Stanley, J., *Hello Sailor! The Hidden History of Gay Life at Sea* (London, 2003), p. 116

**45** Troncy, E. (ed.), *Pierre et Gilles: Sailors and the Sea* (London and Cologne, 2008)

**46** Crisp (1985 [1967]), p. 98

**47** Snaith, G., 'Tom's Men: The Masculinization of Homosexuality and the Homosexualization of Masculinity…, *Paragraph*, 26, 2003, pp. 77–88

**48** Geczy, A. and Karaminas, V., *Queer Style* (London, 2013); Cole (2000), p. 119; Baker and Stanley (2003), p. 13

**49** See also, Provencher, D., *Queer French: Globalization, Language, and Sexual Citizenship in France* (Aldershot, 2012), p. 66 onwards

**50** Loriot, T-M. (ed.), *The World of Jean Paul Gaultier* (London, 2011), p. 265

**51** Blum (2003), p. 115

**52** Loriot (2011), p. 222; see also McDowell, C., *Jean Paul Gaultier* (London, 2001), pp. 54–55, 59

**53** Blum (2003), pp. 20–24

**54** White, P., *Elsa Schiaparelli* (London, 1995), p. 62

## CHAPTER 3, THE FISHERMAN

**1** Shakespeare, *Pericles, Prince of Tyre* (New York, 2011 [c. 1607]), p. 49

**2** Stevenson, S., *Facing the Light: The Photography of Hill & Adamson* (Edinburgh, 2002), p. 108

**3** Whaler's caps at the Rijksmuseum, Amsterdam, object NG-2006-110-4; cotton and linen trousers, *c.* 1810 at the NMM, Greenwich, London, object UNI0092

**4** NMM, Greenwich, object TXT0381

**5** *The Fairchild Books Dictionary of Textiles* (New York, 2013), p. 125

**6** *Les Marins Font la Mode* (2009), p. 17. Thanks also to Agnès Mirambet-Paris and Karine Blancher at the Musée national de la Marine in Paris, as well as Sjoerd de Meer at the Maritiem Museum Rotterdam for providing additional information.

**7** Ivanov, A. and Jowett, P., *The Russo-Japanese War 1904–5* (Oxford, 2004), p. 46; McNab, C., *Modern Military Uniforms* (Leicester, 2000), p. 77

**8** Turnau, I., *History of Knitting Before Mass Production* (Komorów, 1991), p. 29

**9** Turnau (1991), p. 63; Jenkins, D.T. (ed.), *The Cambridge History of Western Textiles Volume 1* (Cambridge, 2003), p. 579

**10** Jean Paul Gaultier in Loriot (2011), p. 222

**11** Bowles, H., *Balenciaga and Spain* (New York, 2011), p. 24

**12** Blackman, C., *100 Years of Fashion Illustration* (London, 2007), p. 70

**13** Charles-Roux, E., *The World of Coco Chanel* (London, 2005), p. 108

**14** British and US *Vogue* cited in de la Haye (2011), p. 31

**15** de la Haye (2011), p. 41; Charles-Roux (2005), p. 290

**16** de la Haye (2011), p. 24

**17** See for example, Walton, J., 'Port and Resort: Symbiosis and Conflict in "Old Whitby", England, Since 1880', in *Resorts and Ports: European Seaside Towns Since 1700* (Bristol, 2011)

**18** Blume (1992), p. 42

**19** de la Haye (2011), p. 41; Picardie, J., *Coco Chanel: The Legend and the Life* (London, 2010), p. 176

**20** Rothschild, D. *Making it New: The Art and Style of Sara and Gerald Murphy* (Berkeley and London, 2007), p. 81; Picardie (2010), p. 177

**21** Fitzgerald, F. Scott, *Tender is the Night* (London, 2004 [1934]), p. 236

**22** Blume (1992), p. 75

**23** Ibid. p. 71; Rothschild (2007), pp. 81–82

**24** Schuyler Lynn, K., *Hemingway* (Cambridge, MA, 1995), pp. 362, 542

**25** Hemingway, E., *The Garden of Eden* (New York, 2002), pp. 5–6

**26** Blume (1992), p. 102

**27** French *Vogue*, January 1932

**28** Schoeffler & Gale (1973), p. 358

**29** Wayne, K., 'Villa America in Context' in Rothschild (2007), p. 190

**30** Wigal, D., *Jackson Pollock* (New York, 2012), p. 226

**31** Tickner, L., 'The Popular Culture of *Kermesse*: Lewis, Painting and Performance 1912–13' in Smith, T. (ed.), *In Visible Touch: Modernism and Masculinity* (Chicago, 1997), pp. 146–147. See also 'L'apache est la plaie de Paris' on the cover of *Le Petit Journal*, 20 October 1907

**32** Silver, K., 'The Murphy Closet and the Murphy Bed' in Rothschild (2007), pp. 111, 117

**33** Nevill, B., 'Bernard Nevill on Op Art and the Abstract Revival', British *Vogue*, 15 September 1965, p. 18

**34** Cunnington, P. and Lucas, C., *Occupational Costume in England from the 11th century to 1914* (London, 1967), pp. 56–57

**35** Shrimpton, J., *British Working Dress* (Oxford, 2012), p. 16

**36** Cunnington and Lucas (1967), p. 62

**37** British *Vogue*, 7 August 1929, p. 26

**38** 'Regional Knitting in the British Isles and Ireland', V&A Museum, www.vam.ac.uk/content/articles/r/regional-knitting-in-the-british-isles-and-ireland, accessed 26 May 2014

**39** Thanks to Penelope Hemingway for her research into regional fishing knits.

**40** Ibid.

**41** Thompson, G., *Patterns for Guernseys, Jerseys and Arans* (New York, 1979), p. 6

**42** Black (2012), pp. 161, 157

**43** Tuite (2014), pp. 115–16

**44** Jenkins (2003), p. 569

**45** *Men's Wear*, 10 September 1924, p. 36 in Schoeffler, and Gale (1973), p. 49

**46** Tuite (2014), p. 104

**47** de la Haye (2011), p. 41

**48** Black (2012), p. 165

**49** 'Regional Knitting in the British Isles and Ireland', V&A Museum

**50** Schoeffler and Gale (1973), pp. 5 93

**51** Smylie, M., *Herring* (Stroud, 2004), p. 149, Shrimpton (2012), p. 19

**52** Rowland, P., *A Dash of Daring: Carmel Snow and Her Life in Fashion, Art, and Letters* (New York and London, 2005), p. 364; Ballard, B., *In My Fashion* (London, 1960), p. 93

**53** Arzalluz, M., *Cristóbal Balenciaga* (London, 2010), pp. 86, 109

**54** Bowles (2011), p. 188

**55** Miller, L., *Cristóbal Balenciaga* (London, 1993), p. 36 and Bowles (2011), pp. 19, 188

## CHAPTER 4, THE SPORTSMAN

**1** Knox-Johnston, R., *The History of Yachting* (Oxford, 1990), pp. 8–9

**2** Jno. J. Mitchell Co., *Men's Fashion Illustrations from the Turn of the Century* (New York and London, 2012), p. 25

**3** Carlson, J., *Rowing Blazers* (London, 2014), p. 12

**4** Reefer was also the name for a naval overcoat similar to the pea coat.

**5** *Men's Wear*, 1 December 1926, p. 70, cited in Schoeffler and Gale (1973), p. 49

**6** *Gentlemen's Quarterly*, 1971, in Schoeffler and Gale (1973), p. 467

**7** Clemente, D., *Dress Casual: How College Students Redefined American Style* (Chapel Hill, NC, 2014), p. 48

**8** *Vanity Fair*, 30:4, 1928, p. 98

**9** 'No wind that blew dismayed the crew', British *Vogue*, 24 July 1929, p. 48

**10** de la Haye (2011), pp. 82–84

**11** Amory, C., 'Palm Beach', *Life*, 21 January 1952

**12** Maglio, D., 'Peacocks in the sands: Flamboyant men's beachwear 1920–30', *Critical Studies in Men's Fashion*, 1:1, 2014, pp. 23–38

**13** *Men's Wear*, 1928, in Schoeffler and Gale (1973), p. 50

**14** Hawes, E., *Fashion is Spinach* (New York, 1938), p. 256

**15** Bowles (2011), p. 109

**16** Hawes (1938), p. 86

**17** Rennolds Milbank, C., *Resort Fashion* (New York, 2009), p. 137; Stewart, M.L., *Dressing Modern Frenchwomen: Marketing Haute Couture, 1919–1939* (Baltimore, MD, 2008), p. 113

**18** Much information here drawn from Dawson, P., *The Liner* (London, 2007)

**19** Tolini Finamore, M., *Hollywood Before Glamour* (Basingstoke, 2013), pp. 64–65

**20** Stewart (2008), p. 84

**21** Yohannan, K., and Nolf, N., *Claire McCardell* (New York, 1998), p. 81

**22** For more see Arnold, R., 'Looking American: Louise Dahl-Wolfe's Fashion Photographs of the 1930s and 1940s' in *Fashion Theory*, 6:1, 2002, pp. 45–60

**23** Bettina Ballard, quoted in Polan, B. and Tredre, R., *The Great Fashion Designers* (Oxford, 2009), p. 116

**24** Hilfiger, T. and Keeps, D., *All American: A Style Book by Tommy Hilfiger* (London, 1998), p. 20

**25** Interview with Jaana Jätyri, 26 January 2014

**26** McDowell, C., *Ralph Lauren* (London, 2002), p. 38

**27** Hilfiger and Keeps (1998), pp. 4, 18
**28** Ibid., p. 46
**29** Rosenblum, E., 'The J.Crew Invasion', *Business Week*, 27 November 2013
**30** Ibid.

## CHAPTER 5, THE PIRATE

**1** Cordingly, D., *Life Among the Pirates* (London, 1996), pp. 6–8
**2** Travers, T., *Pirates* (Stroud, 2007), pp. 11–12
**3** Cordingly (1996), p. 21; Travers (2007), p. 7
**4** Wilkinson-Latham (1977), p. 24; Travers (2007), p. 37
**5** Cordingly (1996), pp. 2, 22
**6** Buckland, K., 'The Monmouth Cap', *Costume*, 13: 1, January 1979, pp. 23–37
**7** Brooke, I., *Dress and Undress: The Restoration and 18th Century* (London, 1958), p. 21
**8** Newark, T., *Brassey's Book of Uniforms* (London, 1998), pp. 12, 21
**9** Pomerantz, D., 'Disney Hits Pause Button on Pirates of the Caribbean 5', *Forbes*, 9 October 2013
**10** Barrie, J.M., *Peter Pan in Kensington Gardens and Peter and Wendy* (Oxford, 2008), p. 115
**11** Cordingly (1996), pp. 22–3
**12** Davis, R.I., *Men's 17th and 18th Century Costume, Cut and Fashion* (Studio City, CA, 2000), pp. 2, 61
**13** Ibid., p. 64; Brooke (1958), p. 25
**14** Newark (1998), pp. 10, 13, 21
**15** British *Vogue*, 25 December 1929, p. 29; British *Vogue*, 16 October 1929, p. 37

**16** McLaren interview by Chris Salewicz, *The Face*, May 1981, p. 42
**17** Discussion with Young Kim, 28 January 2014
**18** Wilcox, C., *Vivienne Westwood* (London, 2004), p. 16
**19** 'Style: The Gold Rush', *The Face*, May 1981, p.14; 'The New Direction', British *Vogue*, August 1981, p. 46
**20** 'Westwood ho! To winter on the Youth Wave', photographed Bruce Weber, British *Vogue*, August 1981, pp. 98–101
**21** William Congreve in *Love for Love*, quoted in Brooke (1958), p. 23
**22** 'Beauty and the Blouse', *Harpers & Queen*, February 1981
**23** Westwood quoted in Savage, J., 'Rich Pickings at the World's End', *The Face*, January 1981, pp. 25–6
**24** Crowdy, T., *French Revolutionary Infantrymen 1791–1802* (Oxford, 2003), p. 60
**25** Ribeiro, A., *Fashion in the French Revolution* (London, 1988), p. 85
**26** Ribeiro (1988), pp. 39, 117
**27** Cordingly (1996), p. 23; Travers (2007), p. 14
**28** Savage (1981), p. 25
**29** Ibid.
**30** Cordingly (1996), pp. 2, 19; Stanley, J. (ed.), *Bold in her Breeches: Women Pirates Across the Ages* (London, 1995), p. 165
**31** Cordingly (1996), p. 20
**32** Ibid., pp. 135–42
**33** 'Natural Dis-Tinction, Un-Natural Selection' collection, spring/summer 2009

**34** Watt (2012), p. 137
**35** Blanks, T., Style.com review, 3 October 2011, www.style.com/fashionshows/review/S2012RTW-AMCQUEEN, accessed 29 May 2014
**36** See 'The Tattoos of Early American Seafarers 1796–1818' in Dye, I., *Proceedings of the American Philosophical Society*, 133:4, December 1989, pp. 520–54
**37** Dye (1989), pp. 537, 542
**38** Ibid., p. 531
**39** Govenar, A.,'The Changing Image of Tattooing in American Culture 1846–1966', in Caplan, J. (ed.), *Written on the Body: The Tattoo in European and American History* (London, 2000), pp. 213–14
**40** *Les Marins Font la Mode* (2009), pp. 166–67
**41** Ibid., p. 168
**42** Thanks to Dr Matt Lodder, art and tattoo historian, for his help and advice in these areas
**43** Bradley, J., 'Body Commodification? Class and Tattoos in Victorian Britain' in Caplan (2000), p. 146
**44** Ibid., p. 146
**45** Stephen, R.J., 'Tattooed Royalty: Queer Stories of a Queer Craze', *Harmsworth Magazine*, December 1898
**46** DeMello, M., *Bodies of Inscription: A Cultural History of the Modern Tattoo Community* (Durham, NC, 2000), pp. 63, 73
**47** Holt, A., *Fancy dresses described* (London, 1896), p. 199
**48** British *Vogue*, August 1929, p.45

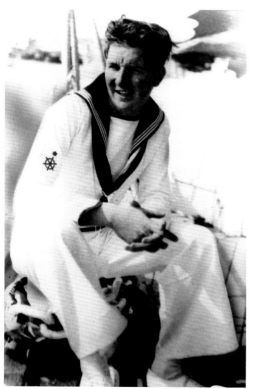

*Able Seaman Anthony Frank Randle in white working dress serving on HMS Chevron, stationed in Malta. Hand-tinted photograph, c.1951.*

## ACKNOWLEDGMENTS

My heartiest thanks to the following for helping me to batten down the hatches aboard the Good Ship Nautical:

Becky Conekin, Guy Hobbs and Gail Prince; Laura Potter, Frances Ambler Anna Perotti and Maria Ranauro. For information and images: Jelka Music (Jean Paul Gaultier), Cécile Goddet-Dirles (Chanel), Kim Stringer (Prada), Alicia de Toro (Yohji Yamamoto), Yumiko Hayashi (Sonia Rykiel), Ulrica Bogh-Lind (Gant), Shona Heath and Kathryn Scahill, Sylvie Flaure (Pierre et Gilles), David Sassoon, Olympia Le-Tan, Nicole Conallin (Woolmark), Mark van Beek and Len Litchfield (Gloverall), Nigel Calladine (Original Montgomery), Eric Musgrave (EMAP), Terry and Liz de Havilland.

Naval twitterstorians: Dr Phil Weir, Nicholas Blake, Dr Steven Gray, Dr Sam Willis, Samuel McLean and Lorna Campbell.

Staff at Lowestoft Library, especially Ivan Bunn; Colin Dixon, Lowestoft

Maritime Museum; Amy Miller, Dr James Davey and Melanie Vandenbrouk, National Maritime Museum; Agnès Mirambet-Paris and Karine Blancher, Musée national de la Marine, Paris; Sjoerd de Meer, Maritime Museum Rotterdam; Peter Tilley, Gieves & Hawkes archive; Rob Jeffries, Thames River Police Museum; Jane Holt, London College of Fashion archive; and Robert Waters for Gaiety Girls expertise.

For specialist knowledge: Dr Matt Lodder, Young Kim, Shaun Cole, Sally Pointer, Penelope Hemingway, John-Michael O'Sullivan, Naomi Thompson, Liz Tregenza, Jaana Jätyri, Helene Thian, Lorene Rhoomes, Jane Dolby, Nancy Bruseker, Phil Bush, Deborah Woolf, Sadie Doherty, Sally and Spencer Green, Joe Neve and wife, and Mel Hales.

And, of course: Rachael, Dana, Nisha, Marawa, Mum, John, Toby and Rob Flowers.